"Our health system must achieve better care, better health, lower costs, and the best possible patient experience through innovation and spreading proven results. Drs. Steele and Feinberg eloquently describe the Geisinger journey, and the story serves as a guiding light for everyone in our health system who wants to achieve better results. The book should be read by everyone who is focused on health system transformation, improvement, caring for patients, and innovation."

—Patrick Conway, MD, MSc
Deputy Administrator for Innovation and Quality and Director,
Center for Medicare and Medicaid Innovation, CMS*

"A must-read for anyone interested in understanding how changing the way care is provided can unlock value in healthcare. Written by the former and current CEOs of Geisinger, it is a readable explanation of the importance of clinical leadership and integrated health systems in creating value. The discussion and experience with ProvenCare will be especially helpful to clinicians, while the financial outcomes of Proven-Care will capture the attention of system CFOs."

—Gail Wilensky, PhD
Economist and Senior Fellow, Project HOPE

"An aging population with multiple chronic conditions, coupled with increased consumerism as patients become more involved in their healthcare decision making, means hospitals and health systems are examining their care processes as they grapple with these new challenges. David and Glenn provide a how-to manual on improving access to care and the quality of care, while lowering costs, in their extraordinary new book. Their fresh approach is based on their leadership of one of the country's leading health systems. A must-read for everyone interested in advancing health in America."

—Rick Pollack
President and CEO, American Hospital Association

"Great leaders, to paraphrase Napoleon, must define reality and then give hope. *ProvenCare* accomplishes both of these objectives, and provides a road map for improving healthcare outcomes that is fact-based, and battle-tested. This is fundamentally a story about leading change in the very complex field of healthcare. The results achieved within the Geisinger system are inspirational, compelling, and relevant."

—L. Kevin Cox
Chairman, Health Transformation Alliance; and
CHRO, American Express Company

The quote represents Dr. Conway's personal views and not necessarily the views or policies of the Centers for Medicare and Medicaid Services.

"*ProvenCare* explores common myths about healthcare in America, and exposes the fallacy that more care is better, along with the tragedy of how many in our country are underserved by our medical system. Glenn Steele and David Feinberg argue that the patient must always come first, and demonstrate that it is through coordination and collaboration, as well as a singular focus on outcomes, that we can improve care while lowering costs. This excellent book is both an exposé and personal guide that provides powerful support for the collaborative and evidenced-based approach to practicing medicine championed by Geisinger, an approach that is leading the way in the transformation in American healthcare."

—Ann Lamont
Managing Partner, Oak Investment Partners

"*ProvenCare* beautifully illustrates how, together, Dr. Steele, Dr. Feinberg, and Geisinger have created proven strategies that balance innovative, integrated technologies with high-touch personal care. ProvenCare, where care and caring go hand in hand, is a model for the future that can be implemented today. PeaceHealth looks forward to adopting Geisinger's approach to care delivery to further our own patient-centric focus on transforming the health and well-being of our patients and communities."

—Liz Dunne
President and CEO, PeaceHealth

"Drs. Steele and Feinberg provide a rare blend of visionary thinking and practical and tactical acumen. Our cooperative of America's leading self-insured health plans benefits immensely from Dr. Steele's leadership. This book is focused on our transformational mission, but also zooms in on the healthcare problems of today and offers solutions to them."

—Rob Andrews
CEO, Health Transformation Alliance

"Grounded within the context of our rapidly changing healthcare landscape, Drs. Feinberg and Steele offer a thought-provoking look at Geisinger's pioneering approach to reengineer care management and improve health outcomes for patients. The lessons learned from Geisinger's innovations to truly integrate care offer new insights to help tackle the fundamental challenges of access, quality, and cost in healthcare that have remained with us for decades."

—Sheila Burke, RN, MPA, FAAN
Senior Public Advisor, Baker, Donelson, Bearman,
Caldwell & Berkowitz; and Adjunct Lecturer
in Public Policy, Harvard University

"Regardless of what happens in Congress or state legislatures, the healthcare industry is in the throes of massive transformation. For leaders of health systems, as well as clinicians trying to lead successful transformation, *ProvenCare* is a terrific playbook that shares the insights and passion of Drs. Steele and Feinberg, who have positioned Geisinger as a role model for what is needed in American healthcare. The book is full of insights into the who, what, when, why, and how of this transformation. It is not a coincidence that many Geisinger leaders have moved on to have significant impact at many prominent healthcare organizations, and now xG Health Solutions, the Geisinger spin-off, is assisting others. Follow the journey and use the insights gained to help accelerate the transformation taking place across this industry."

—Lee B. Sacks, MD
EVP and Chief Medical Officer, Advocate Health Care

"Dr. Glenn Steele and Dr. David Feinberg, well known for their creativity and leadership in helping to solve the complexities of providing value and quality in healthcare, have provided valuable insights into the success of Geisinger as a delivery model for today and tomorrow. Beyond telling the story of the success and creation of the care model with thought and creativity, the lessons learned can be adapted not only to larger systems but also to our struggling rural hospitals. Refreshingly straightforward and practical."

—Lou Hochheiser, MD
Professor Emeritus, University of Vermont; and
former CEO, St. John's Medical Center

"Steele and Feinberg have given us a timely and inspiring procedural on how to improve clinical outcomes and patient satisfaction and reduce the cost of healthcare. *ProvenCare* is a must-read for anyone who desires to fix our broken health system."

—George F. Lynn
President Emeritus, AtlantiCare; and former
Chairman, American Hospital Association

Proven Care

How to Deliver
Value-Based Healthcare
the Geisinger Way

Glenn D. Steele Jr., MD, PhD

David Feinberg, MD, MBA

New York Chicago San Francisco Athens London Madrid
Mexico City Milan New Delhi Singapore Sydney Toronto

1 2 3 4 5 6 7 8 9   LCR   22 21 20 19 18 17

ISBN   978-1-259-64228-9
MHID   1-259-64228-3

e-ISBN   978-1-259-64229-6
e-MHID   1-259-64229-1

Library of Congress Cataloging-in-Publication Data

Names: Steele, Glenn, 1944- author. | Feinberg, David T., author.
Title: Provencare : how to deliver value-based healthcare the Geisinger way / by
   Glenn D. Steele, Jr. and David T. Feinberg.
Description: New York : McGraw-Hill, [2018] | Includes bibliographical
   references and index.
Identifiers: LCCN 2017027131| ISBN 9781259642289 (acid-free paper) | ISBN
   1259642283 (acid-free paper)
Subjects: LCSH: Medical economics--United States. | Medical care--Cost
   effectiveness--United States. | BISAC: BUSINESS & ECONOMICS /
   General.
Classification: LCC RA410.53 .S74 2018 | DDC 338.4/73621--dc23 LC record
   available at https://lccn.loc.gov/2017027131

McGraw-Hill Education books are available at special quantity discounts to use as premiums and sales promotions or for use in corporate training programs. To contact a representative, please visit the Contact Us pages at www.mhprofessional.com.

To all our Geisinger patients and insurance members,
it is our privilege to care for you.

And to everyone in the Geisinger family who
works daily to care for the people we serve.

CONTENTS

PREFACE   vii

ACKNOWLEDGMENTS   xvii

1 Why Geisinger?   1

2 The Problem   15

3 The Fix   25

4 Effective Governance   39

5 Getting Started   49

6 Enabling Change   63

7 ProvenCare Acute: Taking It to the Next Step   79

8 ProvenCare Chronic   105

9 ProvenHealth Navigator: Geisinger's
   Advanced Medical Home   127

10 Leading and Managing a Successful
   Practice Transformation   151

11 ProvenCare Biologics   165

12 ProvenExperience   187

13 Future Vision   213

   NOTES   231

   INDEX   237

PREFACE

The fundamental challenges in healthcare have not changed significantly in the nearly five decades of our involvement in health system leadership. Access, quality, and cost have always represented the underlying combination of intersecting and sometimes conflicting goals.

During President Lyndon B. Johnson's Great Society and the inception of the public payer with the introduction of Medicare and Medicaid in the 1960s, the focus was solely on ensuring adequate access for the elderly and poor citizens who could not then afford available insurance either on their own or through their employers. Interestingly, the opening lines of the Medicare law asserted that the new entitlement would not in any way influence how medicine should be practiced. Through the "Hillary care" debates in the 1990s and into the new millennium, it became obvious to the entire nation and even more so at the individual state budget level that increased access to care without formal expectation of better outcome would drive societal cost to unsustainable and uncompetitive levels.

Amazingly, state and federal regulations continued to demand unfettered fee-for-service reimbursement, as it was felt to be critical to maintain the sacrosanct relationship between patients and providers. Implicit in all of this was the fantasy that all doctors were practicing optimal caregiving and all hospitals were uniformly motivated to do what was right for patients, not what was most convenient and financially beneficial for the hospitals themselves.

Inevitably, the percentage of U.S. gross domestic product (GDP) spent on healthcare grew into double digits and is now approaching 20 percent. And as the public payer has expanded to represent more than 60 percent of the provider payment mix, the question of what everyone is getting for their money has become as important, if not more so than access. The original Dartmouth College studies in the 1970s through the 1990s first reported there was no apparent relationship between cost of care and short- or long-term quality outcomes. Most notable was a region-to-region variation in frequency and cost of most diagnostic and therapeutic interventions.[1]

At Geisinger and other innovative integrated systems, particularly those with insurance and provider components in the same fiduciary structure committed to working together to analyze total cost of care for their mutually shared populations, a relationship between cost of care and quality outcome was established. The link at first, though, seemed counterintuitive. Almost always, the highest-cost patients were those with the least acceptable short- and long-term health outcomes. In a very important way, this inverse relationship helped those of us who were leading the transformation to high-quality, low-cost care to establish a rationale to fundamentally reengineer hospital and ambulatory care to achieve better outcomes for patients and not focus primarily on extracting cost. If unnecessary or hurtful care was removed, a better outcome would result.

Healthcare professionals are motivated to do things differently by knowing that the changes are better for patients—not merely saving money for the insurance company, hospital, or purchaser. So much the better if the reengineering results in increased quality with lower cost as a side effect. That's a double value win. And since professional pride of purpose is what truly motivates the needed behavior change, it was key that the rationale for change focused on patients achieving better outcomes.

All of this created a natural progression in the discussion of how expanding Medicare and Medicaid could influence the access, quality, and cost triangle. Then came the turbulence of our society's attempt to provide insurance for a majority of the 45 million Americans who were uninsured prior to the inception of the 2010 Patient Protection and Affordable Care Act (ACA). Although the primary intention of Obamacare was to decrease dramatically the number of uninsured, there were many incentives to move the provider system as quickly as possible away from what was acknowledged as the key promoter of unhelpful or hurtful costs: fee-for-service reimbursement.

The two main components of the soon-to-be 20 percent U.S. GDP commitment to healthcare spending were higher prices compared to any other developed country in the world and a dominant fee-for-service payment incentive. This incentive based financial success on number of units of work performed, adding irrational momentum to producing more and more units, regardless of whether those units of work helped patients. If pressure successfully pushed down the price per unit, the rational response of any successful provider system would be to produce more units, whether or not that work helped to achieve better patient outcomes.

Depending on political point of view, one could argue whether ACA/Obamacare achieved even its primary goal, but it definitely altered the unsustainable trajectory of significantly rising medical utilization and expenditure. And whatever comes next post-ACA will have to address the same fundamental interplay of access, quality, and cost. Nothing has changed in these fundamentals, and we believe that nothing has diminished the value of the lessons learned at Geisinger summarized in this book. As turbulence in the public payer undoubtedly will increase with the Trump administration's commitment to repeal the ACA, we believe financial pressure will increase on providers facing an uptick of uninsured patients for whom they still are obligated to provide care. Cost shifting will not be the usual easy way out, as commercial payers increase their leverage through continued consolidation. Even the large self-insured employers are banding together—for example, the Health Transformation Alliance and Pacific Business Group on Health—to begin to define high-performing provider networks or centers of excellence to transact value-based healthcare for their employees. Quite simply, these big companies do not want to be the last standing redistribution engines providing caregivers high margins as all the other payers squeeze down.

What do these changes mean in the face of unchanging fundamentals in caregiving, payment for care, and our society's continued expectation of improved health status? And who should be held responsible for its improvement? We believe that unlocking value by changing how care is provided and received remains the only serious way to improve access and quality while lowering cost. This is not easy to transact, but nevertheless is doable as we have seen with the ProvenCare innovations at Geisinger.

The following chapters are designed to provide tangible, practical learnings, and four transformational themes underpin nearly all of the straightforward innovation road tests. The first and most basic transformation is our definition of an integrated health system. In a truly integrated health system, all employees—pharmacists, nurses, administrators, desk clerks, security guards, engineering, food services, employed and nonemployed associated physicians, specialists, subspecialists, PCPs, trainees, and even financial officers—know they are working together and are incentivized to ensure that everyone is focused on benefiting individual patients.

During Dr. Steele's tenure, it was with great pride, and some occasional anxiety, that job applicants were invited to randomly stop any Geisinger employee—pushing a food cart, providing security in the parking lot, or sitting behind a reception desk—and ask what it was like to work at Geisinger and what was the employee's mission. Almost always, the answers to these questions from the frontline workers carried more weight than anything the CEO said about shared mission and staff morale. And the answers most often were about true integration; everyone involved understood how what they did made a difference in achieving optimal patient outcomes. Without this basic definition and understanding of integration, most so-called integrated delivery networks are really no more than financial contrivances to obtain better rates in the capital markets. Without true integration, none of the innovation road tests we describe here could have happened.

Second and even more unique to the Geisinger concept of integration was the unusual structure where both the insurance company and all of the providers involved in caregiving ultimately are overseen by a single parent fiduciary. Numerous attempts to create new models of the Geisinger vertical integration, either real or virtual integration between payer and provider, have proliferated over the past decade. Hospital-centric integrated delivery networks have created new insurance companies. Large independent insurance companies have purchased doctor groups and even hospitals. Nonfiduciary partnering has been structured between large independent insurance payers and a variety of provider systems throughout the country. And of course, the whole concept of accountable care organizations is based on payer and provider working together to benefit their mutual constituency. How many of these actually will achieve higher quality outcome and lower cost is unknown, but the prognosis is not good when the main currency of interaction is simply a change in reimbursement incentives.

True transformation in the Geisinger vertical integration represents a fundamental change in the relationship between payer and provider, sharing information as well as financial risk and, most important, sharing a joint mission to improve health outcomes for individual and populations of patients. Whether this new relationship can be scaled will definitely be affected by the radical change under way in our political environment. It remains to be seen exactly how and when this change will happen.

At Geisinger, because of our unusual payer/provider structure and century-old culture, it really doesn't matter which component of the system does better financially as long as patient outcomes improve and costs decrease. We have the ability to focus together on total cost of care, with access to healthcare delivery data as well as insurance claims data, because patients we care for also are, by and large, those we insure.

A third critical transformation on the provider side of Geisinger was our concept of leadership. We assumed that the combination of a great clinician, great teacher, great administrator, great financial mind, and great innovator would be rare indeed in any single human being. Historically, the most important pillar of credibility at Geisinger always had been to be a great clinician, so that was our starting point. But we insisted that the great clinical leader be paired with a great administrative partner or partners. If the facility or service was large enough or critical to our clinical mission, we often added a financial expert to the leadership team. These leaders together were held responsible for strategic plans, operating budgets, performance metrics, and performance evaluations. Leadership partners also were celebrated together when success occurred. Clinical leaders either learned to share the spotlight or were replaced.

We were trying to change behavior in all of our care reengineering processes. Doing a simple inventory of the details of each care process at the initiation of reengineering was eye-opening. During Dr. Steele's three-day hospitalization for his heart surgery, 147 different individuals legitimately logged in to his electronic health record. The complexity of changing processes and behaviors among everyone involved in the care process was hard enough, but even more difficult was the subsequent transformation in the relationship between caregivers and patients. Fundamental to most of our innovation efforts was an attempt to create an active and much more symmetrical interaction between patient and provider, whether in the context of an acute care episode or when reengineering the management of chronic diseases.

The progression from activated patients and more symmetrical interactions between caregivers and patients to Dr. Feinberg's focus on achieving extreme patient satisfaction is natural. This is not just about the quality and temperature of the food provided in the hospital. It isn't just about having aesthetically pleasing and functional facilities. And it's not simply about giving patients exactly what they want even when that doesn't make sense. It is about understanding that the ultimate choice in the patient/provider transaction is in fact the patient's choice. Getting to an optimal outcome depends critically upon a unique blending of provider expertise and an activated, fully engaged patient who feels every interaction with Geisinger and our people is beneficial.

Most recently, as mentioned earlier, the purchaser of care has been added to the traditional patient, provider, and payer triad. Not just the Medicare and Medicaid public payers, but also the self-insured employers who represent the buyer of healthcare for about 169 million U.S. workers and retirees[2], are demanding better outcomes for their sponsored employees and are pushing their employees to better understand and choose real value in maintaining optimal health or getting better when they are sick.

A fourth and final transformation underpinning the kind of continuous innovation that Geisinger is about is the need not only to create value from the care reengineering process (higher quality and lower cost) but also to ensure that the benefit is distributed to the patient, to the provider, and back to the purchaser. All of these stakeholders have to experience direct benefit from the value created. If there is no sustainable benefit (or sustainable business model in the case of the provider) plus some allowance for innovation failure, good intentions alone or an altruistic mission will not survive. Innovation stops if all of the value is perceived as going exclusively to one stakeholder in the system, such as the insurance company. And if the patient can't feel a tangible benefit in service, decreased aggravation, and improved outcome, he or she will have no motivation to seek out value-based innovative systems. Instead, the patient will continue to demand access to the best-known brands, regardless of whether those brands have anything to do with higher quality at lower cost. Finally, for the purchaser who is footing a significant amount of the bill in either direct or indirect costs, recruiting and retaining the best and healthiest group of employees (and keeping them as healthy as possible) is an absolutely critical factor in staying competitive, particularly in an increasingly global market.

So the fundamentals are exactly the same pre- and post-ACA. Higher quality at lower cost, plus access to health insurance, are critical and intersecting goals. And the transformational themes will continue to cut across all of the necessary innovations in which we take great pride at Geisinger.

Going from innovation—even continuous innovation, which is hard enough to systematize—to scaling innovation is a huge leap. But scaling is what we need as a society, not just more boutique innovation efforts. What we've learned at Geisinger and at Geisinger's scaling engine, xG Health Solutions, about the dynamics of scaling, the very different areas of expertise required, the differences in market forces between for-profit and nonprofit settings, and the importance of committed leadership in both the payer and provider components of the healthcare system could fill a book. But that would be the next book, not this one. What we attempt to do here is describe how we've innovated at Geisinger and our first scaling attempts outside of our system. We hope you will take what seems interesting and applicable to your own organization, modify it, customize it, even claim it as homegrown if necessary, and begin to see the value proposition work. We stand ready at Geisinger and at xG Health Solutions, should you need any help.

ACKNOWLEDGMENTS

Many people did the work we are summarizing in this book, but some deserve special mention. Most important were those who created the innovation infrastructure and those in the various clinical and health plan units that created the individual care reengineering examples detailed in these pages.

The initial rebuilding of Geisinger's physician leadership, the organization's evolution from discipline-based to interdisciplinary service line-based caregiving, and the transformation from "piecework" payment for each unit of work (RVU-based compensation) to physician compensation based on strategic goal achievement began under the leadership of Dr. Bruce Hamory and Dr. Joseph Bisordi, and subsequently was supervised by successor chief medical officers Dr. Howard Grant, Dr. Albert Bothe, and Dr. Steven Strongwater. Interestingly, Dr. Bisordi became chief medical officer of Ochsner Health System, Dr. Grant became chief executive officer of Lahey Clinic, and Dr. Strongwater became CEO of Arius following their times at Geisinger.

The establishment of our "Skunk Works" innovation group was initiated by Geisinger's first chief of innovation, Dr. Ronald Paulus, who is now CEO of Mission Health in Asheville, North Carolina. His key recruits, Meg Horgan and Seth Frazier, helped expand the enabling capabilities of this nonclinical unit and helped create a separate transformation group committed to scaling innovation throughout all of the Geisinger clinical operations. Seth Frazier became a key principle of Evolent, an organization like our own xG Health Solutions committed to scaling the volume- to value-based healthcare transformation throughout the country.

The innovation and transformation groups both reported to Joanne Wade, Geisinger's first executive vice president for strategy. Joanne and Dr. Steele justified the resource commitments and the patient quality and value returns on those commitments to the management and compensation committee of the Geisinger Health System Foundation (now Geisinger Health Foundation) board of directors. Without this innovation and transformation infrastructure, none of the specific payer or provider side innovations would have occurred. Taking a chance on this investment before there was any substantive evidence of return, both in terms of benefit for patients and a viable business model, was a function of three key Geisinger board members: Frank Henry, our chairman at that time; William Alexander, then our finance committee chair; and Allen Deaver, management and compensation committee chair.

As explained in the text, the key structural advantage for innovation to occur at Geisinger was the interaction between Geisinger insurance and Geisinger clinical care. The most important proof of this possible payer/provider synergy was led by Dr. Norman Payson. Although we only "rented" his expertise and credibility, the time he spent with us, as well as the ramifications of the new Medicare Advantage reimbursement rules in the 2003 Medicare Modernization Act (MMA) budget process, and the initiation of the Hierarchical Condition Categories (HCCs) all solidified the fundamentally positive interaction that began to occur between our payers and providers for the 50 percent of patients we both cared for and insured. An equally important contribution from Dr. Payson's interim GHP leadership was our recruitment of his immediate successor, Dr.

Richard Gilfillan, as the Geisinger Health Plan CEO. Dr. Gilfillan and Dr. Duane Davis, our insurance company chief medical officer, became the critical translators of what was known as the Geisinger payer/provider "sweet spot," making the concept of payer and provider entities working together for the benefit of their mutual constituents real. Dr. Gilfillan subsequently became head of the innovation center (CMMI) at CMS and later CEO of Trinity Health. Dr. Davis became chief executive officer of the Geisinger insurance entities.

Additional critical enablers of our acute and chronic care reengineering included Geisinger's two IT leaders at the inception of ProvenCare, Dr. James Walker, chief medical information officer, and Frank Richards, chief information officer. Without these two visionaries, the embedding of our reengineering content into the Epic electronic health record system would not have happened, and routine care would not have changed without the embedding of the new care pathways. Jean Adams, Joan Topper, and Tammy Anderer were key translators of both the internal IT content embedding and our new outreach to many non-Geisinger, nonemployed provider partners in the innovation experiments. As senior leaders strategized, conceptualized, and articulated the need for fundamental change in employed and nonemployed provider behavior, they translated the necessary infrastructure modifications so caregivers could provide added value to their patients and our insurance company members. Karen McKinley, Scott Berry, Janet Tomcavage, and Dr. Thomas Graf were critical leaders in redesigning community practice and the interaction among our 55 community-based sites and the hospital-based specialists and subspecialists. Without these valuable, committed, and aspirational leaders and doers, none of the specific innovations would have happened.

Based largely on the good clinical leadership of Dr. Al Casale, chief of cardiothoracic surgery and co-chair of the heart care service line, Dr. James Blankenship, chief of cardiology at Geisinger Medical Center, and Michael Doll, cardiothoracic surgery chief physician assistant, our first acute care episode reengineering—elective interventional heart care—assured the success of our original heart surgery "warranty" and significant internal and external affirmation. Extension of ProvenCare acute reengineering to other hospital-based interventions including hip and knee replacement and spine surgery has been led most recently by Dr. Michael Suk, chairman of the department of orthopaedic surgery, and Dr. Jonathan Slotkin, director of spinal surgery.

The predicates for success of our commitment to bundled best practice in reengineering care for patients with prevalent chronic diseases should be credited to Dr. Steve Pierdon and Lee Myers, the "founders" of Community Practice Service Line (CPSL), Geisinger's first and most innovative service line. This initial interdisciplinary approach to caregiving was subsequently expanded to 27 other service lines. Dr. Thomas Graf and Dr. Suzy Kobylinski followed Dr. Pierdon as CPSL leaders, ensuring the Geisinger patients first and continuous innovation commitments. Dr. Fred Bloom, now the chief medical officer at Guthrie Healthcare System headquartered in Sayre, Pennsylvania, was the key leader of much of our Proven-Health Navigator medical home reengineering efforts, along with Janet Tomcavage and Dr. Duane Davis from Geisinger Health Plan. These leaders created a fundamentally different interaction among our caregivers largely located in the community sites, the hospital-based specialists and subspecialists, and our Geisinger insurance plan. Major leaders on the specialty side of these new relationships included Dr. Eric Newman, head of rheumatology and vice chairman of medicine; Dr. John Kennedy, head of endocrinology; Dr. Paul Kettlewell in child psychology; Dr. Edward Hartle, chairman of medicine; Dr. Jonathan Hosey and Dr. Steven Toms in the neurosciences; and Dr. David Franklin in surgery. Dr. Hosey, Dr. Toms, and Dr. Franklin have all assumed leadership positions at other academic or integrated delivery systems.

Most recently, the extension of Geisinger reengineering to specialty drug purchasing and management has been led by Michael Evans, Deb Templeton, and Dr. Robert Weil. In addition, Dr. Ray Roth, who was the GHP chief medical officer at that time, was critical in partnering with Mike Evans and Janet Tomcavage in coordinating both the Geisinger insurance platform and the clinical enterprise in all of the organization's drug purchasing and caregiving reengineering. Dr. Weil is now chief medical officer of Catholic Health Initiatives.

Two individuals who were major contributors during Dr. Steele's tenure as CEO and continue to be the key translators of Dr. Feinberg's ProvenCare patient experience are Dr. Greg Burke, chief patient experience officer, and Susan Robel, executive vice president and system chief nursing officer.

Most of the ongoing innovation at Geisinger and most of the bets on future innovation are under the direct supervision of Dr. David Ledbetter, Geisinger's chief scientific officer; Dr. Alistair Erskine, chief informatics officer; and Dr. Greg Moore, who initiated the Institute for Advanced Application and is a senior leader at Google.

The strategic goal of innovation was broadened during the last five years of Dr. Steele's tenure at Geisinger to include scaling and generalizing both within Geisinger and outward into non-Geisinger systems and markets. It soon became clear that scaling was significantly more complicated than innovating, particularly when extrapolating from the ideal Geisinger culture, fiduciary structure, and market demography and penetration into more complex milieus. Dr. Earl Steinberg is Dr. Steele's partner in founding and running our primary scaling engine, xG Health Solutions. xG would not exist without Dr. Steinberg's vision and resilience, the confidence of the Geisinger board of directors, and the literal buy-in of our private equity partner, Annie Lamont of Oak Investments. Colleagues pirated from Geisinger to lead the xG efforts include Meg Horgan, Dr. Steven Pierdon, Dr. Ray Roth, Joanne Wade, and many individual Geisinger subject matter experts whose commitment to spreading the Geisinger model has led to significant successes in California, Delaware, rural Illinois, Maine, New Jersey, northern Virginia, Washington state, West Virginia, Wisconsin, and even Singapore, to name a few client locations.

Finally, a huge debt of gratitude to David Jolley, who co-wrote much of this work, mitigating almost all of Dr. Steele's idiosyncratic and self-adulating writing. And most important, a debt of gratitude to Nicole Lucas, who singlehandedly managed the manuscript process at the same time she managed Dr. Steele through this latest project.

And, of course, our thanks and admiration to the more than 30,000 members of the Geisinger family—our employees—who work night and day, seven days a week and on holidays, to provide professional and compassionate care to our patients and members. They are front and center in everything we do and all of our success.

1

Why Geisinger?

The little boy was essentially dead. He had no heartbeat, no breathing, and an extremely high blood-acidity level. But the team at Geisinger's Janet Weis Children's Hospital and Level One Pediatric Trauma Center refused to stop efforts to save his life. It was amazing that the toddler had made it even this far, pulled from an icy stream hours earlier.

Paramedics started CPR almost immediately after a neighbor found little Gardell unresponsive in the water. That effort continued as the boy was taken to an excellent independent hospital in Lewisburg, Pennsylvania, and then transported by Geisinger's Life Flight helicopter to our advanced trauma center close by in Danville.

Frank Maffei, vice chairman of pediatrics, knew it didn't look good for Gardell, but he and more than 30 colleagues continued CPR, inserted a breathing tube, and worked to raise Gardell's body temperature, which had fallen to 77 degrees. An hour and 41 minutes passed before the boy's heart started beating again, a long time for his brain to be without oxygen. Dr. Maffei told Gardell's mother that he was alive, but there was concern about his brain function. That concern faded over the next few days as Gardell awakened and progressed. A week later, he was back home playing, acting as if nothing had happened.

The teamwork in this case was incredible, from the on-site paramedics to the community hospital emergency staff, Geisinger's Life Flight team, and colleagues at Geisinger Medical Center and Children's Hospital. No one gave up, and we have a happy ending to what certainly could have been a tragedy.

Geisinger regularly celebrates miracles such as this, patients who overcome amazing odds to recover from a wide variety of devastating illnesses and injuries. Similar lifesaving heroics occur daily at healthcare organizations across the United States and abroad.

However, Gardell's care, coupled with efforts to provide it cooperatively, efficiently, innovatively, and economically, highlight why Geisinger increasingly is considered the example of how healthcare can best be provided, not just in Pennsylvania, but throughout the nation and, indeed, the world.

Our innovative approach is known as ProvenCare®, and it is about ensuring that quality, cost-efficient care comes standard. Throughout our organization, we strive to deliver the right care at the right time and to treat everyone as though they were a member of our own family.

Systematically applying national guidelines and results from clinical trials and our own care reengineering studies, Geisinger team members work together to discover what kind of care works—and doesn't—and to develop reliable healthcare methods that improve quality, maximize safety, and get patients feeling better faster. For 10 ProvenCare acute and chronic services, we charge a flat fee that in essence includes a commitment or "warranty" to cover complications and readmissions for 90 days. Our value reengineering has revolutionized healthcare, increasing quality while decreasing cost.

Consider, for example, our anticoagulation therapy management service, which recently achieved best-in-world scores[1] for creating and offering an effective and safe anticoagulation plan for patients, an accomplishment that has caught people's attention far and wide. The experience of an elderly farmer who limped into Geisinger's primary care practice in rural Lewistown at 6:30 p.m. one evening demonstrates our high degree of care coordination. Within two hours, the patient was diagnosed as having deep vein clots in his legs and examined by ultrasound performed at the site but read in central radiology at Geisinger Medical Center in Danville. The patient was immediately started on an anticoagulation protocol designed and administered by the Danville anticoagulation clinic but performed on-site in Lewistown. By 9:00 p.m. he was back home with instructions to follow up with his primary care doctor, and a health navigator from Lewistown visited him the following day. His ultrasound images and interpretation, visit summary, therapeutic recommendations, and future course of treatment all were recorded directly in the patient's electronic health record (EHR) and sent with his permission to a daughter in Texas.

Other achievements of ProvenCare include:

- For coronary artery bypass graft surgery (CABG), a 67 percent decrease in mortality, a 4.8 percent decrease in cost per case, and a 17.6 percent increase in contribution margin
- With ProvenCare Perinatal, a decrease in C-section rates from 28 to 20 percent and a reduction in neonatal intensive care unit admissions from 9.4 percent to 5.9 percent
- With ProvenCare Knee, a reduction in average acute and rehabilitation time from 16 to 9.9 days

Since our founding in 1915, Geisinger has evolved from the original George F. Geisinger Hospital in Danville to become one of the nation's largest health systems—a physician-led, vertically integrated system with some 30,000 employees, including nearly 1,600 employed physicians, 13 hospital campuses, two research centers, a 583,000-member health plan, and Geisinger Commonwealth School of Medicine, all of which leverage an estimated $12.7 billion annual economic impact in central, south central, and northeast Pennsylvania and most recently in New Jersey.

Coauthors Glenn D. Steele Jr., who served as Geisinger president and CEO from 2001 to 2015, and David T. Feinberg, who in turn began his tenure as Geisinger's top leader in May 2015, both were attracted to the organization for the opportunity to accomplish real change to help patients. Dr. Steele became convinced that Geisinger could become a national laboratory for healthcare innovation not previously conceived or transacted anywhere, then oversaw a 15-year groundbreaking evolution. Dr. Feinberg perceived an opportunity to begin Geisinger's second century of service capitalizing on a legacy of innovation and elevating the patient experience to historic levels.

HEALTHCARE'S VALUE REENGINEERING CRUCIBLE

Geisinger's growth and success in healthcare value reengineering are due in large measure to:

- A systemwide culture of innovation and early adoption of best practices
- Pioneering implementation of the EHR

- A stable, loyal patient population
- The ability to permit and recover from failure
- An embedded health insurance unit partnering with clinicians to improve outcomes

Bedrock Culture of Innovation

Put simply, Geisinger does things differently. Our organization began a century ago, when Abigail Geisinger founded the Danville hospital in memory of her husband. Her charge to "make my hospital right, make it the best" defined the organization's founding mission and set the tone for a culture of caring and a never-ending quest toward perfection that continue to this day. Mrs. Geisinger modeled her hospital after Mayo Clinic and recruited her first chief medical officer, Harold Foss, who was on his way to private practice in Philadelphia following a fellowship with founder Will Mayo. Mrs. Geisinger insisted on an employed physician group, although today Geisinger has both employed and independent physicians on staff. Even over a hundred years ago she was concerned about cost and each day discussed with Dr. Foss the detailed expenses that patients in her hospital had to pay. With her directive to make it the best, Mrs. Geisinger inspired Dr. Foss to create a healthcare system grounded in the concepts of group practice and an interdisciplinary approach to patient care. A century later, Geisinger remains rooted in Mrs. Geisinger's vision of an organization unwilling to be bound by convention.

This propensity to innovate surfaced multiple times throughout Geisinger's history, including the development during the mid-1970s of our vertically integrated payer/provider fiduciary, Geisinger Health Plan (GHP). It was also during this time that CEO Henry Hood negotiated an important agreement with Geisinger's trustee so that our board of directors could select its chair instead of the trustee's chairman automatically serving as our board chair, a change Dr. Hood and his leadership team felt necessary for swift and appropriate forward movement. To better assist other hospitals approaching us for administrative and management advice, we formed a for-profit management corporation in 1978. Through regional expansion in the 1980s, we ensured that no matter where patients lived, they were within a half hour of a Geisinger doctor, and we attained the first certified adult and pediatric trauma center designation in a rural setting in 2002.

Vanguards in the Electronic Health Record

Geisinger's leadership made an incredibly wise and fortunate choice long ago to partner with Epic as the organization's EHR vendor. Quite remarkable in 1995, we decided to employ the EHR in the ambulatory setting before implementation in our hospitals, and Epic was the only EHR that had our desired functionality. Only after the ambulatory EHR was fully installed throughout Geisinger's 78 ambulatory sites in 42 counties were the two major inpatient facilities at that time converted from paper. There were growing pains, of course, with patients complaining that their caregivers were constantly pecking away at computer keyboards. But implementation became an efficient stabilizer and drove the reengineering that provided major productivity increases. Our EHR continues to be an important tool helping to drive innovation, and as Geisinger has expanded, we now work with both Epic and Cerner regarding EHR functionality.

Our EHR is a critical success factor in ProvenCare, providing the important information for clinicians to interact appropriately with patients. Histories, test results, and physician notes all are readily available, as well as best practice reminders to ensure that every patient receives the same level of care. For example, the EHR reminds clinicians about beta blockers and aspirin therapy for heart patients and ensures that we talk with patients regarding annual flu shots and other preventive care. And through our web-based portals, patients can connect easily with clinicians and access information to better understand and participate fully in care.

A Patient Population Unique in Stability and Loyalty

The population, particularly in central Pennsylvania around Geisinger Medical Center, is older, sicker, and poorer than just about any demography in the United States outside of the Deep South. It is extraordinarily homogeneous and stable, with approximately 15 percent of our patients being second and even third generation. The ability to change care and determine long-term effects over generations is a unique advantage that allows Geisinger to have a remarkably long vision.

In addition, the social values in the Geisinger patient population are traditional, old-time ones. Most of the men and women in this economically deprived area are incredibly family-oriented, see Geisinger as a great strength with significant credibility as both provider and payer, and still respect caregivers. Almost all of Geisinger's constituents are remarkably willing to participate in a variety of forward-thinking approaches, whether they involve attempts to change how Geisinger cares for type 2 diabetes or to create a new best practice for heart surgery. Patients readily accept Geisinger's assurances regarding genome sequencing that the information will remain confidential and be shared with them and their families, regardless of whether there's something that immediately affects how they live or should be cared for in the future.

The Ability to Permit and Recover from Failure

There are a number of other factors that enabled Geisinger to begin its ProvenCare innovation journey. For instance, our physician group is highly stable, with only six leaders in 100 years. We were one of the nation's first regional health systems and pioneers in the design of a rural hub-and-spoke delivery system, with primary care in 50-plus community sites throughout our service area. We made the transition from discipline-based physician care to 28 cross-disciplinary service lines with a patient-centered approach, not based on how specialists and subspecialists wanted to deliver care but on how patients and their families wanted care to be delivered. In the 1980s, we established clear-cut self-replicating governance for the entire entity.

However, among the most critical factors is a subtle institutional advantage: the ability to permit and recover from failure.

To illustrate, at the time of ProvenCare's inception, Geisinger had merged with Penn State Hershey Medical Center, from which we painfully demerged three years later. The period had been marked by lost clinical leadership and three years of posturing to see which culture would predominate, followed by a subsequent focused strategic intent to dissolve the marriage as quickly as possible.

The separation was a perfect time not simply to rebuild, but to do so in a way that would have a positive impact on healthcare throughout Geisinger and beyond. As we emerged from this failure, we asked, what could Geisinger do to help define a new vision for healthcare as it shifted from payment for volume to payment for value, particularly for a population of patients?

A consistent operational return was imperative to fund innovations to enhance patient care. We knew that not every innovation would be successful and that we would no doubt spend time and money on ideas that would not succeed. Operational recovery allowed Geisinger to develop and implement a set of radical innovations, where 15 to 20 percent failure could be allowed without putting at risk the balance sheet, operations, expansion, morale, or credibility with the Geisinger board of directors. We were able to remain true to our fiduciary responsibility, which then translated into improvements over time to our primary mission of taking better care of our patients. It would have been most difficult, for example, to cover the costs for complications without an overall strong organizational bottom line. Ultimately, our innovations all have been about doing what is right and best for patients. It has been our operational recovery and sustainability, though, that makes such enhancements possible.

Geisinger's Sweet Spot

Geisinger started an insurance company in the mid-1970s. Over the past 15 years in particular, we have attempted to change how our insurance company could work with its providers and members to move to higher quality at lower cost. While Geisinger contracts with most major insurances, and GHP contracts with numerous non-Geisinger providers, the sweet spot is those patients who are cared for by the Geisinger employed physicians and insured by a Geisinger insurance product. We were able to move ProvenCare forward because GHP partners with Geisinger clinicians to improve outcomes.

Our experiment worked out incredibly well, and we delivered on providing better care at lower cost. We set up a quality fund that was able to transfer literally tens of millions of dollars from the return on investment in attacking total cost of care. This was an immediate gain for the patients, decreasing the need for hospitalizations and rehospitalizations due to inadequately treated chronic diseases. It came directly back to the insurance company because of decreased costs, and those savings could be transferred to the providers (primary care and specialists) who were doing a better job taking care of their patients with illnesses such as diabetes, congestive heart failure, or chronic obstructive pulmonary disease. The internal transfer pricing allowed the benefit of the financial model to be redistributed to those who actually changed for the better how care was given. This all led to better outcomes and decreased need for acute care, which was the first major benefit in mitigating the total cost of care.

ACCLAIM FOR THE GEISINGER MODEL

When we started an effort to achieve nine best practice goals for our 30,000 type 2 diabetes patients, for example, we initially focused on the usual intermediate markers like hemoglobin A1C, microalbumin, pneumococcal vaccination, cholesterol, and blood pressure. What we really were interested in, however, was the actual long-term benefit to our diabetes patients who had been included in the improved bundle of best practices. We were pleased to find that there were 306 prevented heart attacks and 141 prevented strokes, compared to what would have been predicted, and 166 prevented cases of retinopathy, simply by having the patients cared for within our best practice value reengineering change.

Results such as these have drawn the world's attention and emulation. For example, the Commonwealth Fund, a private foundation dedicated to promoting a high-performing health-care system with improved access, quality, and efficiency, was well aware of what was taking place in Pennsylvania. The fund inventoried healthcare quality and value throughout the United States and made worldwide comparisons, consis-tently referencing Geisinger as one of the few high-quality/ low-cost delivery systems.[2] This is particularly noteworthy given Geisinger's medically needy, rural, and postindustrial market.

In 2007, the *New York Times* reported on the Proven-Care approach to CABG surgery in a major feature article.[3] "Geisinger's effort is noteworthy as a distinct departure from the typical medical reimbursement system in this country, under which doctors and hospitals are paid mainly for deliver-ing more care—not necessarily better care."

In 2009, President Barack Obama cited Geisinger before a joint session of Congress on healthcare.[4] "We have to ask why places like Geisinger in rural Pennsylvania . . . can offer high-quality care at costs well below average, but other places in America can't," he observed earlier that year in a Green Bay, Wisconsin, town hall meeting.[5]

In the June 11, 2012, *TIME* magazine cover story "How to Die: What I Learned from the Last Days of my Mom and Dad," political columnist Joe Klein described Geisinger as a model for providing better care in an economic manner and Geisinger physicians as understanding, compassionate, profes-sional, and intent on doing what was best for the patient, rather than driving revenue-producing volume.[6]

On November 11, 2015, *U.S. News & World Report* cited our commitment to refund all or part of the copay for spine and bariatric surgery to patients dissatisfied with their care, calling this "the latest, and perhaps most radical, innovation of a system recognized for continually reinventing medical care."[7] Feedback and service recovery are processed via a mobile app.

As other healthcare organizations became interested in Geisinger's unusual success in changing how care was delivered, they initially doubted that our innovations could be applied and sustained in their particular cultures, fiduciary structures, and demographics. This trepidation about scaling and generalizing elsewhere has evaporated, and our care reengineering and population health techniques have been adopted by health systems outside Pennsylvania.

Several clients across four states all have shown similar results to what was achieved in Geisinger's traditional service area with our unique structure and sociology. For example, the accomplishments of one Virginia client partnered with Geisinger include growing the health system from four to seven hospitals; integrating the medical group and expanding it to more than 450 physicians; establishing 32 advanced patient-centered medical home sites that have improved physician productivity; optimizing payments with managed care and the Centers for Medicare & Medicaid Services, increasing downstream revenues, decreasing downside risk by reducing 30-day readmission rates from 2.96 percent to 0.82 percent, and securing managed care contracts for medical home; implementing ProvenCare Navigator CABG at two hospitals; and securing risk-sharing contracts with three major insurers.

This book is about how Geisinger has reengineered healthcare value and quality. We demonstrate that our principles are applicable anywhere, tell you how we did it, share our success secrets as well as what didn't work, and reveal where we're going next. The goal is nothing short of a complete transformation of the U.S. healthcare industry into one that provides affordable coverage for all, payment for value rather than volume, care coordination, continuous improvement and innovation, and empowered patients and their families who are active partners in care. Join us in the revolution!

2

The Problem

"Aunt Mary" enjoys a big celebratory meal on Thursday evening while visiting with her extended family. But because the 75-year-old woman—who suffers from chronic congestive heart failure—doesn't take her diuretic as directed that day, along with 14 other medications, she gains 5 to 10 pounds of water weight. Sometime on Friday she becomes short of breath and calls 911.

Paramedics rush her to a local hospital's emergency department, where she is treated and stabilized by well-meaning doctors who have never treated her before and can't access her medical records. They aren't in touch with Aunt Mary's primary care physician, so the doctors admit her for a few days to be "tuned up," just to be extra careful. She returns home without genuinely understanding her new medication instructions. So Aunt Mary ignores her congestive heart failure until she finds herself in another emergency situation, and the cycle repeats.

Patients with chronic diseases, such as congestive heart failure, coronary artery disease, diabetes, and hypertension, and the often-accompanying depression, are the 10 to 20 percent who account for 80 to 90 percent of healthcare spending,[1] simply because their care is not optimal.

Wouldn't it be better to manage these "Aunt Mary" patients proactively in a true provider/patient/family partnership to improve their health and health outcomes, while utilizing fewer inpatient services and decreasing the family's, as well as society's, costs? In short, increasing healthcare's value?

Geisinger has consistently pursued the answer to this question.

CHAOS IN U.S. HEALTHCARE

Two factors intersected to set the stage for Geisinger to lead: a chaotic U.S. healthcare environment and our system reeling from a failed merger.

Well before passage of the Patient Protection and Affordable Care Act (ACA) in 2010, U.S. healthcare needed fundamental redesign: the system cost too much, had no wide application of best practice or evidence-based care, and all too often provided care that did not benefit patients.

In addition, under the traditional fee-for-service, payment-by-volume system, healthcare providers actually generated more revenue when patients experienced complications requiring additional care. Most crassly, this was getting as many "heads in beds" and performing as many tests and procedures as possible, regardless of whether they made a difference. In addition, some insurers were reluctant to dive headfirst into payment-for-value, because they were doing so well in the fee-for-service system, particularly as leverage in decreasing payments to providers per unit of work was growing due to insurance company consolidation.

Conversely, a relatively small group of value-driven providers, including Geisinger, was involving patients and families as partners in maintaining health and in obtaining healthcare. Their focus was on wellness and prevention, ensuring that patients received the care they needed when and where they needed it, and on healthcare value, meaning better outcomes and lower cost. The question was whether these interesting and promising models could be scaled and generalized.

Then there were the health policy experts, regulators, and well-meaning government administrators who understood that healthcare needed to change, but carried with their good intent the challenges often present when government intervenes. So Washington took action and passed the ACA, which is essentially health insurance reform. It began to address the need for everyone to have insurance, which is an appropriate and admirable goal, but core issues remain regarding how care is provided and financed. The post-ACA environment continues to be turbulent because of new leadership in Washington, D.C., as well as changing expectations among patients, caregivers, healthcare payers, and taxpayers.

U.S. healthcare's transformation should include:

- Affordable health insurance coverage for all
- A move to payment for value and outcome, rather than volume
- Best practice, coordinated care
- Continuous innovation
- Patients and their families empowered and active partners with providers in managing health and getting care

TURMOIL WITHIN GEISINGER

Separate from the chaos in the overall healthcare environment in the years leading up to the ACA, we had our own problems at Geisinger. We were among a handful of providers attempting consolidation in the 1990s, along with the predecessors of Partners HealthCare in Boston, Mount Sinai and New York University hospitals and schools of medicine in New York City, and the University of California San Francisco and Stanford University medical schools in the Bay Area. There was tremendous national buzz around these unusual, and largely doomed, marriages.

We had a full-asset merger with Penn State Hershey Medical Center, including the medical school. It did not go well.

The merger was strategically sound, combining Geisinger's clinical strengths and significant provider and payer market share in rural Pennsylvania with the strong, aspirational medical school culture at Hershey in a good demographic cohort in south central Pennsylvania. But the lack of understanding regarding how to mesh two very different institutional cultures and create a constituent governance led to a dysfunctional three-year marriage. The combined Geisinger–Penn State board had the temerity to make the big bet in the first place and the wisdom to end the merger quickly when the transaction began to blow up.

Our financial condition at the time of the demerger was bleak, caused by a number of factors including no strategic program plan, ill-defined leadership roles, inadequate capital resources, no accountability, no incentives based on accomplishment, and the constriction of clinical delivery resources for a number of years. In addition, our insurance company had only two products: Geisinger Gold, a Medicare HMO product with year-over-year low federal reimbursement increases of 1 to 2 percent, and a commercial HMO offering. Not only were two of the three Geisinger operating businesses (the hospital and clinic) sustaining significant operating losses, the purported success of the third operating business (the insurance company) in fact was due to internal transfer pricing and moving as much of the risk as possible to the providers during the annual budget process.

In addition, Geisinger suffered from institutional post-traumatic stress that dated back even before the merger and accelerated during the three-year dysfunctional marriage, and this went way beyond low morale. A number of excellent clinical leaders at Geisinger, fearing that Hershey would dominate in the merged entity, had left the organization. Numerous clinical training programs either degenerated or were shut down in anticipation of new consolidated programs based in the Hershey Medical School academic departments. The repetitive implementation of inflexible expense management templates also contributed mightily to the institutional malaise.

Personal and group aspirations were slumping in a sort of mediocrity-driven quid pro quo for presumed quality-of-life gains. Some were willing to work for less (not simply money, but also lower group goals) in order to live in a perceived lower-stress, higher-quality-of-life environment.

Although we were structured as a truly vertically integrated system, including the insurance company and all providers in our combined fiduciary, we didn't function in an integrated way. Instead, the insurance company saw the providers and hospitals as the enemy and vice versa. Each constituency was vocal in its opinion regarding the best way to fix the organization. "Sell the insurance company," said the doctors. "Get those doctors under control," said the insurance company leaders.

MOVING FORWARD TO
SEIZE THE VALUE SPACE

This environment turned out to be an ideal starting place to reinvent the organization. In such a setting, people are more likely to welcome new ideas and new goals, so it's easier to introduce and implement a new set of aspirations and, in our case at that time, a new compensation plan.

Strategic discussion focused on determining whether Geisinger would be a local/regional system or whether we could foster national and even international aspirations. While remaining true to our local and regional service area, new leadership at Geisinger saw the opportunity to make a positive difference beyond our traditional geography.

Two critical factors drove much of Geisinger's commitment to innovate: a RAND study published in the *New England Journal of Medicine* in 2003[2] and the data from Arnold Milstein, cofounder of The Leapfrog Group and the Consumer-Purchaser Disclosure Project in the 1980s and '90s, demonstrating that there was no relationship between the cost of care and quality-of-care outcomes in the United States.[3] These were personal epiphanies for Dr. Steele that informed his understanding of how healthcare should be reengineered to unlock a significant amount of value. As CEO, he used these findings as the predicates for all the subsequent acute care and chronic disease management changes that would cascade throughout the organization and create the momentum for doing something at Geisinger that could not easily be done in nonintegrated healthcare systems.

The *NEJM* article was particularly telling. The researchers looked at prevalent hospital-associated care episodes in different U.S. markets and concluded that almost 45 percent of care was suboptimal, evenly split between too much, too little, and the wrong care.

Geisinger perceived this as a major opportunity. One-sixth of the U.S. economy was healthcare related, and if up to 45 percent of the cost did not bring benefit to those served, or, in fact, may have harmed those served, we could create value simply by extracting some significant amount of this unnecessary or hurtful cost.

Our second belief was an evolution from Dr. Milstein's thinking that there was no relationship between healthcare cost and quality to an understanding that the relationship between cost and quality actually was inverse. More often than not, patients with the worst outcomes were those whose costs were highest. We were able to define populations of patients who had the worst outcomes based on patients who had the highest costs. Clearly, the table was set to improve care in a cost-effective way.

These two beliefs led to a remarkable convergence in our professionals' motivation to reengineer care fundamentally. We knew that posing the transformation challenge as a cost-cutting maneuver would not engage our physicians. So instead, we used high cost as a surrogate for poor outcome and focused reengineering efforts on achieving better outcomes for patients, with decreased costs as a collateral benefit. Thus it was professional pride of purpose that energized the Geisinger clinicians.

With the unlocked value from removing useless or hurtful cost in healthcare delivery, we were not simply aspiring to grow into a larger version of a good community hospital; rather, we created a truly integrated healthcare delivery organization committed to healing, teaching the next generation of providers, discovering new knowledge through translational research, and serving patients and the community as a national model for innovation.

Our approach to rebuilding was to develop clinical programs and market share, with the overall mission of improving healthcare value. We would:

- Build more specialty and subspecialty programs and demand, both of which were remarkably absent in the central and northeast Pennsylvania markets
- Solve substantial access issues and stop the leakage of referrals out of Geisinger
- Open the organization's payer mix to Blue Cross of Northeastern Pennsylvania (now part of Highmark), Capital BlueCross, Coventry Health Care, and Highmark
- Incentivize physicians who wanted to take better care of patients
- Expand the organization's research and education initiatives through a redeployment of unlocked value

While the alternative of starting our value reengineering projects with less well-led services, such as perinatal care and bariatric surgery, was considered, we chose to identify high-probability early wins that would establish quickly what was possible at Geisinger and eventually could be developed into a national model. We would build momentum by beginning with programs or services that already had excellent clinical leadership and good outcomes prior to reengineering. We settled on coronary artery bypass grafting as our beta test. Success ultimately resulted in the full portfolio of 25 Geisinger Proven-Care Acute, ProvenCare Chronic, and ProvenHealth Navigator programs.

The considerable enthusiasm and excitement around what could be accomplished at Geisinger to enhance healthcare value and help solve the nation's healthcare challenges aided us in recruiting strong new leaders who surrounded themselves with associates truly motivated to deliver superb care. We attracted highly accomplished physicians from across the country and beyond to come to central and northeast Pennsylvania, in large part because they saw we were being innovative and getting results. Geisinger was viewed as one of the most exceptional models of care in the world due to our reengineering vision and its transaction.

Given the increasingly complex nature of healthcare, we implemented triad leadership partnerships: physician, administrative, and financial leaders working together and accepting joint accountability for a service line or hospital platform's operational performance, on both the revenue and the expense sides. Leaders conceptualized their areas of responsibility as small businesses and ran them accordingly. This partnership model enabled physicians to lead by practicing great medicine. When you have compelling physician leaders who expertly perform cardiac surgery or manage a complex chronic disease constellation, for example, you want them to continue to have adequate time and energy to care for patients and not be consumed analyzing a P&L statement or human resource policy. But they need to be surrounded by the necessary administrative and financial expertise.

This clear strategy for organizational recovery resulted in sustained operational gains, fueled in large part by our rebuild of the clinical caregiving capacity, the new hospital-based specialty and subspecialty programs, and huge productivity increases for the population care delivered by our community practice service line. Within two years postmerger, the three major businesses were in the black and our financial trajectory was extraordinarily positive. We then began thinking more and more about how innovations at Geisinger could be scalable and generalizable elsewhere. Our health system was well on its way to making a positive difference beyond central and northeast Pennsylvania.

LESSONS LEARNED

- Suboptimal care drives healthcare cost.
- Patients with the worst outcomes usually have the highest costs.
- Removing unnecessary or hurtful care creates value.
- Physician leadership is critical in reengineering care.
- Physician leaders must be respected clinicians and should be surrounded by administrative and financial partners.
- Focusing on providing the best care when and where patients need it drives physician performance.

3

The Fix

It's helpful to think about Geisinger after the turn of the millennium in terms of three five-year plans. Our first five-year strategy (2001–05) centered on getting operations in order post-demerger, and we achieved this in about half the time. The accelerated success allowed us to start discussion early regarding the second five-year plan (2006–10), which focused on fundamentally changing care delivery and developing and implementing innovative approaches to providing additional quality and value for patients and insurance company members. After successful and sustainable innovation within our own system, we then began to concentrate on scaling and generalizing to other systems and markets in our third five-year plan (2011–15).

Laying the groundwork for our three plans started with systematic and extensive Geisinger-wide conversations with almost all employees. We talked about who we were and who we wanted to be. We discussed what was different and unique at Geisinger and what we could do that other well-meaning organizations would find difficult, even though they too had good people, strong commitment, and unique excellence.

OUR SINGLE MOST IMPORTANT DECISION

It emerged that the most obvious difference in our structure and a potential advantage was having both the provider and payer functions within one organization. Geisinger was one of the first to build out a payer from its provider structure, initially in partnership with Capital BlueCross in the 1970s and then solely as a stand-alone insurance company.

This vertically integrated payer/provider model had begun to be questioned in the 1990s. For nearly a decade, many respected, well-known consulting firms made the rounds to various provider-associated and provider-owned insurance companies recommending that the two businesses be disconnected. The stated rationale was that the business models in insurance and clinical caregiving were generally 180 degrees off cycle. If the insurance company was making money, the providers were not; if the providers were transacting a huge amount of health-care and making money, the insurance companies were getting hurt financially. The unstated rationale was that provider-owned organizations just didn't have the skills to run insurance companies.

No one had intuited the benefit of a functional payer/provider overlap in the reengineering of care or the possible synergies of payer and provider working together not only to align incentives, but to maximize data exchange pinpointing hospital-based and ambulatory patients most likely to benefit from care reengineering.

The concept of bilaterally attacking total cost of care by improving patient/member outcome was unheard of. Naturally, the financial benefit of any decrease in total cost of care would come to the insurance company. But since both payer and provider at Geisinger were in the same organization, it didn't matter who won financially as long as patients benefited. We could get the financial affirmation back to whomever deserved it by internal transfer pricing, and if the total cost of care went down, we could remain insurance-market competitive by lowering prices of insurance premiums.

Many organizations structured like Geisinger, including Virginia Mason Health System in Seattle, were convinced to sell their insurance companies at the time, and we too took steps in that direction, upon the recommendation of a respected consulting firm.

However, after determining the value of our health plan for a possible sale, we decided to build the value of the insurance products ourselves before any subsequent reconsideration of selling. Additionally, we began to speculate that a fundamentally different payer/provider partnership might be the key to an unprecedented bilateral payer/provider approach to reengineering care for prevalent hospital-based and ambulatory diseases. Keeping the health plan was the single most important strategic decision we made.

MOVING THE CULTURE

Our conjoined payer/provider engine in time fundamentally changed how we produced value for all patients, but the evolution was not inevitable. Moving the culture from our polarized payer-versus-provider battle was the key. In 2001, there were basically only two health plan products at Geisinger, both classic HMOs: a commercial HMO and a Medicare Advantage Plan. There was no PPO product, despite almost all of our business clients and potential individual members being interested in something other than a classic restricted-provider HMO network. Our health plan basically was showing a profit only because it shifted most of the risk to our doctors and hospitals. The plan reimbursed both Geisinger and non-Geisinger providers as little as possible, despite the credibility of the Geisinger brand to patients and insurance company members. We were despised widely among both employed and nonemployed providers at the start of 2000, and we were undoubtedly the lowest-priced medical insurance product on the market. This was not a good place to be.

Upon changing the insurance company's leadership and introducing a variety of new products and market pricing strategies, GHP actually made a profit. This improved the longstanding antagonistic relationship between the insurance company and both employed and nonemployed providers, since their reimbursement improved. Only after all of this occurred could we ask the essential question: What can Geisinger do because of our unique fiduciary structure, culture, demography, and informatics that other well-intentioned, committed health systems could never do?

Of course, Geisinger also benefited from the Medicare Advantage reimbursement increases that were built into the Medicare Modernization Act (MMA) in 2003 and the year-over-year risk severity increases built into something called Hierarchical Condition Categories (HCCs) that began even before the MMA. The HCCs singlehandedly changed the Medicare Advantage business model. It meant that instead of avoiding the sickest members, plans like the Geisinger Gold Medicare HMO could enroll high-severity and high-acuity members, take better care of them, and do well financially.

This was the perfect business model for us to begin our attack on the 30 to 40 percent of unnecessary costs routinely built into healthcare delivery and shown to be either unhelpful or even hurtful to patients. With both payer and provider in the same fiduciary assuming population risk sharing, this remarkable confluence of internal commitment to value reengineering and external good fortune proved a perfect time to test the concept of achieving better outcome at lower cost.

The insurance company baseline for developing our sweet spot was built on two fundamental concepts. The first was that every product developed by GHP needed to float on its own financial bottom. The second was that each of the products had to bring something special to the provider/payer joint commitment to reengineer care toward higher quality at lower cost.

We initially focused almost all of our care and payment innovations on the 50 percent of patients we treated as well as insured. This was the perfect pilot for subsequently changing all hospital-based and ambulatory care to increase quality while decreasing cost. The CEO of insurance operations at Geisinger was also an executive vice president of the overall Geisinger organization, including the provider side. This intentional overlap in titles and responsibility meant that this senior leader had two explicit obligations: one to the sustainability and dynamism of the insurance operations and the second to the holistic effects of the insurance operations plus the clinical enterprise on Geisinger's overall strategic plan accomplishment.

HIGHER QUALITY AT LOWER COST

Our second five-year plan explicitly concentrated on fundamental care redesign based on the new payer/provider sweet spot concept. It must be emphasized that best practice reengineered care was provided to all patients regardless of whether they were insured by a Geisinger insurance product. This was consistent with our commitment to innovation no matter who insured our patients or whether they had insurance.

Within Geisinger's fiduciary structure, it didn't matter who made the profit as long as the patients and insurance members received higher quality at lower cost. Both payer and provider sides of the organization were committed to benefit our mutual constituency. The ability to perform internal transfer pricing if we achieved a significant decrease in total cost of care allowed us to move as much of the added value as needed to whatever provider component deserved it. This was a huge functional and structural advantage in the iterative processes of clinical innovation. We were not locked into long-term negotiated contracts between payer and provider in the usual way, where the big question always was which side could out-game the other side financially. And we were not worried about which part of the organization won and which lost financially in the reengineering process.

We were concerned only with giving better care at lower cost. The best way to make a systemwide profit was to decrease the total cost of care. The proximate benefit almost always went to the insurance company, but we could redistribute an appropriate part of this value creation back to the part of the system that actually created the value. In addition, a portion of the value was redistributed to the buyers of our clinical services by competitive market-based pricing of insurance premiums.

There were two other significant advantages in moving from conceptualization of the payer/provider sweet spot to its actual transaction. The first was the substantial strength Geisinger had on both the provider and payer sides. This was a function of the credibility of the holistic Geisinger brand.

People we served believed in Geisinger and were willing recipients and participants in our care-delivery reengineering because they trusted us. A second significant advantage was Geisinger's ability to feed almost real-time data from both the payer and provider sides back to the providers at the point of care. This was an extension of Geisinger's long-term commitment to an electronic health record (EHR). Reengineering would have been impossible without near real-time data enabling provider behavior change.

Fundamental apps, data warehousing, data analytics, customization of payer/provider data for immediate and easy use by providers, and new evidence of interoperability between various information technology systems continue to be critical enablers to help us change the behaviors of both caregivers and patients. The ability to use predictive analytics from insurance company claims data and to customize and present utilization variance data to providers in a way that is not only timely but immediately usable has been key.

At the beginning of the new relationship between our payer and our providers, the doctors were surprised to learn that there was important information other than reimbursement to be obtained from the insurance company, including data regarding which patients were the highest utilizers during a given year or which physicians were using the most resources and not following protocols. What is now taken for granted, that the patients who were the highest utilizers in the past year likely would be the highest utilizers in the coming year, was a breakthrough thought at the time. Predictive analytics using insurance company claims data allowed us to target specific groups of neediest patient populations and calculate where we would have the highest probability of changing the worst outcomes. We used this information to stratify the most intense care for the highest utilizers. Our Geisinger version of advanced medical home care, ProvenHealth Navigator, focused first on the highest-utilizing, sickest members. We used a different ratio of nurse practitioners or care managers when caring for patients defined by insurance company claims analyses as being less sick. Real-time data from our EHR data warehouse ensured that providers were following best practice protocols every time. The design of that best practice approach and our assurance that it actually was being carried out was dependent on both insurance company and provider data availability. With Geisinger having payer and provider in the same organization, we were able to ensure that this process worked, a feat not easily accomplished in non-vertically integrated payer/provider relationships.

LINKING INCENTIVES AND FUNDAMENTAL CHANGE

Our ongoing systematic strategic prioritization process was linked early on to an evolving approach to compensation for providers as well as clinical and administrative leadership. Initially, we felt the need to change incentives to address the post-demerger operational malaise and get Geisinger's three major businesses (hospitals, clinics, and insurance company) financially viable and sustainable. When the operating trends became extraordinarily positive, the strategic focus turned to quality and innovation as an added and important part of affirmation and compensation.

Innovation was defined at Geisinger as fundamentally changing how we cared for patients with prevalent diseases, not simply checking off quality metrics boxes on the margin. Quality was defined as fundamental change in morbidity and mortality, cost, and patient and professional satisfaction outcomes. Our assumption was that fundamentally changing much of what we did in our routine clinical caregiving would improve process metrics. But being subservient to metrics was not the intention. We were not "teaching to the test." Rather, the intention was to fundamentally change how care was given to the benefit of patients with acute and chronic diseases. We were striving to create Geisinger as its own new model of a continuous innovation machine, not simply attempting to be a mediocre version of an academic medical center or a larger version of a good community hospital.

A new compensation plan was designed so that all physicians and leaders within the organization understood they would do better if they achieved their part of the overall system's strategic aims. Accomplishments and rewards were linked directly to innovation. The choice of specific innovation or quality projects for each of the service lines, hospital platforms, discipline-based entities, or insurance company components was a discussion that began with the frontline caregiver or insurance leader. Some 20 percent of total compensation was linked to achieving specific strategic goals, as opposed to simply seeing more patients, having a bigger panel of patients, or performing services with higher relative value units. More than 20 percent of total compensation for leadership was based on whether various strategic aims were achieved.

How we paid our employees was the engine ensuring that the strategic plan would be aligned and affirmed throughout the organization. We believed it was critical that everyone felt evaluated in the same way, achieving not only standardized productivity benchmarks but also the strategic innovations that would make the Geisinger brand well known and perhaps unique over time.

ROLLOUT OF THE STRATEGIC VISION

To obtain employee buy-in, Dr. Steele made it a personal priority to deliver the strategic vision by interacting with as many members of the organization as possible. This led to between 55 and 65 annual town hall meetings with every conceivable component of both the provider and payer sides of Geisinger. We regularly communicated with support services, patients, insurance company members, and local community leaders in each major market. It was important for the CEO to be seen and to have the opportunity to tell employees and others why we needed to innovate, why Geisinger was the perfect place to innovate, and why really good people at other good organizations might not be able to do what we were doing.

Our first strategic vision presentations began by referring to our touchstone, founder Abigail Geisinger. Geisinger's "heal, teach, discover, serve" mission was applied as the core of our new endeavors. Discussions with various operating and support units started with where we were at the time of demerger, a summary of the unique demographics in our distinct market areas, what was special about Geisinger, and how we might build a strategy and program portfolio that would utilize our special structure and culture to differentiate us from other great organizations.

Our thought here was that success was most likely if expectations were tailored to specific strengths and structural/ cultural aspects of Geisinger. Although fundamental change would be required, we wanted the process to honor the heritage of our founder, who a century ago demanded, "Make my hospital right, make it the best."

The development of our strategic vision began with a repetition of a completely unaltered Geisinger mission: "to enhance the quality of life through an integrated health services organization based on a balanced program of patient care, education, research, and community service." We then linked the mission to four golden rules: quality, value, partnerships, and advocacy. With a minimum of top-down manipulation and a huge amount of bottom-up socialization, our first four strategic aims became:

- Grow the clinical enterprise
- Innovate healthcare delivery
- Expand and focus research and education
- Provide a national voice for rural healthcare

These aims were contextualized as what Mrs. Geisinger would want us to do. They were connected to significant resources already committed in our expanding utilization of the EHR, and they publicly acknowledged an immediate need for developing innovative ways to reengineer care.

The progress report in our annual strategic vision presentations became the backbone of our communication strategy. We wanted everyone at Geisinger to know what the mission and strategic aims were, and how each individual's work connected to our overall successes and challenges. It didn't matter if we were talking with heart surgeons, neuroscientists, food service employees, or members of our security team. Everyone was included, and everyone was part of the Geisinger story. We would succeed or fail together.

We could not start the fundamental care innovation without changing our operational trajectory. As we grew our way out of the postmerger malaise, we began the second systematic strategy discussions in anticipation of new operational health.

The ultimate goal was to provide significant and increasing benefit to those we served from the clinical enterprise as well as from the payer side of the organization, our patients and insurance members. Expanding into ever-greater operational strength and higher operating margins, although an exciting change for us, was not our primary purpose. It was the new operational strength that enabled us to finance our risk-taking care reengineering and innovation.

The second five-year strategic aim set, again evolving from an extensive and systematic discussion with as many Geisinger employees as possible, coalesced as:

- Strive for perfection in quality
- Expand the clinical market
- Sustain innovation
- Secure the legacy

All of these were direct extensions or modifications of our first five-year goal set, and all were predicated on continuing operational success. We insisted on aggressive growth and adequate performance to budget. A fundamental change from the first to the second strategic vision set, however, was growing recognition that Geisinger quality targets, and in particular our nascent national reputation for innovating how we provided care, were rapidly improving our brand. This allowed us to more aggressively recruit and retain employees, since we were now recruiting from a national market. The people we recruited and retained were key to building our conventional as well as our more innovative programs.

Finally, our third five-year strategic aim set was a direct extension of our previous four strategic aims. We already had achieved major national recognition. We already had built ProvenCare Acute and ProvenHealth Navigator, as well as the bundled best practice ProvenCare Chronic innovation portfolios. We combined quality and innovation into a single top strategic aim. Market growth was modified into something more nuanced, and we thought more sophisticated, called market leadership. Plus, a substantive component of that market leadership aim now committed us to scaling and generalizing the Geisinger innovations outside Pennsylvania.

Without a doubt, scaling and generalizing was the biggest aspiration. Many organizations and individuals visiting Geisinger over the past decade had seen progressive credibility and sustainability in the value reengineering accomplished in our traditional service area. But they almost always ended their stay in Geisinger Shangri-La by claiming that nothing they saw could ever be accomplished in their particular market with their particular fiduciary structure or culture.

We became progressively more frustrated with the skepticism, especially given that Geisinger was being touted as a model for healthcare reform in the great Obamacare debates. We almost felt compelled to include scaling and generalizing as a logical next specific aim under our market leadership strategy. This led to the question of how to transact scaling and generalizing, which in turn led to three separate scaling and generalizing operational engines at Geisinger.

The first was our merger and acquisition activity. Could we do in Wilkes-Barre/Scranton and eventually Harrisburg, Pennsylvania, and in Atlantic City, New Jersey, what we had done in the Danville, Pennsylvania, Central Susquehanna region of the Geisinger payer/provider sweet spot? A second scaling and generalizing engine was our insurance operations moving beyond Pennsylvania and attempting to do with non-Geisinger providers and in non-Geisinger markets what we had accomplished with our value reengineering in our traditional service area. Finally, the third engine was the establishment of xG Health Solutions, a for-profit Geisinger spin-off joint venture committed to spreading our intellectual property in population health, value reengineering of acute and chronic care, and reformulation of the payer/provider relationship.

LESSONS LEARNED

We can't overemphasize the importance of communication in achieving our goals. Communication was repetitive and progressively simplified, delivered to a larger and increasingly complex organization. Approaches have evolved: for example, Geisinger grew from approximately 7,000 to about 30,000 employees during the past 15 years, making town hall meetings more challenging and time-consuming. However, CEO visibility is essential to demonstrating the importance of targets and operational successes that enable achievement of long-term strategy. The concrete link between strategic goal accomplishment and payment incentives throughout the organization is equally important.

In summary:

- Good operational performance is a necessary foundation for innovation.
- Know your special culture, structure, market demography, and pedigree.
- Build from what is special (and felt to be special).
- Capturing attention and establishing a strategy in a large, complex organization is easier after an institutional near-death experience.
- CEO communication is imperative.
- As the organization becomes larger and more complex, the strategy aim set must become more repetitive and simpler.
- All organizational members need to be aligned in achieving individual and group success.

4

Effective Governance

A team is only as good as its ownership. This is especially true in times of great change, stress, cultural transformation, and innovation. Geisinger's board structure over the years serves as a good case study for the importance of effective governance, adapting to major changes in the organization and in the healthcare industry. Geisinger's evolution from a regional provider to a nationally recognized, vertically integrated health services delivery and payer model could not have happened without a simultaneous evolution in board composition, structure, and aspiration.

The fundamental Geisinger governance structure and function was first set up in 1981 with the creation of a single functional governing board, which became the Geisinger Health System Foundation (now Geisinger Health Foundation) Board, a self-replicating, single fiduciary that serves as the parent for the entire organization. Under this structure, all other Geisinger boards were controlled by the foundation board. This straightforward, single fiduciary ensured that there would be no silo thinking at the top of the organization. What mattered most was what would enable Geisinger as a holistic system to deliver the best quality and best value care. At least at the governance level, it mattered less how the various components of the system—hospitals, doctor group, and insurance company—stacked up against each other in the annual budgeting and capital allocation processes. This single, all-inclusive fiduciary integration remained our core bellwether of "systemness" until the 2014 merger with Holy Spirit Health System in Harrisburg, and subsequently the merger with AtlantiCare in New Jersey, when the foundation board needed to delegate some components of its fiduciary responsibility to local market system boards and became, to an extent, a holding corporation.[1]

During the unsuccessful three-year merger (1997–2000) between Geisinger and Penn State Hershey Medical Center, the merged-entity board, although a single unified fiduciary, was constituent-based with a 50-50 split between appointments from Penn State Hershey and appointments from Geisinger. Unfortunately, the cultural disparity of the two systems, plus the constituent governance model with 50-50 participation, quickly led to polarization.

Two conclusions can be drawn from this brief, unhappy episode. First, the Geisinger board could take major chances on fundamental transformation. Second, when failure became obvious, the board wisely and quickly unwound the merger before mortal damage was done to either institution. While the Geisinger board felt seared by this merger experiment and avoided complex new fiduciary structures in the near term,[2] the merger and its interim constituency governance did not fundamentally change the unique integrated fiduciary structure that had been in place since 1981. Simple, straightforward governance remained a core strength that helped bring Geisinger back to operational health and to its core mission.

Sustained, effective board leadership started at the top with a well-respected chairman, whose credibility was so great that he remained the chairman before, during, and after the unsuccessful merger. At the time of the demerger, and with an interim CEO holding down the fort, the Geisinger board found itself in the unenviable position of serving in a much more operational role than intended or appropriate. Board committees were involved with granular management issues that are important functions, but not true fiduciary responsibilities.

During the immediate postmerger malaise, the board met monthly, focused on details such as the number of charts that remained to be dictated by the discharging physicians, and typically ended the meetings with a review of medical malpractice cases, which was not an inspiring way to move forward. During the three-year dysfunctional marriage, the only strategic goal had been to get divorced as soon as possible. Management was focused only on preparing for each month's board meeting, rather than attempting to develop a new strategic vision or looking at the fundamentals necessary to turn the operations around. Changing the board meeting frequency first to every other month, then quickly to a quarterly schedule was a function of increased management credibility as a positive operational performance trajectory became evident.

More important than the change in board meeting frequency were changes in committee structure and functions, board culture, composition, and agendas. All of this was intended to conform to what was becoming a much more strategic management and board alignment. The key to the transformation was a unified stance in the critical leadership partnering between board chairman and CEO. In any complex organization, but particularly in a nonprofit entity undergoing a massive transformation, there can be no space between the chair and the CEO. Strategic agreement, confidence in each other's tasks, and response to setbacks all demand leadership unity. Not once in the almost 15 years Dr. Steele shared with two board chairs was he ever distracted from the fundamental work to improve healthcare value. At the CEO transition to Dr. Feinberg, it was up to the board to determine the direction of the next leg of the system's journey.

Within one year post-demerger, Geisinger had expanded the audit, management and compensation, and nominating and governance committees; created a medical affairs committee; and changed the function of the investment committee from hiring and firing fund managers to creating and monitoring the rules for and hiring of an outsourced chief investment officer. The finance committee assumed responsibility not only for annual budgets, but also extensive long-range financial modeling and planning.[3] The new strategic plan was linked to this rolling three-year financial model as the organization stretched to meet aspirational, innovative goals ensuring that we would maintain a sufficient annual operating margin and rebuild the balance sheet overall.

The management and compensation committee, along with senior management, instituted fundamental change in how we paid doctors and how we held all Geisinger employees accountable for achieving strategic goals, not just increasing units of work. The link between board-level supervision of the new incentive plan and management's ability to transact the new strategic aim of innovating healthcare delivery became critical.

Through our medical affairs committee agenda, we ended each board meeting with data and examples reminding everyone what we actually were most dedicated to: caring for patients and improving the health status of insurance company members. This routinely brought all of us, including the board members, back home to the meaning of all of the fiduciary tasks. Most important, we ended each board session with a presentation by clinical caregivers about something innovative, high-quality, challenging, or new related to one of our strategic aims. Most often, these vignettes exemplified the new cooperative interaction we were struggling to affirm between the payer and the provider sides of the Geisinger system.

In addition to focusing on our core mission of caring for people, these presentations exposed providers and sometimes even patients to the board directors, which was remarkably gratifying to all involved. Those who presented were celebrated, and board members could see the incredible dedication, quality, and accomplishments of our team members, as well as the success of our recruitment efforts.[4]

Geisinger governance, of course, is blessed (or further complicated) by the fact that the health system includes not only a clinical enterprise, but also an insurance company. As Geisinger Health Plan grew in membership and expanded its product offerings, it soon became apparent that the fiduciary of the foundation board and the fiduciary of the insurance company board needed to be redesigned.

In addition, the Allina Health System legal challenge in 2002 brought the matter of potential conflict in all vertically integrated health organizations to a head when the Minnesota attorney general indicted Allina for having insufficient fiduciary separation between the insurance and provider sides of its fiduciary structure and insufficient oversight of purported or real conflicts of interest.[5] While our situation and structure was quite different, we sought outside legal advice to optimize our fiduciary template, which led to significant changes in the composition and function of the Geisinger Health Plan board.

The balancing act was to ensure independence of the insurance board while building a functional interaction that would permit Geisinger's payer and provider components to work together in the best interests of their mutual constituents. This was accomplished by creating more of an independent Geisinger Health Plan board of directors and establishing a robust committee structure within that insurance board, including nominating and governance, management and compensation, finance, and audit, all independent of the overall Geisinger foundation board committee structure. Thus, the best practice governance we established for our insurance operations became separate from the big board, but still linked by overlapping board membership and by the Geisinger CEO assuming the chairmanship of the insurance board. From the top down, this allowed us to develop a systematic payer/provider "sweet spot" encompassing a commitment to the patients we both cared for and insured and becoming the engine for most of our innovation in caregiving and in how we were reimbursed for it.[6]

There was still a good deal of meshing in the senior management responsibilities between payer and provider and in the specific organizational structures and titles. For instance, the CEO of the insurance operations also was an executive vice president of the entire Geisinger organization. He or she not only reported directly to the Geisinger CEO but also to the Geisinger Health Plan board with the Geisinger CEO sitting as the insurance board chair. This governance solution was critical in terms of ensuring that payer and provider components within Geisinger would no longer be polarized, but would work together without perceived or actual conflict of interest. This most fundamental transformation between the insurance company and the provider group is what enabled our subsequent care innovation and now is being modeled in many real and virtual vertically integrated system experiments throughout the country.

As our aspirations grew from being an excellent regional health model to becoming a national example for healthcare reform, it became apparent that we needed to change the expertise and national visibility of both our foundation and insurance boards. Although the change in board composition hit some speed bumps, we were successful over time and consistent in adding directors with national credibility, special expertise, and admirable personal values.

Quite simply, without this board reconstruction, our innovation journey would not have happened. We ended up with an incredibly aspirational group of directors, who backed management's commitment to change healthcare delivery and payment fundamentally. Our directors once again became risk-takers.

Adding national representation also helped the board become more diverse, both in gender and in politics. Karen Davis, the first woman appointed to lead a U.S. public health service agency as deputy assistant secretary for health policy in the U.S. Department of Health and Human Services, also was the first female to be appointed to the Geisinger board since Abigail Geisinger founded the system in 1915! Gail Wilensky, who directed the Medicare and Medicaid programs in the early nineties and served in the White House as a senior health and welfare adviser to President George H. W. Bush, provided added perspective and great healthcare policy knowledge. Over time, we also added expertise in insurance operations, integrated health system leadership, medical group leadership, and significant entrepreneurial success. All of these individuals were well-recognized regional or national leaders.

Matching our new structure and board composition with significant changes in the board agenda, influenced by repetitive and straightforward presentations of our system-wide strategic vision, resulted in a steady-state, optimally functioning board. And integrating every aspect of our strategy into each of our committee and full board meetings was integral to management's strategic aspirations and absolutely critical in achieving innovation, growth, and continued risk-taking that put our positive operational margins to their appropriate use providing better care to a demography older, sicker, and poorer than anywhere else outside the Deep South. As it should, the board always asks tough questions and often pushes back when our answers are less than crisp. But it has never prevented us from doing what we felt best to grow the organization or distracted us from our real work of making things better for our patients and insurance company members.

Until recently, the Geisinger board did follow a number of traditional governance practices including strict age limits, strict term limits, and regularly scheduled and intrusive external board assessments. The amount of functional demographic and aspirational change managed by the board over 16 years was proof that these external devices did not need to be in place in order for the board to make tough political decisions. In addition, board compensation was limited to travel expense reimbursement. To be part of the governance of a nonprofit organization with such transformative clout was perceived a privilege.

The key leadership relationship in any nonprofit fiduciary is between the CEO and the board chair, and this has been the case throughout Geisinger's history. Mrs. Geisinger, who founded Geisinger Medical Center over a century ago, worked closely with Geisinger's first chief executive, Harold Foss, to ensure that patients were being cared for properly. Mrs. Geisinger visited the hospital regularly, talked with patients, and worried not just about their care, but also about its cost. At the end of each day, she would meet with Dr. Foss and discuss everything that happened in her hospital. A hundred years later, Dr. Steele partnered throughout much of his tenure at Geisinger with Frank Henry as board chair as Geisinger grew in national stature. The ability to focus almost solely on the critical aspects of improving care, not being diverted by the usual political issues in governance, was a blessing. Dr. Feinberg partnered with William Alexander as board chair for the first 18 months of his tenure, and now partners with John Bravman as new treatments, research initiatives, educational programs, and patient experience enhancements are pioneered. Shared vision, good chemistry, and longstanding fiduciary and management relationships allow clear-cut governance and management alignment that has been foundational for Geisinger's operational and strategic achievements.

In the most recent phase of the Geisinger evolution, the system entered into a frenzy of merger and acquisition activity. This has led to significant changes in governance structure, with the foundation board delegating some primary responsibility for operating performance, regional strategic growth, and administrative leadership to local market boards.

LESSONS LEARNED

- Effective governance is integral to organizational risk-taking and success.
- Alignment between management aspiration and board aspiration is critical.
- The most important relationship in any nonprofit organization is that between the board chairman and the CEO.

- Vertical integration between insurance payer and care provider is best accomplished with both components in the same fiduciary.
- Simple, straightforward governance is best.
- As systems get larger and more complex, governance structures most often become larger and more complex.
- Scaling innovation into larger and more complex systems will become a more difficult management and governance challenge.

5

Getting Started

Glenn D. Steele Sr., the coauthor's father, began to experience debilitating angina when Dr. Steele Jr. was in medical school. In the 1960s, coronary artery bypass grafting (CABG) had just begun, and there were only a few medical centers that had reasonable volume. Dr. Steele Sr. and his family chose to go to the center with the most experience and best outcomes.

Convincing the 55-year-old physician that he needed to give up a two-pack-a-day cigarette habit became almost impossible after he met the world-famous cardiologist who performed the diagnostic coronary catheterization. The cardiologist's pack of Lucky Strikes, rolled up in the sleeve of his undershirt, was clearly visible under the operating gown and radiation shield.

The post-catheter discussion was simple: don't leave the hospital until the heart surgery. So the family didn't. Not even for dinner, since at the time there was a razor wire fence surrounding the all-concrete campus. When the next day his wife insisted that the family talk to the proposed surgeon, the floor nurse observed that it probably was best not to do this, since the surgeon chosen (not by the patient) to do the CABG didn't speak English very well. However, he was undoubtedly the "best pair of hands" among the cardiac group.

After waiting in the hospital for about 10 days to have this semi-emergency heart surgery, Dr. Steele Sr. had his procedure on a day when 52 coronary bypasses were performed. He was number 48. At the end of the day, the families of all the heart surgery patients were assembled in a conference room adjacent to the cardiac intensive care unit. A nurse at a podium called out the patient numbers and family names. The family members raised their hands in response. She announced that patient 48 had been returned to the operating room due to continued bleeding, but was doing OK now. At least the family felt a modicum of empathy from the strangers surrounding them as the nurse moderator moved on quickly to number 49. Despite selecting this superb institution based on its high volume and best outcomes of CABG surgery, and despite Dr. Steele Jr.'s presumed insensitivity as an aspiring surgeon in training, he knew the overall experience was not optimal.

This was during the days of full indemnity medical coverage, and when the family received the bill, the insurance company had been charged for two operations: the first one planned and the second one performed to repair problems related to the first. As a budding physician, Dr. Steele Jr. began to think beyond the physiology and anatomy of disease, surgical brilliance, and acute-care responsiveness. How could the system be so screwed up, and what could the quality, cost, and patient experience be if the entire episode were reengineered? Some 35 years later, what better place for this reengineering to occur than Geisinger?

Initiating change is never easy. Coming off the dysfunctional Geisinger/Hershey merger made the operational turnaround at Geisinger easier. But now the institution was getting into the really tough stuff: changing how doctors practiced and had been taught to practice, and altering or at least redirecting some of the fundamental personality traits that got them selected for medical school in the first place: independence, creativity, ability to work incredibly hard, need for autonomy, and belief in the sacrosanct doctor/patient relationship that often celebrated individual variation to a fault. We were questioning how Geisinger providers had done things for most of their careers with good results, most of the time. We were about to suggest in our new strategy that the number one goal was fundamental innovation and continuous improvement in how we provided care. Manipulating the strategic conversation to get apparent buy-in would be easy compared to getting the work reengineered.

WE START WITH HEART

Our choices were intentional regarding how, where, and with whom to begin ProvenCare Acute. We wanted to create a flywheel effect within the organization. If patients were better served through reengineered cardiology care, we felt certain that clinical leaders in orthopedics, gastroenterology, rheumatology, endocrinology, and others would move quickly to join the reengineering effort.

What were the ground rules for our innovation beta test? We wanted to start with something that already was performing well. This seemed counterintuitive to some colleagues who felt we should pick a clinical service obviously in trouble or producing suboptimal outcomes. Our starting assumption, however, was that clinical leadership would likely be the most important lever in getting key professionals to change how they gave care. And we assumed that the best clinical leaders were most likely in the service lines or departments already producing the best results. Credible physician champions would be integral in socializing the new institutional commitment to default best practice every time for every patient. Our intent was to move a service with pretty good outcomes to as close to perfect outcomes as possible.

The most credible non-Geisinger quality outcome metrics at the time were from the Pennsylvania Health Care Cost Containment Council (PHC4), an independent state agency focused on addressing the increasing cost of healthcare. At least theoretically, PHC4 was meant to stimulate competition in the healthcare market by providing individual consumers and group purchasers of health services comparable information about the most efficient and effective healthcare providers and by giving data to providers for identifying opportunities to contain costs and improve care quality.[1] We routinely used these metrics to determine our quality and cost competitive position benchmarked against all other providers in Pennsylvania.

We wanted to pick a high-volume, high-cost, high-visibility hospital-associated episode of care at the top of the PHC4 reports. We would then attempt to encompass in the redesign effort everything from diagnosis through post-acute-care rehabilitation.

Another ground rule was to choose a care pathway in which the main disciplines had established unambiguous indications for the intervention; had evaluated data or actual scientific evidence to achieve consensus on what should and should not be done throughout the entire episode; and, finally, had agreed on short- and ideally long-term outcome metrics.

When we started the ProvenCare Acute process in 2004–2005, there was little best practice or evidence-based consensus process available for off-the-shelf use. No one had attempted to bake it into an entire reengineered care pathway to evaluate whether it could be done or would actually affect patient care quality and/or cost outcomes.

The key postulate to unlocking value would be eliminating unjustified or ambiguous indications for treatment in the first place. We would then apply already-identified, evidence-based or consensus-based best practice recommendations (ideally available from discipline-based study groups) to begin identifying and minimizing unjustified variation for each component of the care. Surprisingly, few professional disciplines had developed any kind of formalized best practice consensus process at the time we started our reengineering, and almost none of the disciplines had established outcome registries. As a result, our choice of clinical service reengineering targets became quite easy. In fact, outside the relatively limited universe of randomized clinical trials (not applicable to most of our patients due to age, comorbid disease processes, and simple lack of geographic access), only cardiology and cardiothoracic surgery had any immediately available consensus processes and readily available outcome metrics. Our choice of heart disease, specifically elective CABG and interventional cardiology for stent placement, took advantage of a combination of Geisinger's strengths in those services plus the readily available best practice recommendations we could bake into attempts at reengineering the treatment episodes.

Once our best-probability reengineering wins were under way, the buzz created by the early results affected our internal Geisinger momentum (the flywheel effect) and had influence on other disciplines' best practice consensus processes and registries, first and most prominently, orthopedics through the Hospital for Special Surgery in New York City and the American Association of Hip and Knee Surgeons.

Our choice of the Geisinger Community Practice Service Line (CPSL) for our first reengineering target in ambulatory care was again quite intentional. CPSL was our first multidisciplinary service line, it was large (composed of approximately 250 primary care physicians in 2001), and it was geographically dispersed, with 55 sites providing care in 47 of Pennsylvania's 67 counties. It primarily was responsible for the care of nearly 30,000 type 2 diabetes patients. And most important, similar to our heart care clinical services, CPSL was incredibly well run and Geisinger's most innovative care delivery group.

SUCCESS FACTORS IN OPERATIONALIZING AND SCALING

Innovation was our top strategic target, so we began to socialize our definition of fundamental innovation in caregiving using a repetitive top-down narrative. But it was the men and women providing care in the service lines or in the discipline-based units who were expected to pick what they most wanted as their innovation targets. The job of leadership was to prioritize a limited number of beta tests believed most likely to succeed in providing real benefits to patients. It probably was a combination of wisdom and luck that led us to choose heart care for the initial ProvenCare Acute reengineering and a reengineered care pathway for type 2 diabetes for the ProvenCare Chronic bundled best practice redesign commitment. Getting early success was our goal. Even with the inefficiencies of any beta test, ProvenCare Heart began to show higher quality and lower cost for the CABG patients within several years. ProvenCare Chronic demonstrated immediate benefit in achieving improved intermediate and process metrics and surprisingly showed dramatic effects in lowering diabetes-related disease effects within three years. As expected, this early success led to incredible internal and much more than expected external affirmation.

Some of this was deserved, such as our American Surgical Association presentation and paper[2] and the *Bloomsburg* (Pennsylvania) *Press Enterprise* editorial on the effect of reengineering on teacher compensation.[3] Some was over the top and focused more on the sexy packaging of our single-priced so-called warranty, as it was referred to in the *New York Times*,[4] instead of the substantive default best practice commitment that was the core of our reengineering from the beginning to end of a particular treatment. But no matter—both the internal flywheel effect and the external affirmation meant scaling within Geisinger became assured.

Of course, learning from our failures also helped us move forward to scale innovation. Our first attempt to reengineer how we cared for autism patients and their families is a good example. Our researchers looked at why there was on average a year-and-a-half wait for an initial appointment. We already had recruited a group of excellent autism psychiatrists and psychologists, but demand was staggering, and the referral lineup and waiting times simply were unacceptable. Our researchers developed an extraordinarily interesting automatic writing device that could transmit a significant amount of information and allow families to provide input to the doctor's office prior to seeing one of our autism specialists. That sounded great, but there was one big problem. The researchers didn't include caregivers in the instrument design and its application into the redesigned clinical pathway. No matter how cool a new device or technology might be, if respected clinical leaders don't buy into the care redesign, it isn't going to happen.

A second example of learning from failure was our redesign of cataract surgery. When Geisinger ophthalmologists presented their reengineering results, it was obvious that patient outcomes before and after redesign were close to perfect. The redesign efforts were worthy in getting the group to move together, but much less so in terms of actually improving the value proposition.

Surprisingly, no one has ever asked us to present our failures and what we learned from them. Outsiders must assume we would either be too embarrassed to expose our failures, or they might suspect we would cloak them as hidden successes. Failures are as important to learning as the successes that receive much more focus.

Discussion leading up to passage of the Patient Protection and Affordable Care Act (ACA) did not directly influence our overall innovation approach and its internal organization successes. But the debate did help, particularly since early on many of our clinical, insurance, and administrative leaders were involved. This was more a function of the Geisinger payer/provider structure than it was healthcare reform altruism. We simply were trying to take advantage of our relatively unique overlap between caring for and insuring the same patients. Our business model and professional pride of purpose were in remarkable confluence. If the patients we cared for stayed healthy, our insurance company made money. If our providers decreased unnecessary or bad care, our patients did better and our insurance company did well financially. Proving this alignment of professional aspiration and business success, first in Medicare managed care, then in commercial managed care, and most recently in Medicaid managed care, has made Geisinger the model for many virtual and real payer/provider vertically integrated models presently being constructed.

At the heart of our reengineering innovation was an intent to use our structure, culture, and unusual payer/provider overlap to obtain benefit for those we served in both the insurance company and clinical enterprise sides of Geisinger. This was something we knew that other providers could not achieve easily.

Changing the compensation plan also was important. Money flowed from the insurance company to the providers as a result of significantly lower total cost of care obtained through fewer complications, decreased test duplications, shorter lengths of stay, and for the patients in ProvenCare Chronic ambulatory reengineering, significant declines in cost of care from decreased hospital admission and readmission rates. If our 30,000 type 2 diabetes patients had significantly fewer strokes, heart attacks, and eye and kidney disease complications because of better care, they were certainly better off, their need for inpatient hospital care diminished, and the total cost of care decreased to the benefit of our insurance company. We could then shift a portion of that unlocked value through internal transfer pricing to our people who had actively changed how they provided care to patients in order to continue improving outcomes.

The compensation plan was redesigned to set aside 20 percent of total compensation for clinicians based upon their achievement of specific patient care benefits. These were linked annually to the organization's strategic aims, primarily innovation, and not to relative value units, patient panel size, or other volume metrics. Although compensation incentives were important, clinicians responded more directly to seeing patients do better. For example, our community practice leadership and physicians committed themselves to Geisinger's diabetes care bundle, and the results in their patients (decreased number of heart attacks and strokes, better management of glucose levels, lower risk of developing diabetes complications over their life-times, etc.) furthered professional pride.

If we hadn't seen patient benefit from our redesigns, the compensation plan changes alone would have been ineffective in sustaining long-term buy-in to the continuous innovation strategy. Both Geisinger and non-Geisinger academic and clinical colleagues quickly became interested in knowing how default best practice could be socialized among a group of highly productive and rambunctious specialists (even ortho-pedists) without our being accused of dictating cookbook medicine or managing to a static process nonresponsive to the rapid advances regularly being claimed and sometimes validated in diagnostics and therapeutics.

Another key to our initial and ongoing ProvenCare success was finessing false polarities and showing them to be non-stoppers in our commitment to reengineering. Two prominent examples were "You're making us practice cookbook medi-cine," and "New discovery is changing medical care too fast to commit to any best practices for any period of time." The way false polarities were finessed was extraordinarily important. We quite simply allowed people to make exceptions to what-ever was in the best practice algorithm as long as they justified those exceptions in real time to their professional colleagues. In addition, we allowed revision, updating, or modification to the best practice default algorithm at any time, and the discussion to socialize change could be called by any of the people involved in the episode of caregiving. The changes had to be socialized in a consensus process similar to the socialization of the original best practice algorithm.

But getting better outcomes at lower cost through care reengineering was the heart of the matter and the target of our internal and external professional interests. Most healthcare economists and public policy mavens were focusing on the problem of high price per unit in healthcare delivery. Geisinger was focused on removing unnecessary or hurtful units of work. As our early Geisinger reengineering road tests were expanded and sustained, we began to hear the next logical level of questioning. If the process worked at Geisinger, and if the results benefiting patients as well as the business model were valid and sustainable at Geisinger, could ProvenCare be applied elsewhere?

External affirmation also was important, and we insisted that whatever we did strategically needed to create national excitement in order to recruit and retain the kind of Geisinger family members necessary for long-term growth. Some of the external affirmation was the more typical muted academic publication and presentation of truly remarkable results, and some was beyond anything possible in the academic or professional venue. Increasing quality and lowering cost by diminishing unjustified variation was old hat in most industries, but revolutionary in healthcare, and it caught the attention of Reed Abelson of the *New York Times*. When her article on heart care at Geisinger[5] appeared above the fold on the front page, it produced a tidal wave of recognition and affirmation. Subsequent positive articles and commentary emphasized many of our other value reengineering efforts, and a growing number of peer-reviewed publications began spreading the word among academics about our successful attack on total cost of care and the real benefit of better outcomes for patients.

Such peer-reviewed and popular press articles built significant momentum. The timing of this attention was propitious since it coincided with the two-year run-up to the ACA. The Geisinger model began to be touted as one possible template that could succeed in the non-fee-for-service world proposed in the provider reform parts of the ACA. During the end of the ACA run-up, U.S. President Barack Obama mentioned Geisinger and our remarkable value reengineering innovations in his 2010 State of the Union address. Although he mispronounced our name the first time (he got better after that), the attention from the White House added significantly to our brand-building story.

Geisinger also became a source of leadership for other organizations aspiring to be innovative or attempting the transformation from volume-based to value-based or population-risk-sharing reimbursement. What we achieved were real-world road tests of fundamental care redesign and change in the payer/provider interaction, not just conceptualizations. What was happening at Geisinger in the 2004–08 period was not happening most anywhere else, and candidates at all levels of experience began to seek us out. This momentum from both our internal and external buzz enabled early success in beta tests to lead to enthusiastic expansion of the innovation portfolio within the Geisinger family. Externally, it led others, and ultimately it led us, into asking and then beginning to answer the more important question. Could our results be scaled and generalized outside of Geisinger?

We were extraordinarily blessed to recruit and retain remarkably articulate and substantive colleagues who could both do the work of innovation and tell the story internally and externally. In addition to the CEO providing congressional testimony, Geisinger speakers commonly were found at various national meetings of professional healthcare associations and societies, where we let our road tests and results lead, not our opinions. Subsequently, interesting early evidence of scalability and generalizability in non-Geisinger markets such as Delaware, Maine, New Jersey, northern Virginia, and West Virginia became a larger part of our external narrative.

Without our Geisinger family of totally committed, incredibly productive men and women sharing a compelling vision and making it real, there would have been no story to tell.

LESSONS LEARNED

- Start with a compelling shared vision.
- Fit the vision to the structure, culture, and unique capabilities of the organization.
- Allow workers to decide how to make their own contributions to the vision.
- Link success in achieving the vision to everyone's well-being (both compensation and pride of purpose).
- Start with the highest likelihood of success.
- Get good results quickly and learn from mistakes.
- Utilize clinical leaders.
- Keep refining, but repeating, internal and external narratives.
- Make patient benefit the key goal.
- Accept the good luck that comes along.

6

Enabling Change

The operations were humming, and the financial trajectory was positive. Leadership and key employee recruiting had recovered well from Geisinger's demerger malaise. And the strategic discussion was coalescing nicely around how optimal healthcare could be delivered and paid for, which was uniquely testable in our structure, sociology, and market context.

But how could strategic commitment to continuous innovation be enabled throughout Geisinger at the front lines of caregiving to ensure broad success? Simple, repetitive communication of the strategic goal was key, but not enough. Neither was the obvious Geisinger advantage of a systemwide, standardized electronic health record (EHR).

We created an infrastructure to serve as a bridge between aspiration and continuous innovation, one that was pragmatic, instructive, and efficient and would eliminate the need for reinvention every time we scaled and generalized ProvenCare. This infrastructure has evolved over the years as we took Geisinger value reengineering into new markets within our own expanding health system as well as into new non-Geisinger markets.

DRIVING DESIGN PRINCIPLES

In almost every aspect of the Geisinger story of the past 16 years, our focus on desired patient outcomes was the driving force. Without the energizing professional pride of purpose, improving patient outcomes would not have happened. Our priority was to target the hearts first, then the minds, and finally the wallets of the entire Geisinger family. Without all three, and without sequential focus on the first two motivators, the compensation plan alone would not be an effective lever.

In addition, we believed that top leadership should not interpose itself between clinicians and their patients, but rather should motivate, coalesce, cheerlead, and empower caregivers themselves to establish improvement targets and best practice defaults. Leadership's job was to enable, not to showboat.

Leadership's enabling started by choosing areas most likely to create recognizable quality improvement quickly. Our choices ranged from programs with documented good outcomes and good clinical care leadership in place to programs with relatively bad outcomes and no reasonable clinical leadership in place. Despite the latter appearing to be the obvious improvement candidates, we always chose to go from good to great, assuming that with internal and external affirmation, we could more easily recruit better leaders into the clinical problem areas.

Clinical leadership was always key. No one was going to change anything at Geisinger without a respected clinician at the head of the transformation effort. Even at the CEO level, clinical credibility enabled questioning why and how things were done and exploring how they could be changed without losing the troops in either hospital-associated treatment areas or the ambulatory setting.

We also realized that most successful, busy clinicians were not competent financial or operational experts. So we included in our design principles a dyad or triad approach to clinical service-line and discipline-based leadership roles, with the clinical leader, operational leader, and/or financial leader working together. We did not wish to dilute a great clinician's credibility and productivity by asking him or her to obtain additional operational or financial training. However, we did require that our clinical leaders agree to equal input from coleaders with specific financial and/or operational expertise. While this may sound straightforward, we often found that a clinical leader simply could not or would not acknowledge the necessary added expertise, nor celebrate the visible coleadership of the other members of the dyad or triad. In these cases, we replaced the clinical leader. We were also willing to replace the nonclinical partners if they viewed themselves simply as suppliers of data rather than key members of the accountable leadership duo or trio.

Another major design principle became obvious early on as we simultaneously grew our geographic reach and market share and began to transact the innovation strategy. At issue was what we came to call the dominance of the day-to-day operational crisis. In both for-profit and nonprofit settings, increasing growth, complexity, and stringency of the payer and provider markets created so many legitimate operational and even existential challenges that leaders became completely reactive to the momentary crisis or the particular stimulus at the time. The confluence of these factors became a catalyst for leaders to shift their focus away from strategy to almost exclusively operational emergencies.

Advances in communication technology compounded the problem, as thought was supplanted by action, thoughtful action was replaced by motion, and discussion was replaced by transaction. Human interactions were interrupted by the telephone; the telephone was replaced by e-mail, then text messaging and tweeting. Writing with punctuation disappeared, and thinking was diluted by multitasking. Thinking and discussion with others was replaced by chaotic social media. It was imperative to slow this decline into chaotic activity, which we did through intentional structural design.

ELEMENTS OF OUR STRUCTURAL DESIGN

Most important was leadership recruitment, in our case an executive vice president for strategy and strategic program development. Interestingly, at the time none of our benchmarking data contained any such job category. This individual focused exclusively on helping to establish, maintain, update, and transact the strategic plan and became the most important colleague of the CEO and the chief medical officer (CMO). The position maintained the CEO's critical process map, ensuring that the journey reached its desired endpoint.

A second part of our intentional structural design was to force overall institutional attention to strategic accomplishment and to mitigate the operational dyads or triads being too focused on operational issues when allocating their limited time and energy, even with 20 percent of total compensation based on achievement of strategic goals.

We took inspiration from three models of innovation in other industries during some extraordinarily progressive transformational eras: the Institute for Advanced Study, associated with Princeton during the era when computational data analysis was combined with nuclear physics; Bell Telephone

Laboratories and the old AT&T when communication, physics, and mathematics were producing the first high-tech revolution; and the Skunk Works at Lockheed Martin Corporation that combined breakthrough science and engineering to develop magnificent new products.

To foster continuous innovation, we committed space and resources that permitted people to think about new ways of doing things and new scalable enabling ideas and products without the continuous distraction of running an operating unit in our hospital, provider group, or insurance company. We called this Geisinger Innovations and recruited the second-most-critical colleague in our top leadership team, our chief of innovation, who reported to the strategy EVP. At the outset, the chief of innovation position also had no basis in benchmark data.

During the next five years, Geisinger Innovations built up key staffing that helped design, transact, and update the Geisinger continuous innovation process and expand our healthcare value reengineering into the ProvenCare Acute and ProvenCare Chronic portfolios. The group included key nurse leaders on both the provider and payer sides of Geisinger. We also recruited and expanded the physician assistant leadership crucial in ensuring that real-time data was collected and initially fed back manually to clinicians through parallel non-EHR systems. The group also included IT experts seconded from other parts of our system to design best practice templates to be embedded into our EHR. Finally, Geisinger Innovations enabled interaction with key health economists whose input was critical to analyzing and eventually publishing the patient outcome benefits, as well as the cost consequences, of our value reengineering efforts.

This innovation structure justified a separate budgeting process for the start-up costs, which had two distinct advantages.

First, we could define the costs. Second, we didn't have to make individual return on investment arguments at the operating-unit level to prioritize resources that would be in competition with more immediate and operationally pressing clinical operating needs. The innovation budget was determined by the CEO and the EVP for strategy, managed by the chief of innovation, and justified to the Geisinger board of directors by the CEO, who could tout innovation as the main enabler of the strategic plan's top priority.

OPERATIONALIZING THE INNOVATION FUNCTION

Here's how our innovation process worked. The CEO and/or the strategy EVP began a discussion with the leadership duo or trio in a clinical service line or discipline, for example, cardiovascular, which was a single combined surgical and medical service line at Geisinger. The objective was to obtain baseline data regarding indications for a particular procedure and to inventory the occurrence of unjustified variation in each aspect of routine practice for an episode of care. The leaders of the caregiving disciplines or interdisciplinary service lines simply needed to lead the effort to inventory the baseline data and then to help socialize whatever became the default best practice. All of the data accumulation, best practice template building, transaction detailing, and updating of the rapidly changing knowledge base was done by Geisinger Innovations. Our innovations function was the key driver of increased efficiency and decreased cost in our overall transformation effort.

The clinical leadership narrative, the goal-setting tasks, and the transaction of key innovations were critical and difficult.

For instance, almost all of the CEO's initial ProvenCare Acute proposals were modified significantly from their original high-impact concepts to become more practical, but still substantive and attention-capturing. Similarly, almost all of the initial clinical leadership commitments to default best practice and standardized outcome metrics were modified. Initial bottom-up proposals were identified either as sandbagged or as unlikely to make a real difference in increased quality or decreased cost, or at least not easily perceived by the outside world as making a real difference.

There were basic lessons that, at least in retrospect, seem intuitive. The first was the difficulty of managing a growing budget with the yet-to-be-realized economic return. Second, as the results of ProvenCare accrued and affirmation increased both within the system and externally, many of our best medical and surgical acute care nurses, acute care physician assistants, and insurance company care managers began to prefer the professional trajectory of innovations compared to their core caregiving commitment. Managing this inflow without stripping our clinical leadership was a balancing act.

In addition, every successful non-P&L budget could easily justify infinite growth after several years of expanding our ProvenCare portfolio. So we quickly grew to see the need for a more generalizable and less costly approach to systematic clinical value reengineering, and Geisinger Transformation, a sister non-P&L group, was established. Its mission, first under the Geisinger Accelerated Performance Program and later under the acronym PRIDE, for Proven Innovation Drive for Excellence, was to increase efficiency across our system and extract 15 to 20 percent of our cost structure over three years. This was a scaling effort related to, but not quite the same as, the innovation group's original mission, and initially the head of Geisinger Transformation reported to our chief of innovation.

Another basic lesson learned was the continuing pull of operations, particularly as individual senior leaders contemplated what most likely would be helpful in advancing their own careers. Dr. Steele, a resolute contrarian who put the Skunk Works idea into practice at Geisinger, always maintained that the most difficult job was one in which there was no easy definition of schedule, metrics, or outcome; hence the need to recruit the strongest probable leadership into these usually nonoperational, often nonbenchmarkable jobs. For individuals who could tolerate the uncertainty and ambiguity inherent in the new, highly matrixed positions, there always was the siren song of big operational leadership opportunities, either within Geisinger or outside.

A key evolution in our start-up infrastructure was the consolidation of transformation and innovation and the evolution of innovation into three separate units. One is under the direction of a single leader who is both chief medical informatics officer and chief information officer. This seemed logical given that value reengineering continues to be dependent upon either embedding innovation into transactional EHRs or bolting innovation onto functional applications.

A second innovation center is under the direction of our chief scientific officer, who is responsible for our basic science portfolio, health services research, and a remarkable new effort in population genomics, our version of individualized medicine.

The third innovation component is embedded in a center called the Institute for Advanced Application, focused on bedrock bench-to-bedside translational medicine, doable at Geisinger with an immediacy unavailable in almost any other academic medical center.

SCALING OUTSIDE OF GEISINGER

We established three scaling and generalizing engines at Geisinger, all formulated with the understanding that scaling was quite different from innovating. The first test of our Proven-Care portability was simply the growth of our own payer/provider markets into Harrisburg, Scranton, and Wilkes-Barre, Pennsylvania, and most recently into Atlantic City, New Jersey. We knew that what had been successfully tested and grown in the sweet spot of the Geisinger Central Susquehanna, Pennsylvania, market might not be easily translatable into the quite different sociology of those other markets. In northeast Pennsylvania, for instance, even though 50 percent of the payer market was Geisinger Health Plan, almost 90 percent of the clinical care that occurred in the Geisinger hospital in Scranton was provided by non-Geisinger, nonemployed physicians. Our value reengineering was applied when many of the levers and enablers available among our own doctors were not applicable to our nonemployed caregiving partners.

A second engine for scaling and generalizing ProvenCare was our intentional expansion of Geisinger insurance into Delaware, Maine, New Jersey, and West Virginia, with no intention of any Geisinger provider overlapping expansion. In most of these new insurance markets, working with non-Geisinger delivery systems was enabled by partnering the insurance products with our third scaling engine, the xG Health Solutions consulting group, which was created in 2013 as a for-profit spin-off.

The first evidence of scaling success was with one organization in Virginia and another located in rural Illinois and Wisconsin. These partnerships occurred even before we formalized xG as a for-profit Geisinger spin-off and were instructive in both positive and negative ways. Significant results in redesigning hospital-based care, changing the fundamental doctor-hospital leadership relationship, and decreasing hospitalization needs by improving ambulatory care for patients with multiple chronic diseases were accomplished almost as quickly in the non-Geisinger markets with non-Geisinger providers as they had been accomplished at Geisinger.

This proved to be the case for each of our subsequent experiments in exporting ProvenCare. In the joint Geisinger Health Plan and xG ventures in Delaware, Maine, and West Virginia, quality and cost benefits in managing hospital-associated and chronic disease patient populations became obvious after one year. (See Figures 6.1 and 6.2.)

But limits to the sustainability of the reengineering also were evident after several years. First was the effect of leadership change. Regardless of whether a strong leader left when a system was in disarray or handed over an intact system with a strong operational trajectory, our successful joint experiment would wither quickly if good hospital margins were dependent on fee-for-service and if the leader's successor was not committed strategically to fundamentally transforming how care should be financed. If the hospital-centric CFO saw a volume decrease because the organization was taking better care of patients with multiple chronic diseases, unit prices would rise precipitously. Second, if the dominant payer was in a position to threaten the fee-for-service reimbursement to our provider partner if the Geisinger beta test continued or, even worse, expanded, most system leaders would cave, and we were quickly dismissed. Most important, though, we learned that our costly infrastructure used to initiate and enable our initial innovation engine did not need to be reproduced in our forays into these non-Geisinger markets.

FIGURE 6.1 Significant Reduction in Utilization at Client A

SERVICES DEPLOYED IN 2012–2014	RESULTS: REDUCTIONS IN UTILIZATION	SAVINGS
• TPA services • 5 patient-centered medical homes • Trained and supervised embedded case managers • Population health analytics • Best practice sharing	• 32% Med-Surg Admits/1,000 • 72% Med-Surg Readmits/1,000 • 7% ED Visits/1,000	• $8.6 million reduction in total cost of care

FIGURE 6.2 Significant Reduction in Utilization at Client B

SERVICES DEPLOYED IN 2012–2014	RESULTS: REDUCTIONS IN UTILIZATION	SAVINGS
• Third party administrator (TPA) services • 3 patient centered medical homes (PCMHs) • Embedded case managers • Pop. health data analytics • Utilization management (hospitalizations, high end radiology; transitions of care) • Condition management	• 17% Med-Surg Admits/1,000 • 20% Med-Surg Readmits/1,000 • 33% 1-day Med-Surg Admits/1,000 • 10% ED Visits/1,000	• $3 to $6 million reduction in spending + additional $1.4 to $2.8 million in savings due to increased worker productivity

xG HEALTH SOLUTIONS

As word of our ProvenCare success spread throughout the healthcare industry and the country, many leaders from integrated delivery networks and organizations that wanted to become integrated delivery networks visited Danville to discover firsthand the Geisinger approach to innovation. The number of visit requests became so great that we initiated quarterly innovation conferences where we explained the Geisinger innovation portfolio and its key infrastructure. Attendees were impressed with our structure, culture, innovations, and sustainability; however, they often felt what they learned at Geisinger could not be replicated in their particular organization or geography.[1]

We pushed back with those visitors who believed our innovations could not be exported outside of Geisinger. As healthcare in the United States entered a period of unprecedented turmoil and opportunity, particularly with the ACA, many policy makers and integrated provider system leaders came to believe the Geisinger model and innovation accomplishments were well positioned for the move from volume- to value-based reimbursement. To us, the situation provided an attractive business opportunity to assist providers who wanted to operate successfully in a value-based payment environment. We determined we could export the following:

- Customization of the Geisinger electronic health record
- Bolt-on or embedded software programs to enhance primary care and subspecialty work flow in clinical decision support
- Data warehouse updating in near real time from both the electronic health record and claims data

- Extensive data analytic algorithms to enable change in managing individual patients and populations
- Evidence and consensus-based care pathways integrated into clinical work flows
- Multidisciplinary clinical service lines with leadership teams to ensure how care should be given
- Fundamental change to ensure caregivers all operate at the top of their license
- Care management partnering between our payer and provider components targeted to patients and issues that yield the greatest benefit (for example, concierge care for the sickest patients)
- A curriculum and incentive system affirming and promoting continuous care innovation[2]

Rather than assign responsibility for scaling to our leadership team's already long list of responsibilities, we decided to recruit new team members devoted specifically to this effort and to position them in a new entity that could control its own resources rather than compete with other parts of Geisinger. And while launching an entity to help other healthcare delivery systems improve their performance was similar to our not-for-profit mission, the goal of creating a meaningful financial return to Geisinger through this endeavor could best be realized through the creation of a for-profit entity, particularly if we partnered with a credible and repeatedly successful private equity co-investor. We also felt it would be easier and require less investment to recruit and maintain the caliber of talent required for a new entrepreneurial venture to be successful if the venture was a for-profit entity in which employees could be incented primarily through equity self-interest.[3]

While the Geisinger board agreed to invest the required capital, we looked for an outside partner to affirm our business model, bring market-based discipline, add significant subject matter expertise and market networking, and increase the likelihood of success while at the same time reducing Geisinger's financial risk. Through a process assisted by JP Morgan, which had been Geisinger's banker for more than 30 years, Oak Investment Partners became co-investor and xG Health Solutions was launched in 2013 as an independent, for-profit company. Although the Geisinger board understood it could not possibly know what intellectual property the health system would produce over the next decade, it also recognized there would be substantial cost related to finding potential commercialization partners and negotiating and renegotiating license agreements if it decided to license each intellectual property separately. We agreed to a perpetual license agreement, allowing xG Health to retain its rights over the long term even if it was acquired by another entity, and with a noncompete provision to ensure that Geisinger would present a single face to the marketplace for selling its innovations outside of its traditional service area. In addition, the license was exclusive for a specified period of time and reciprocal—xG Health Solutions licensed to Geisinger any derivative work and new intellectual property that xG Health acquired or developed. Governance and management structures have ensured a close working relationship between xG Health and Geisinger, and the product portfolio has been sharpened over the past three years. xG Health's client base has been broadened to include significant distribution channel opportunities by embedding content into high-market-share electronic health records, becoming the design architect of a new cooperative of 40 self-insured companies intent on working together to purchase value-based healthcare for their employees, and continuing to accrue provider clients.[4]

LESSONS LEARNED

- Assigning responsibility for strategy is key to attaining an important strategic destination.
- Making space and resources available for innovation as a nonoperating unit is important to start the process.
- Pairing great clinical leaders with administrative and/or financial coleaders creates an accountable team.
- The enabling structure varies over time and should become less costly.

7

ProvenCare Acute:
Taking It to the Next Step

At age 63 and as CEO of Geisinger for seven years, Glenn Steele believed he was in good health. Although he was working 24/7 and under a good deal of self-imposed stress, he was running several miles a day, maintaining strength and flexibility, and skiing regularly. All of Dr. Steele's male family members died of heart or peripheral vascular disease at a median age of 50, but they all had smoked cigarettes or cigars, never modified their predominantly meat-based protein diet, and believed that deep fried meant great taste. In addition, they all had vigorous and stressful professional or business careers. It had been 40 years since his father was among the first generation of patients having the groundbreaking coronary artery bypass graft (CABG) procedure for occlusive coronary artery disease.

Annual wellness exams and cardiac stress tests were all normal, but Dr. Steele saw his general internist and a cardiologist after noting a significant change in his resting pulse rate.

Nothing else—no pain, no change in exercise tolerance—just a pulse rate of 85 when it previously had been 60. In retrospect, there were some brief unexplained episodes of shortness of breath, as well as some decrease in speed and intensity when skiing during the past few years.

Dr. Steele's coronary angiogram showed occlusions not easily corrected by angioplasty or stent placement. Shopping for the desired opinion and a less invasive approach would have been possible, but the combination of internist and cardiologist opinion and Internet literature search all pointed to the preferred therapeutic approach, open heart surgery.

As a physician and healthcare leader, Dr. Steele had extensive access to publicly available and private data on cardiac surgery outcomes at all the best places and on the world's best cardiac surgeons. He was well known enough that he would have been treated as a VIP (not necessarily a good thing in getting the best care) no matter where he decided to have his care.

Why did he choose to stay in his own system? With comparable individual outcome numbers for the best institutions and the best individual practitioners, what differentiated one institution from another in this superb group? It was how explicit the system was in ensuring that it actually functioned as a system.

What was the evidence, from the time of diagnosis through rehabilitation and into secondary prevention of an ongoing chronic disease, that everyone involved was incentivized, enabled, and motivated to work together to achieve an optimal outcome? What was the evidence that the system not only was committed to but actually had achieved continuous improvement, not just in the setting of a formalized, randomized clinical trial but all the time? What was the evidence that the fundamentally asymmetric relationship between caregiver and patient had begun to change to achieve a true therapeutic partnership, so that even if a bad outcome occurred, the patient would understand that both partners had worked together to minimize the chances of complication and, in the case of Geisinger's ProvenCare, that the caregiver would fix the problem at no extra charge?

All of these components critical to achieving the highest probability of best outcome were built into Geisinger's design and transaction of ProvenCare. The ProvenCare method is a structured approach to provide quality care at a reduced price for acute hospital-based surgical procedures and for select chronic diseases managed in an ambulatory setting. ProvenCare incorporates current evidence-based best practice elements into the work flow to reduce unwarranted variation in indications for a test or procedure and in the delivery of care processes. The goal is to extract the 35 to 40 percent of services and costs that do not produce benefit or may actually harm those served.

Return on investment in ProvenCare includes (1) improved clinical outcomes; (2) increased efficiency in resource use and patient throughput; (3) reduced total cost of care; (4) enhanced patient and provider satisfaction; and (5) program differentiation. We assumed that doing this care design reengineering would give us a market share advantage because of the unlocked value produced.

GETTING STARTED

To establish a baseline before care reengineering, the easiest way to learn how much unjustified variation is built into any routine caregiving is to ask a simple question at a key site of care. For hospitalized patient interventions, the recovery room is one of the most critical sites. Determinants of good outcome following most major surgeries are prevention of infection and blood clots that migrate from the leg veins to the lungs.

To determine the degree of care variation following surgery, ask the recovery nurse, "What's the antibiotic protocol being used? Or what's the blood-clot prevention protocol?" If the nurse asks you to wait a moment to check who the patient's doctor is, that is all you need to know! This is straightforward confirmation of no consensus driving best practice and of continued "seat of the pants" non-evidence-based healthcare delivery. Providing care is similar to every other complicated task in life; the more unjustified variation is involved in the process, the more cost will be incurred and the higher the probability of a bad outcome.

Consider the following attributes of typical acute care in America today:

- Uncertain appropriateness
- Limited patient engagement
- Unreliable compliance with evidence-based guidelines
- Lack of accountability for outcomes and quality
- Incomplete communication across the continuum of care
- À la carte payment for services
- Perverse incentive with more payment for more complications
- Stunning geographic disparities in frequency of care
- Widely variable outcomes not explained by severity stratification
- Often an inverse relationship between quality of care and cost of care

Compare this to the attributes of a high-performance health system, where U.S. healthcare desires to be:

- Designed to achieve high-quality, safe care
- Access to care for all people
- Efficient, high-value care
- Capacity to continuously improve

How do we get from where we are to where we want to be? The following classic approaches are no longer reasonable or effective: overdependence on diligence and hard work; benchmarking to the mean (which ensures mediocrity); permissive clinical autonomy; and inadequate use of human factors knowledge in reliability science (understanding human error).

ProvenCare is a formalized process initiated to document appropriateness of care; establish evidence- or consensus-based best practices for all high-frequency services; reliably deliver default best practices by redesign of complex clinical systems that embeds new behaviors into everyday patient flow; activate patients and their families and engage them in the care processes as symmetrical partners with caregivers; and provide a packaged price for the episode of care, including a so-called "warranty" that transfers the risk for the financial effects of preventable complications to the caregiver.

There are six core components to our ProvenCare Acute program (reengineering of hospital-based or hospital-associated episodes of care): (1) documenting the appropriateness of care; (2) establishing all key elements of evidence-based or consensus-based best practices; (3) socializing and making routine the complex clinical systems that embed default best practices into new provider behaviors for everyday patient flow (the new care processes must be easier than what's being replaced); and (4) activating patients and families so they are fully engaged in the care process redesign and implementation (caregivers and patients working together to achieve optimal outcomes). The last of the ProvenCare components comprise the product packaging: (5) negotiating a single bundled price for the entire episode of care with the payer or the actual buyer of the care, in the context of an employer self-insured buyer; and (6) transferring risk for the financial effects of preventable complications to the provider and to the health system via the bundled payment.

There are seven stages in the implementation of Proven-Care Acute:

1. Start-up
2. Literature review, best practice elements identification
3. Current state
4. Process redesign and electronic health record (EHR) tool development
5. Database and report build
6. Soft go-live
7. Go-live

Best practice elements are derived from evidence-based literature or from the consensus of the in-house multidisciplinary team. A given best practice is included only if there is 100 percent provider agreement to include it. At any time, a member of the multidisciplinary team can request changes in the best practice elements.

Performance measure sets embedded into the team's work flow, through the EHR or bolt-on EHR applications, and all-or-none compliance for each patient is monitored in real time. For example, the appropriate antibiotics begun at the appropriate time preoperatively and stopped at the appropriate time postoperatively.

The structure of the team is critical to socializing the behavior change, and the weekly time commitment for the various team members must be made explicit for the reengineering to succeed. Consider the weekly time commitment various team members must make for the reengineering to succeed. (See Figure 7.1.)

FIGURE 7.1 Reengineering Implementation Time Commitments

TEAM MEMBER	PRE-IMPLEMENTATION STEPS 1–5 (~6 TO 8 MONTHS)	POST-IMPLEMENTATION STEPS 6–7 MONITORING (~1 TO 3 MONTHS)
Clinical Champion	6 to 10 hours (1 hour weekly meeting plus coordination and communication)	4 hours (Weekly huddles)
Operations Leader	6 to 10 hours (1 hour weekly meeting plus coordination and communication)	5 hours
Physicians	4 to 8 hours (1 hour weekly meeting plus homework)	4.5 hours
Nursing	4 to 6 hours (1 hour weekly meeting plus homework)	4.5 hours
Electronic Health Record Staff	14 weeks—1 full-time employee (FTE) (1 hour weekly meeting until the EHR build)	10 hours
Reporting Analyst	14 weeks—1 full-time employee (FTE) (1 hour weekly meeting until the report build)	10 hours
Project Facilitator	10 hours (1 hour weekly meeting plus coordination and communication)	4–5 hours (for continuance of project)

It's important to understand operational complexity in the current care pathway before redesigning the process. Two preexisting beliefs represent the most frequent objections to change. The first is, "We do not have unjustified variation here. Our providers are driven by common goals and shared value systems, and we come to consensus on a regular basis." The second is, "We already have informally established our best practice consensus, and we are certain it is uniformly applied by our superbly trained, highly productive specialists, hence our good outcomes."

Inventorying the actual breadths and depths of variation in performance and the lack of knowledge of this variation begins the behavior change process. For example, when beginning our inventory of the indications for surgery and best practice elements throughout the treatment process, our seven cardiac surgeons couldn't imagine there was significant variation. That was until we discovered all the differences in antibiotic usage and timing of antibiotic treatment and the variety of opinions about routinely obtaining carotid ultrasound before elective CABG and the benefits of routine continuous blood glucose monitoring. It was eye-opening when even these closely knit, incredibly collegial cardiac surgeons understood how they individually varied and what they each thought was the default best practice for their own patients. Process redesign for the defined care pathway begins with eliminating non-value-added work. We prefer work that can be performed using technology and, whenever possible, work is delegated to trained nonphysician staff. For example, nurse specialists are assigned to follow the patients' continuous blood glucose and begin educating patients at the end of the inpatient stay to attempt to influence patient behavior for those found to be prediabetic. New work flows are incorporated into the practice and hardwired with reminders through either EHR tools or bolt-on apps to enhance reliability and efficiency of care.

Most important, patients and their families are activated as essential partners in the redesign and implementation processes.

Specifically, patients and families were involved in the group that constructed the best practice algorithms, and potential patients are asked to commit to a "patient compact" under which they are part of the best practice default monitoring process and agree to stop smoking cigarettes or cigars prior to surgery. Patients above their ideal body weight commit to altering their diet and activity levels, both before and after elective surgery.

Databases are created that permit real-time monitoring of all-or-none compliance with the best practice elements in each patient, including financial metrics allowing cost analyses before and after redesign and providing immediate justification for individual provider deviation from a given best practice. Largely to defend against the accusation of forcing "cookbook medicine," we allow provider variation from default best practice as long as the provider documents the variation and justifies it to his or her professional colleagues. Most individualized and non-evidence- or consensus-based variations in key elements are a function of learned behavior or idiosyncratic beliefs held by the provider. Neither of these justifications stand up to peer scrutiny.

It took 18 months from the time we defined our first ProvenCare design process through a soft go-live and ultimately a fully automated process implementation. The time was condensed as we added more care episodes to the redesign portfolio and as success with increasing quality and decreasing total costs of care became obvious to the clinical leaders. Throughout the effort, administrative and clinical commitment to attacking unnecessary, redundant, or hurtful care became almost a religious belief in striving for higher quality and has remained the most important success factor. Otherwise, too many other priorities would have taken precedence.

BETTING ON
IMPROVED OUTCOME

The bundled payment package became a financial bet that care redesign would significantly decrease the cost structure while increasing quality outcomes by reducing complications. We looked at all complications during the 90 days after a given acute care episode and calculated our total costs for caring for these bad events, regardless of whether they were causally related to the original treatment episode. We simply negotiated a discount into the single price for the initial episode, including the costs of tests, interventions, the pharmacy, doctors, the hospital, and the post-acute phases of the care pathway. To articulate the single price, we needed to know the pre-redesign cost of care for the episode and either know the individual key element costs or assume that by removing unnecessary key elements the postdesign costs would be significantly less. The bet on how much improvement would occur from diminished complications was simply a negotiation. We halved the cost number that was ascribed to historical complication rates and the cost for treating those complications. Thus the care redesign had to improve the outcome by a factor of two for us to break even.

Negotiations with non-Geisinger payers have been based on our knowledge of how low our price could go and still allow us to make a margin, assuming our care redesign would be as effective in increasing quality and decreasing complications as it was during the beta test. The other aspect of negotiations with non-Geisinger payers was how low a price they needed to take the risk of incentivizing their members or employees to travel to a distant center of excellence for purportedly higher-quality, lower-cost care.

Another important aspect of our so-called "warranty" in a single-priced package was its simplicity. As providers, we were taking financial risk for the quality of our caregiving and, over time, acknowledging that the unlocked value in the reengineering process itself allowed for some of the value to be kept for the system's sustainable business model, some of it to go directly back to the buyer of care, and some to go to the men and women who had changed their behaviors, leading to better quality at lower cost for our patients.

Another critical success factor in implementing the ProvenCare redesign process was linking our system's top-down strategic commitment to innovation to the bottom-up individual service line commitments to ProvenCare goal setting. We used a reliable, consistent set of individual compensation metrics as an engine for affirming success in improving both quality and cost outcomes. We revised our professional compensation plan at the beginning of the care redesign era to link 20 percent of our providers' total compensation to strategic goals only and not to relative value unit (RVU) type of productivity. We chose the 20 percent arbitrarily, and the non-RVU component easily could have been a higher percentage or significantly less. The importance was that a significant portion of our clinical leadership's and the actual caregivers' financial well-being was now tied to accomplishing the redesign of care pathways and sharing the benefit with patients and with the buyers of care.

ProvenCare would not have happened at all or would have been an evanescent innovation at best without this combination of leadership commitment to redesign, an almost religious belief in unlocking value through care process improvement, the professional pride of purpose in our clinicians seeing significant quality benefit coming to their patients, and redistribution of some of the unlocked value to those paying for the care.

EARLY SUCCESS

Fortunately, the first of our hospital-associated value reengineering projects, ProvenCare CABG, turned out to be a home run in every way. We chose this as our initial high-volume, high-impact bundled episode of care because we thought it had the greatest probability of quick success. Most importantly, we had motivated clinicians who already had established enthusiastic and effective clinical leadership throughout Geisinger in both cardiac surgery and cardiology. Our outcomes for elective CABG were already excellent, as defined by the external benchmarking Pennsylvania Health Care Cost Containment Council database, and robust systems collecting outcome data already existed both within Geisinger as well as nationally.

Significant volumes of care and an understanding of adverse outcomes, both for the patients and the financial aspects to the system, allowed rapid assessment of impact on quality and cost. Most of the analysis, either evidence-based or consensus-based, of what should be done every time for every patient from the diagnosis of coronary artery disease through rehabilitation had already been processed by the cardiology community and the cardiac surgery disciplines. What had never been done was a systematic care pathway reprogramming, enabling all of the best practices to be the default for every patient who was diagnosed with coronary artery disease and proposed to be a candidate for CABG. So ProvenCare Acute really began as a sociology experiment.

One of the most important aspects of systemizing care is documenting the appropriateness of the proposed care intervention in the first place. Once again, CABG was an excellent beta test, because there were unambiguous, authoritative criteria of absolute indications for intervention (Class I appropriate);

ambiguous indications but still legitimate circumstances (Class IIa and IIb criteria); and unambiguously non-indicated intervention (Class III).[1] So the process at the beginning formally could exclude individual patients when there was evidence-based or consensus-based lack of indication for the procedure, obviously the easiest way to eliminate unnecessary or harmful cost.

The next important step is establishing the team to do the hard work. Our teams include a clinical champion, typically the leader of the discipline or service line; an operations leader, the administrative partner of the clinical champion; all physicians who participate in the actual episode of care; all nursing staff and their surrogate leadership who participate in the care; EHR staff, who determine where the behavior changes are embedded, either directly or through bolt-on applications; a reporting analyst; and a project facilitator.

The process begins with establishing the best practices; identifying the population, disease, and procedures to be reengineered, as well as when the episode begins and ends; selecting which hospitals are involved (initially at Geisinger, a combination of owned and nonowned); deciding whether the reengineering includes the post-acute care rehabilitative process; and determining how much responsibility is taken for some or all complications over how long a period of time following discharge from the acute intervention.

Literature then is searched for guidelines and outcome metrics from all appropriate authoritative sources. For example, CABG sources included the American College of Cardiology, Society of Thoracic Surgeons, Agency for Healthcare Research and Quality, and American College of Surgeons National Surgical Quality Improvement Program. Straw man guidelines are documented if guidelines from the literature search are not readily available. An advocate is assigned to each guide-line believed to be key in impacting patient outcome. Validation is done through critique of the literature, advice of experts, and a consensus-driven process among all members of the team. It is critical to translate from generalities in the guide-lines to specific ProvenCare behavior: What behavior needs to be accomplished? When in the care episode does it need to be accomplished? Who is accountable for the behavior? What is the process to track the care in real time? What are the opt-out provisions for justified variation from the default best practices?

The review team established its own commentary on the American College of Cardiology Foundation/American Heart Association Task Force guidelines for CABG indications. The surgeons on the review team vetted and validated each of 12 Class I and Class IIa guidelines, translated 40 verifiable, actionable behaviors with clear-cut accountability and time-line definitions, and achieved unanimity and complete buy-in to default best practice to be accomplished every time for every patient. The recommendations that became key default best practices in version one of ProvenCare CABG are found in Figure 7.2.

But did ProvenCare CABG really work? There was only one way to know, as far as Dr. Steele was concerned: He had to try it. He was patient number 86.

The prehospital physical and educational preparation, the hospital acute care redesign, and the default best prac-tices, plus his motivation to be out of the acute care setting as quickly as possible, resulted in a two-and-a-half-day hospital stay. So Dr. Steele felt very busy most of the time as an inpa-tient. When the transitions of care nurse visited him on the way into the post-acute setting, he was pretty well exhausted. And when told that continuous blood glucose monitoring indicated

FIGURE 7.2 ProvenCare CABG Recommendations

ACC/AHA CLASS I RECOMMENDATIONS	ACC/AHA CLASS IIA RECOMMENDATIONS
• Pre-op antibiotics	• Pre-operative use of a CABG operative mortality risk model
• Pre-op carotid Doppler studies	
• Aspirin	• Anticoagulation for recurrent/persistent postoperative Afib
• Epiaortic echocardiography to identify atherosclerotic ascending aorta	• Anticoagulation for postoperative anteroapical myocardial infarction (MI) with persistent wall motion abnormality
• Aggressive debridement and revascularization for deep sternal wound infections	• Carotid endarterectomy for carotid stenosis that is symptomatic or greater than 80 percent
• Perioperative beta blockers (or amiodarone) to reduce atrial fibrillation	• Intra-aortic counter-pulsation for low LV ejection fraction
• Statins	• Blood cardioplegia
• Smoking cessation education and pharmacotherapy	• Delay operation for patients with recent inferior MI with significant RV involvement
• Cardiac rehab	
• No Clopidogrel for five days pre-op	• Tight perioperative glucose control
• Left internal mammary artery as graft for the LAD	

probable prediabetes, he finally gave in to stimulus overload and responded flippantly that at his age, pre-anything was a victory!

There were 144 separate entries into his EHR, all audited and legitimate, an incredible biopsy into the number of caregivers uniformly intent on achieving a perfect outcome. Everything observed during Dr. Steele's care journey and documented as results afterward would be used to improve the next patients' care process. Knowing that many fellow Geisinger family members had seen him in his medically neediest moment, and in a skimpy hospital gown, was a small price to pay for being a beneficiary not only of individual commitment and brilliance but of an entire system's commitment to excellence and continual improvement. Dr. Steele was fully functional and back to work in one month. Clinical outcomes and reliability and financial outcome information is found in Figures 7.3 and 7.4.

GROWING THE PROVENCARE PORTFOLIO

With the success of ProvenCare CABG, other service lines at Geisinger were eager to adopt the ProvenCare approach for their particular service. We decided to move forward next with hip surgery. Two separate, but connected, value reengineering approaches were applied to high-volume hip surgery. One patient cohort was the group undergoing elective hip replacement, and the second was hip fracture, most often in elderly patients, the so-called "fragile hip." For these two conditions, the composition of work groups was mostly similar for establishing baseline variation in care processes and developing consensus on default best practices for ensuring optimal care during each part of the patient flow. Since elective hip starts in the outpatient clinic, an important aspect of default best practice starts with a decision to operate in the first place. Since care for fragile hip almost always begins in the emergency room after the hip fracture, the default best practice begins after the indication for surgery. Both of these pathways, however, include default best practice all the way through complete functional rehabilitation. (See Figures 7.5 and 7.6.)

To reiterate, common principles apply to all ProvenCare Acute process redesign projects: eliminating non-value-added work; automating work as much as possible; delegating work to nonphysicians whenever possible so physicians have more time

FIGURE 7.3   Clinical Outcomes Pre- vs. Post-ProvenCare CABG Protocols

	BEFORE PROVENCARE N=132	AFTER PROVENCARE N=715	% IMPROVEMENT
In-hospital mortality	1.5%	0.5%	67%
Patients with any complication (STS)	38%	34%	11%
Atrial fibrillation	24%	20%	17%
Permanent stroke	1.5%	1.3%	13%
Prolonged ventilation	5.3%	4.9%	8%
Re-intubation	2.3%	1.0%	57%
Intra-op blood products used	24%	12%	50%
Re-operation for bleeding	3.8%	2.4%	37%
Deep sternal wound infection	0.8%	0.18%	78%
Post-op mean length of stay (LOS)	5.2 days	5.0 days	4%

FIGURE 7.4   CABG Reliability and Financial Outcomes

Reliability	• 40 best practice elements × 715 patients = 28,600 opportunities
	• 37 missed best practice elements in 24 patients
	• 37/28,600 = 0.13% elements missed
	• (715-24)/715 = 96.6% of all patients had all elements delivered
Financial Outcomes: Hospital	• Contribution margin increased 17.6%
	• Total inpatient profit per case improved $1,946.00
Financial Outcomes: Health Plan	• Paid out 4.8% less per case for CABG with ProvenCare than would have paid without ProvenCare
	• Paid out 28% to 36% less for CABG with Geisinger than with other providers

FIGURE 7.5   ProvenCare Acute Total Hip High-Level Flow

OUTPATIENT CLINIC	→	PRE-SURGICAL EVALUATION/ PRE-ADMISSION VISIT	→	PERIOPERATIVE	→	POSTOPERATIVE
• Documentation of indication for surgery • Smoking cessation counseling • Body mass index (<40) • Blood conservation consult and labs ordered • X-ray/imaging • HbA1c (<7) • Pre-op conservative management • Patient questionnaire/ outcome measures • Patient agreement • Physical exam (range of motion, alignment, ligament stability)		• Pre-op consent completed • Pre-op EKG (within one year) • Pre-op labs ordered and reviewed • Total joint class • *Staphylococcus aureus* nasal screen and decolonization • Chlorhexidine wash/wipe • Screened for anticoagulant use with instructions for pre-op use		• Pre-op antibiotics 60 minutes before incision • Body temperature management • Mechanical deep vein thrombosis prophylaxis (sequential compression devices) • Intraoperative hyperglycemia screening • Correct insulin management (as indicated per protocol) • Hair removal • Universal protocol • Pain management protocol		• Antibiotics discontinued within 24 hours post-op • Neurologic checks q 4 for the first 24 hours, then q8 • Physical/ occupational evaluation/ therapy post-op day 1 • Deep vein thrombosis prophylaxis: mechanical and pharmacologic • Post-op imaging ordered and reported to physician (anteroposterior) • Foley catheter removed post-op day 1 • Pain protocol • Pain assessment protocol— capture at least once/day

TRANSITIONS	→	RETURN POST-DISCHARGE (7–16 DAYS)	→	RETURN POST-DISCHARGE (6 WEEKS)
• Confirm post-op visits • First post-op out-patient therapy appointment made within 7 days of dis-charge OR home health referral OR SNF admission		• Outcomes assessment • Deep vein thrombosis prophylaxis • Therapy/function/activities of daily living • Tobacco screen-ing and counseling • Wound check • Schedule next post-op visits		• Deep vein thrombosis prophylaxis • Therapy/function/activities of daily living • Tobacco screen-ing and counseling • Wound check

FIGURE 7.6 Fragile Hip High-Level Flow

CARE GIVEN IN EMERGENCY DEPARTMENT	→	PERIOPERATIVE	→	POSTOPERATIVE
• STAT laboratory studies to include complete blood count/differential, international normalized ratio, type and screen, basic metabolic panel, ferritin, transferrin, 25 hydroxyvitamin D, thyroid stimulating hormone, urinalysis • X-ray demonstrating fracture antero-posterior pelvis and anteroposterior/lateral of full femur (includes hip and knee) • Orthopedic consult: mechanism of injury, approximate time of injury, neurovascular examination of involved limb, baseline ambulatory status, baseline use of assistive devices, baseline Parker index assessment • Surgery within 48 hours of admission • Surgical consent signed • Deep vein thrombosis prophylaxis • Chest x-ray • Electrocardiogram • High-risk osteoporosis clinic consult if glomerular filtration rate >30 • Care management consult • Clinical nutrition consult • Blood conservation consult ordered • Delirium screen • Smoking history by internal medicine • Skin survey • Appropriate size IV catheter inserted • *Staphylococcus aureus* nasal culture completed and decolonization initiated		• Anesthesia consult • Hair removal (Surgical Care Improvement Project measure) • Pre-operative antibiotics within 60 minutes of incision (Surgical Care Improvement Project measure) • Universal protocol • Intraoperative hyperglycemia screening • Correct insulin management (as indicated by protocol) • Body temperature monitoring (Surgical Care Improvement Project measure) • Mechanical deep vein thrombosis prophylaxis • PACU: anteroposterior/lateral view of hip		• Antibiotics discontinued within 24 hours postoperatively (Surgical Care Improvement Project measure) • Deep vein thrombosis prophylaxis protocol (Surgical Care Improvement Project measure) • Foley Catheter removed post-op day 1 (Surgical Care Improvement Project measure) • Skin survey • Patient out of bed w/ progressive mobility on post-op day 1 by Physical Therapy • Pain protocol • Medication ordered to prevent constipation • Post-op vascular and neurological exam documented within 24 hours post-op • Weight bearing as tolerated ordered • Daily complete blood count • Tobacco screening and cessation • Delirium screen • Inpatient Rx consult for anticoagulation

TRANSITIONS →	RETURN TO CLINIC

• Two-week follow-up orthopedics appointment scheduled before discharge
• Discharge plan completed by Care Manager
• Discharge instructions to include:
  • weight bearing status
  • activity
  • wound care
  • deep vein thrombosis prophylaxis
  • medications: calcium, vitamin D, pain, constipation
	• Patient had 10-14 day return visit
	• Patient had return visit bundle completed:
	  • *Wound check*
	  • *Ambulation assessment*
	  • *Outcome assessment score*
	  • *Deep vein thrombosis prophylaxis decision to continue or discontinue*
	  • *Posture balance and physical activities in daily life assessment*
	  • *Reinforce high-risk osteoporosis clinic plan*
	• Patient had 12-16 week return visit
	• Patient had return visit bundle completed:
	  • *Wound check*
	  • *Ambulation assessment*
	  • *Outcome assessment score*
	  • *Deep vein thrombosis prophylaxis decision to continue or discontinue*
	  • *Posture balance and physical activities of daily living assessment*
	  • *Reinforce high-risk osteoporosis clinic plan*

for direct patient care; incorporating new work flows into the practice; hardwiring with EHR tools or bolt-on applications to enhance reliability and efficiency of care so the new behavior becomes easier than the old behavior; and activating the patients and their families so they become partners in striving for perfect outcomes.

The starting point for ProvenCare Hip and ProvenCare Fragile Hip was different than ProvenCare CABG because, at that time, uniform agreement on indications for elective hip replacement surgery through how and where the post-acute rehabilitation should be accomplished was nowhere to be found in any of the discipline-based consensus arenas. Even national registries collecting a standard set of success metrics post-hip and post-knee replacement were not established until the past few years, to some extent catalyzed by the ProvenCare CABG results. In addition, the extraordinarily close connection between device manufacturers and their sales organizations has led to many orthopedists in a number of systems (not Geisinger) to prefer specific devices because of financial self-interest, not necessarily because of what is a consensus best practice for their patients.

As a result, socializing the best practice default in hip took significantly more committed clinical and administrative leadership, particularly at the start of the process. The consensus was that determining default best practice was much more of an internal process than simply modifying and applying off-the-shelf, already available discipline-based rules regarding who should have surgery, what devices should be used, and how and where all the key best practice elements were required every time for every patient. Even before the present orthopedic registries were initiated, the work was accomplished and the benefit to patient quality and patient cost outcomes was apparent.

Uptake on the all-or-none process changes was similar to what we experienced with ProvenCare CABG, but with optimal performance that never reached 100 percent physician compliance. This was undoubtedly a function of the internal socialization process that until recently was without significant external validation or help from discipline-based off-the-shelf outcome metrics or best practice evidence or consensus.

Reengineering sustainability has come most importantly from sharing the improved patient outcomes, which affirms professional pride of purpose. In addition, the benefit in lowering the total cost of care has enabled additional throughput at lower cost per patient, potentially increasing market share, and enabling redistribution of some part of the unlocked value back to those who provided the improved care processes. This was accomplished as a direct add-on to the non-RVU total compensation, the 20 percent linked to achieving individual and service line components in the overall system's strategic commitment to innovation. Our Geisinger data on ProvenCare Hip clinical and financial outcomes is found in Figures 7.7 and 7.8.

Expansion of the initial ProvenCare hospital-based redesign pathways now includes a wide spectrum of high-volume interventions and high-volume hospital-associated care pathways. Our ProvenCare portfolio includes ProvenCare Autism, ProvenCare Bariatric Surgery, ProvenCare Cellulitis, ProvenCare Chronic Obstructive Pulmonary Disease (COPD), ProvenCare Coronary Artery Bypass Graft (CABG), ProvenCare CNS Mets, ProvenCare Epilepsy, ProvenCare Fragile Hip Fracture, ProvenCare Heart Failure, ProvenCare Hepatitis C, ProvenCare Hysterectomy, ProvenCare Inflammatory Bowel, ProvenCare Lung Cancer (Commission on Cancer Collaborative), ProvenCare Lumbar Spine, ProvenCare Migraine, ProvenCare Multiple Sclerosis, ProvenCare Percutaneous

FIGURE 7.7 Clinical Outcomes: Hip

COMPARISON OF BEFORE (N=267) AND AFTER (N=797) PROVENCARE (MARCH 2007–JANUARY 2010)
58% reduction in readmissions within 30 days
49% reduction in deep vein thrombosis (DVT)
67% reduction in pulmonary embolism
40% overall reduction in perioperative complications

FIGURE 7.8 Financial Results: Hip

	BASELINE (FY2006)	LOOK BACK (FY2010)	VARIANCE
Cases	267	373	106
Length of Stay (LOS)	5.19 Days	4.37 Days	(0.82)
CM Per Case	8,976	10,140	1,164
Net Revenue per Case	$19,932	$22,823	$2,891

Coronary Intervention, ProvenCare Perinatal, ProvenCare Psoriasis, ProvenCare Rectal Cancer, ProvenCare Rheumatoid Arthritis, ProvenCare Total Hip, and ProvenCare Total Knee.

SCALING AND GENERALIZING WITH PROVENCARE LUNG CANCER

The success of ProvenCare Lung Cancer is especially compelling, because of huge variation and noncompliance nationally with the most important staging and preoperative requirements for potentially resectable lung cancers of specific histologic types. Patients were not receiving generally agreed-upon evidence-based care, as defined by a number of national discipline-based and cancer-based organizations.

Since 2010, Geisinger's ProvenCare template for surgical treatment of lung cancer patients has been piloted by a dozen hospitals of different sizes and models and with more than 2,000 patients through the Commission on Cancer's ProvenCare Lung Cancer Collaborative.[2] The study involves patients with non-small cell lung cancer who are candidates for lung resections.

Participating hospitals provide treatment according to Geisinger's ProvenCare Lung Cancer care pathway, containing 38 standardized elements that cover everything from antibiotic administration and pain management to mediastinoscopy and lymph node sampling. Results show compliance with the 38 elements rising to nearly 90 percent from below 40 percent when the study began and similar to what we experienced at Geisinger.

Researchers now are utilizing the findings, amassed in the Society of Thoracic Surgery National Database, to determine five-year clinical oncological outcomes of these patients, including staging accuracy, interoperate lymph node yield, and pneumonia and other respiratory complication rates before, during, and after the ProvenCare journey. The collaborative expects to see improvement in outcomes as a result of institutions following the ProvenCare pathway.

A new phase of research is looking at all stages of lung cancer. The program will now involve multiple departments at eight hospitals, including medical and radiation oncology, and encompass 53 elements as opposed to the 38 we started with, everything from diagnosis to staging, treatment, survivorship/palliative care, and end of life care related to lung cancer.

At the very least, we have demonstrated that the application of the process goes well beyond a single committed institution and is motivated by clinical leadership and pride of accomplishing real improvement in patient care, since none of the non-Geisinger institutions have the advantage of a payer/pro-vider partnership that built in a pricing component as a part of the effort.

LESSONS LEARNED

- Continuous improvement is possible in routine clinical practice.
- Default best practices can improve quality and lower costs.
- Unjustified variation can be mitigated without resorting to "cookbook" medicine.
- Scaling to other institutions is promising.
- Professional pride of purpose and clinical leadership are the key success factors.

8

ProvenCare Chronic

By the time 74-year-old Arthur went to his first appointment with a Geisinger endocrinologist in 2009, he had had angioplasty twice to open blocked coronary arteries. His hemoglobin A1C was 9.6 percent when he began cardiac rehab, met with a registered dietitian and certified diabetes educator, and started to limit his carbohydrates to no more than 45 grams per meal. He followed his prescribed medication regimen and worked hard to manage his blood glucose levels, and in September 2010 underwent coronary artery bypass grafting (CABG) with placement of an implantable cardioverter defibrillator.

Arthur began growing vegetables, first for himself and his wife, then for family and friends. His garden became so prolific that he brought fresh vegetables to doctor visits during growing season each year. He had 31 appointments with a diabetes educator or endocrinologist from 2009 to 2015, approximately one visit every three months. He lost 18 pounds, maintains his low-density lipoprotein (LDL) or "bad" cholesterol at 72, and has persistent total cholesterol elevations in the 200 to 300 range, despite a combination of atorvastatin, Fenofibrate, and fish oil.

Arthur has maintained his hemoglobin A1C at or below 7 percent from 2011 to 2015 and his blood pressure at 124/58 with medication. Now age 80, he enjoys an active retirement and visits from his grandchildren and plans to continue his lifestyle changes for many years to come. Despite the challenges of his disease, our ProvenCare Chronic Diabetes program has enabled him to maintain an active and enjoyable lifestyle.

The 2006 expansion of our value reengineering portfolio from ProvenCare Acute to ProvenCare Chronic made sense for several reasons. After the success of elective heart surgery and interventional cardiology acute care reengineering and the significant amount of external validation, in both the academic arena and the popular media, our hoped-for flywheel effect occurred dramatically. Additional Geisinger service lines and discipline-based areas of the organization wanted to get in on what they could do for their patients to attack both total cost of care and suboptimal outcome issues. Our success also improved our ability to recruit extraordinarily bright people to join the Geisinger family and further our innovation machine.

Many hospital-based service lines, including our most innovative first service line, community practice, began to contribute their own ideas about fundamental reengineering of care for the most prevalent diseases in their patients. This was welcome for two reasons.

First, it demonstrated that our major strategic goal of fundamental innovation could in fact be disseminated into the various discipline-based and multidisciplinary service lines. Not only was there top-down demand to achieve a common high-level strategic aim, there was bottom-up demand regarding goals for individual caregiving entities. The entire effort could not have been done without combined top-down strategic discussion and agreement and a bottom-up ability to define specific goals that were compelling to our people who were actually taking care of the patients. In addition, affirmation in both professional pride of purpose and total compensation was uniform and aligned throughout the entire organization. The top-down strategic insistence plus the bottom-up buy-in to individual provider-led patient care reengineering was the winning combination for getting everyone throughout the organization incentivized and energized to the Geisinger concept of a healthcare innovation engine.

The second reason we welcomed the enthusiasm for reengineering the management of prevalent chronic diseases was that almost every acute care episode was a window into a much larger, ongoing chronic disease management problem. Quite simply, doing an effective coronary artery bypass or placing a stent for a clogged coronary artery relieved the immediate problem, but did not change the overall challenge of long-term outcome in patients with systemic vascular disease. The interventional surgery was not a reset button, and it did not change the ultimate biology that caused the blockage. Only the combination of the effective intervention plus a fundamental reengineering of the patient's and the doctor's approach to the chronic disease would ultimately expand life and functionality.

Because ProvenCare Chronic would require close cooperation between primary care physicians (PCPs) and specialists, we sought assistance from our community practice service line (primary care) leaders to help identify the specific chronic disease we would tackle first.

COLLABORATING ON CHANGE

As with ProvenCare CABG, we wanted to start our chronic disease reengineering effort with a high-impact, high-probability winning result. There is strong incidence of diabetes in the Geisinger service area, nearly one million adults age 18 and older, according to the Pennsylvania Department of Health.[1] Our community practice doctors were caring for approximately 30,000 type 2 diabetes patients, and we had just recruited a full complement of excellent endocrinologists at our two hospital hubs.

Type 2 diabetes was challenging because it involved a number of departments and caregivers not typically collaborating to benefit patients, including endocrinologists, PCPs, pharmacists, nutritionists, general internists, and nurses, among others.

Our starting point was to entice the hospital-based specialists to open their hospital-based clinic schedules to diabetic patients in crisis. But our aspiration for ProvenCare chronic disease management went well beyond simply opening up schedules and being responsive, because it's unacceptable that patients must travel from wherever they are and from whomever is taking care of them to see hospital-based specialists.

The endpoint for ProvenCare Chronic reengineering for care of all chronic conditions was to identify ahead of time the patients at most risk for medical crisis and fundamentally change our care for them before they go into crisis. We wanted to get as much collaborative best practice care to patients near where they live, with the entire provider group (and at Geisinger, the payer as well) committing to achieve a common metric of all-or-none best practice bundle-of-care measures delivered to the patient in the community setting. Some of these best practices are taken from the discipline-based evidence and consensus process led by the specialty societies, and some are decided upon internally as part of the default best practice socialization process.

The reengineering approach to chronic disease care requires a fundamentally different interaction between specialists and PCPs. From the beginning of the reengineering effort, we insisted on bringing care to patients with extraordinarily difficult type 2 diabetes management, rather than demanding that they come to us. Instead of opening up schedules for these patients to be seen when necessary at the endocrinology-based clinics typically near our hub hospitals, we systematically took our endocrinology expertise out to the community practice offices. This fostered interaction between endocrinologists and our PCPs when patients with type 2 diabetes were in or approaching a crisis.

The only way bundled best practice works, and to some extent it's used as a forcing function, is if data from payers is used to stratify which chronic disease patients need the most intense care. Initial redesign for all type 2 diabetes patients would have been useless and incredibly costly. For the most fragile diabetes patients, for example, our initial goal was to hone in on those patients requiring the most intense care and to meld the rapidly changing specialty knowledge of the endocrinologist with the access, general management, and credibility in the community-based practitioner. This was a superb way of creating more patient-centric care delivery without sacrificing the expertise that prior to our bundled best practice and care reengineering demanded that patients physically move from their community practice-based interaction to the specialists in or near the hospital hubs.

We took a similar approach to congestive heart failure, involving hospital-based cardiology specialists and community practitioners in a way that enabled a significant amount of caregiving for the most difficult patients to be provided in the community practices near where patients lived, as opposed to simply opening up schedules and demanding that patients and their families travel to hospital-based hubs. Almost 80 percent of the patients normally referred for specialist visits could be cared for much more efficiently by having specialists available to the PCPs in our 55 community practice sites. Our outcome metrics are decreased acute care needs, decreased frequency of secondary disease consequence, and decreased cost of care over time, the ultimate increased value outcome.

There's another compelling reason for specialist and PCP collaboration in reengineered prevalent chronic disease care. Without making the most expert opinion available to front-line caregivers and caring for both healthy and sick patients, we could not feel confident that the best care was delivered in the most convenient way to our sickest patients. Working together toward this goal was directly correlated with the 20 percent innovation-related compensation targets for the specialists as well as the PCPs.

PERFORMANCE MEASURE SET

The ProvenCare approach to diabetes management is a team-based model of care that uses the ProvenCare methodology to help practitioners manage type 1 and type 2 diabetes patients in the primary care setting. The three-pronged approach combines work flow improvement, information technology (IT) optimization, and performance measurement. The system helps caregivers proactively manage their patient population's compliance with a set of nationally recognized performance measures. Based on these measures, providers can pursue appropriate chronic condition management for their patients. Specifically, the diabetes management system of care includes:

- An all-or-none set of 14 measures for diabetes that tracks patient compliance to evidence-based guidelines. (See Figure 8.1.) The measures provide a consistent way

FIGURE 8.1 Diabetes Patient Compliance Measures

CMS ALL-OR-NOTHING MEASURE	GEISINGER PROVENCARE MEASURES	QUALITY STANDARD
1	Hgb A1C measurement	Every 6 months
2 Yes	Hgb A1C control	Patient-specific goal (CMS <8 percent)
3	LDL measurement	Yearly
4 Yes	LDL control	Patient-specific goal <70 or <100 mg/dl
5 Yes	Blood pressure control	<140/80
6	Urine protein testing	Yearly
7	Influenza immunization	Yearly
8	Pneumococcal immunization	One before age 65, once after 65
9 Yes	Smoking status	Nonsmoker
10	Foot exam	Yearly (may be performed by a provider, advanced practitioner, nurse, or medical assistant)
11	Retinal exam	Yearly (performed by an eye/vision care provider)
12	ACE inhibitor/angiotensin II receptor blocker (ARB) use in nephropathy	Patients are excluded if they have a contraindication to the drug
13	ACE inhibitor/ARB use in hypertension	Patients are excluded if they have a contraindication to the drug
14 Yes	Aspirin use	Daily aspirin use for patients with diabetes and ischemic vascular disease

to manage the diabetes patient's health based on best practice care, and all measures are required in the all-or-none measure set.[2]

- Clinical process redesign to eliminate, automate, delegate, incorporate, and activate.
- Clinical decision support through the electronic health record (EHR) at clinic nurse and provider levels (evidence-based alerts and health management reminders).
- Patient-specific strategies using registry report data.
- Activation strategies such as patient letters and e-mail communication via secure patient portals.

An all-or-nothing measures set raises the performance bar by more closely reflecting the interests and desires of patients, fostering a systems approach to achieving all goals, and providing a more sensitive scale for assessing improvements. Both patients and physicians want to either slow disease progression or prevent the consequences of additional diseases that might be avoided by more optimal treatment. We presupposed this could happen only if all the known best practices for a given condition were achieved every time for every patient. So we committed to a best practice bundle even though there could be either medical or practical issues mitigating optimal achievement for individual components of the bundle.

Not all patients will achieve each measure; for example, not all will quit smoking. The set of measures offers real-time feedback regarding progress by the patient and in the population. The measures also attempt to stratify the type 2 diabetes patients most at risk and to enable much more proactive input from the endocrinologist in addition to the PCP. Finally, the measures also seek to include patients and their families in a self-care partnering arrangement to achieve the best possible outcomes.

We included patients and families in each of the care delivery reengineering processes, redesigning the care pathways, delineating new responsibilities for providers, patients, and their families in jointly defined accountability to achieve optimal outcome, and fundamentally reframing the relationship between the caregiver and patient. Even giving patients and their families access to our progress notes was a fundamental realignment. Finding out how often the patients and their families did not understand or agree with what was documented in their progress notes was eye-opening. Setting a new baseline of mutual understanding and agreement was an important starting point in optimizing chronic disease management.

Our initial approach was to use our EHR, Epic, employed across the entire Geisinger system, to embed the provider prompts and feedback enabling behavior. We now are working on bolt-on and content embedding applications that would enable connections to Epic, Cerner, and Athena Health.

In the beginning, our PCPs and endocrinologists committed to achieve nine best practice goals for the type 2 diabetes patient population. The first few years focused essentially on the usual surrogate markers, such as hemoglobin A1C, microalbumin, pneumococcal vaccination, LDL, blood pressure, and so on. We eventually included 14 best practice measures.

To the aggravation of most community practice leaders, whenever there was a year-over-year improvement in the process or surrogate panel, particularly since it would always meet or beat the innovation requirements for the performance part of compensation, Dr. Steele would ask, "So what?" He was interested in the actual long-term benefit to diabetes patients included in the improved best practice bundle.

Remarkably, it took only three years of this fundamentally changed set of practice incentives and practice enablers to show that the answer to "So what?" meant that there were 306 prevented heart attacks compared to what would have been expected; likewise 141 prevented strokes and 166 prevented cases of retinopathy, simply by having the patients cared for within this bundled best practice value reengineering change.[3] In addition to the patient benefit, bundled best practices significantly decreased the total cost of care. Value was increased by both improving quality and lowering costs.[4] (See Figure 8.2.)

FIGURE 8.2   Diabetes Bundle Exposure Impact on Total Medical Cost of Care ($ per Member per Month)

# MONTHS OF DM BUNDLE EXPOSURE	MEDICAL: OBSERVED	MEDICAL: EXPECTED	DIFFERENCE	% DIFFERENCE	P-VALUE
> 0	630	677	−47	−6.9%	< 0.05
1–12	551	551	0	0.0%	0.99
13–24	520	562	−42	−7.4%	0.21
25–36	513	586	−73	−12.5%	< 0.05
27–48	603	620	−17	−2.7%	0.69
49–60	538	662	−124	−18.8%	< 0.01
61–72	602	706	−104	−14.7%	< 0.01

The bundled best practice sets then were expanded from the initial 30,000 diabetes patients to almost 20,000 patients with coronary artery disease and to more than 260,000 patients who were placed under a series of care best practices for prevention purposes. The specific preventive care metrics depended upon whether the patients were young, middle-aged, or old. Most important was the commitment of PCPs to consider everything known in the literature about prevention as a "must-do" for their patients, with rational compartmentalization regarding what was appropriate for various age groups, lifestyles, and behaviors.

For the type 2 diabetes patients, the most important ramification of our care change was diminishing long-term disease consequences. The economic benefit of decreasing the need for hospital care and treatment for diabetes-related diseases went straight to our insurance company's bottom line. As usual, a financial deal was made between Geisinger as provider and Geisinger as an insurance company, but similar to ProvenCare Acute, the care reengineering was expanded to include all of our type 2 diabetes patients, no matter who insured them.

Based on the ProvenCare Chronic diabetes outcomes, we experienced the following benefits:

- More efficient care processes were created.
- Patients were identified as to when they were likely to need additional care.
- Providers were empowered to carry out their own transformational change as they gained experience and knowledge. Doctors strive to be at the top of a performance list, and when they are in the middle or lower quadrants, there is automatic pressure to improve. At Geisinger, there actually was a best practice competition between community practice sites and among individual providers. We try to understand what is being done better in one group and transmit it to other groups not performing quite as well.
- Patient outcomes were improved with individual measures of care such as influenza vaccination rates, hemoglobin A1C at goal, and LDL at goal. Hemoglobin A1C at goal increased 45 percent over a seven-year period for a study population of 25,000 people, and LDL at goal increased 18 percent over the same period in the same population, even after

establishing more strenuous goals. Most important, there also were reduced rates of stroke, myocardial infarction, and retinopathy in the same population.[5] Most important, these intermediate and performance metrics subsequently were shown to link to better diabetes-related disease outcomes, less need for acute care hospitalizations, and longer, more functional lives.

- Compliance increased across all measures within the set. For the nine original measures (percentage of influenza vaccination, percentage of pneumococcal vaccination, percentage of microalbumin result, percentage of hemoglobin A1C measured and at goal, percentage of LDL measured and at goal, percentage of blood pressure less than 130/80, and percentage of documented nonsmokers), compliance in the study population of 25,000 increased from 2.4 percent to 14.5 percent over a seven-year period. Within the first year of implementation, compliance went from 2.4 percent to 7.2 percent.[6]
- IT was used more fully to reinforce the new roles of practice site staff.

For all of the IT enabling that was part of the care reengineering, the key was to change who did what and how the care was actually delivered to patients. The transactional EHR, the functional content added to it, and the analytics that came from the claims and clinical data were useful only in direct linkage to changing the entire care pathway. Both at Geisinger and in the literature, it was obvious that chaos would ensue if the care pathways were not changed at the same point in time for the increased IT usage.

Further, IT both enabled and reinforced the changing roles of the care team and the changed care pathway. The enabling technology and the new pathway had to be easier than what was done previously, because change would not occur if the pathways were more complex than the ones already in use.

For example, when the suggested new pathway for autism didn't fit this criterion, we accepted it as a failure and did not adopt it. On the other hand, we created and adopted a very successful new care pathway regarding the use of erythropoietin (EPO) in patients with anemia associated with chronic renal disease. The new approach was adopted only when the transactional EHR-enabled best practice algorithm for EPO treatment could be applied to pharmacists and pharmacy techs and withdrawn as a responsibility of the nephrologist. Only through the new approach could significant benefit be shown in tightening indications (for example, using EPO only when iron would not be equally beneficial) and in increasing the efficiency of the actual EPO treatment through algorithm use transacted by techs and supervised by pharmacists and doctors. There are many additional examples of how the best practice bundle was systemized throughout our entire community practice and endocrinology specialists. It could not have been done without strengthening the fundamentally changed care pathway with enabling technology.

PROVIDER PROCESS

To identify a patient with type 1 or type 2 diabetes for inclusion in the diabetes bundle best practice measurement set and to trigger future alerts, the provider must select a diabetes diagnosis and add it to the patient's list of health problems in the EHR. When the diagnosis is entered on the patient's problem list, the patient is automatically in the diabetes registry. The registry for diabetes management lists all patients in the practice who meet the measure set criteria.

The diabetes diagnoses offer caregivers the opportunity to select a specific diagnosis that matches the current state of the patient's condition and allows for patient-specific goal setting. This provides the additional information to ensure accurate measurement.

For example, a typical diabetes diagnosis such as "diabetes mellitus without mention of complication, type 2 or unspecified type, not stated as uncontrolled," will have specific Proven-Care diagnosis options that map to the same root International Classification of Diseases code. Examples of ProvenCare best practice codes include: diabetes type 2, goal A1C < 7; diabetes type 2, goal A1C < 8; diabetes type 2, goal A1C < 9; diabetes type 2, goal A1C to be determined; and diabetes type 2, goal symptom management.[7] The specificity of these Proven-Care codes allows the care team to track the patient's diabetes measure progress and ensures that all staff are aware of the goals for the patient and are focusing appropriately on the problem. In addition, these specific codes are used in the diabetes set of measures reports.

The presence of a diabetes diagnosis in the patient's list of health problems will trigger health management reminders, with the EHR system automatically posting the patient-care activities for the evidence-based protocols. Activities can be reflected as due for care, overdue for care, or care completed. Completion of the activity is captured based on information contained in the EHR or other health tracking tools.

The provider can view a summary report for a particular patient before entering the examination room. This report provides an update of the relevant information for treating diabetes based on care protocols and assists the provider in preparing for the actions that should occur during the particular office visit. The diabetes summary report provides the following information on the patient:

- Allergies
- Current medication list
- Body mass index
- Social history
- Blood pressure, pulse, height, and weight from the past two office visits (if available)
- Diabetes labs for the past three results over two years
- Most recent immunizations/injections
- Summary of patient care activities, indicating via a symbol what is late, due, due soon, or on hold

The provider will address any alerts displayed for the patient. Patients and their family members share information to assist the provider in making complex diabetes care decisions based on combining information from the EHR and/or other clinical systems such as lab values, patient care activities, and the diabetes diagnosis. The provider reviews each alert, selects the appropriate care action, then accepts the alert to satisfy the action. How these specific activities are satisfied is outlined in Figure 8.3.[8]

CLINICAL ORDERS

At the end of the office visit, the provider reviews and signs the orders the nurse has noted as pending during the patient rooming process. The provider has the option to sign all the orders at one time, edit an order, or remove orders that are unnecessary based upon information captured during the office visit.

FIGURE 8.3   EHR Alerts

	MEASURE AND QUALITY STANDARD	HOW TO SATISFY THE ALERTS
1	HgbA1C measurement	HgbA1C resulted in last 6 months Palliative Care Dx on patient health problems list
2	HgbA1C control patient-specific	Goal < 8
3	LDL measurement	LDL resulted in last year Palliative Care Dx on patient health problems list
4	LDL patient specific control	Patient-specific goal; < 70 or < 100 ml
5	Blood pressure control	< 140/90
6	Urine protein testing	Urine microalbumin resulted in EHR in last year Palliative Care Dx on Problem List Manually add HM Plan/Patient Adjuster: • HM Permanently D/C Urine Microalbumin
7	Flu (influenza immunization))	Flu shot documented in immunization record (this flu season) Egg allergy documented in allergies activity Manually add HM Plan/Patient Adjuster: • *Egg Allergy or HM Permanently D/C Seasonal Flu Shot* • To defer alert until next visit, place order: *DEFER SEASONAL FLU BPA UNTIL NEXT VISIT*
8	Pneumococcal immunization	Pneumovax documented in immunization record before age 65 and after age 65 Pneumovax documented in immunization record within the last 5 years Pneumovax allergy documented in allergies activity Palliative Care Dx on Problem List Manually add HM Plan/Patient Adjuster: • *Pneumovax Allergy or HM Permanently D/C Pneumococcal (age 5 years-up)*
9	Smoking status	Non-tobacco user
10	Yearly foot exam	Place order: DIABETES FOOT EXAM Bilateral Amputation Dx on patient health problems list Palliative Care Dx on patient health problems list Manually add patient care plan/adjuster: • Patient care Activity Permanently D/C DM Foot Exam
11	Yearly retinal exam	Optometry/Ophthalmology visit in last year Outside Optometry/Ophthalmology report scanned against order: Diabetic Eye Exam in last year Blindness Dx on patient health problems list Palliative Care Dx on patient health problems list Manually add patient care plan/adjuster: • Patient care Activity Permanently D/C DM Eye Exam
12	ACE inhibitor/angiotensin II receptor blocker (ARB) use in nephropathy	Patients are excluded if they have a contraindication to the drug
13	ACE inhibitor/ARB use in hypertension	Patients are excluded if they have a contraindication to the drug
14	Aspirin use	Daily aspirin use

If not already completed, the provider determines what care is due based on the diabetes protocols. The provider reviews the patient's health problems to decide if the diabetes diagnosis is still applicable and adjusts the treatment as necessary. New problems are added to the patient's problems list in the EHR. For subsequent visits, administrative staff can inform patients that they are overdue for certain care and at the visit prepare orders for the provider. Any appropriate clinical staff members, who also view alerts for best practices, can perform procedures such as diabetic foot screenings.

Performance data for the diabetes management set of measures is displayed in multiple management reports to aid operational and clinical staff in monitoring and addressing performance on a monthly basis. Practice site directors, operations managers, clinic staff, and providers access appropriate reports for the site they are responsible for at the level of detail needed. We obtain individual patient and individual site feedback in near real time and use the variation in performance to determine why one site or one individual is doing better than another. This must be part of the socialization process for provider behavior change to occur.

PATIENT OUTREACH

It's important for diabetes patients to become active partners in their care with the caregivers they see regularly for ongoing diabetes care and other health issues as well, since most diabetes patients have multiple issues. In addition to our clinicians developing such partnerships with their patients during their office visits, Geisinger uses patient self-management and regular chronic disease "communications" (both letters and e-mails) to encourage patient involvement. The self-management messages explain the patient's current diabetes condition and offer suggestions for clinical care. They encourage the patient to become a member of the care team. Much of this outbound communication has been enabled by our Epic patient portal and the recent systemwide rollout of progress notes being available to patients.[9]

The chronic disease communications are designed as targeted outreach to encourage patients to seek care by scheduling an appointment. The communications are automatically generated monthly to patients who meet the following criteria: older than age 65; PCP within the Geisinger system; diabetes diagnosis present on the patient list of health problems or a diabetes diagnosis used more than four times at an office visit; no appointment scheduled with a PCP in the next four months; no chronic disease management visit scheduled in the next four months; did not receive a chronic disease management phone call; and did not receive a chronic disease letter in the past six months.

ACHIEVEMENT

As reported in the *American Journal of Managed Care*, a study of claims data for Geisinger Health Plan (GHP) members meeting the criteria for a diagnosis of diabetes found a "significantly lower risk of macrovascular and microvascular disease end points in the first three years of a diabetes system of care that included an all-or-none bundled measure compared with primary care without this intervention. . . . Perhaps the most notable finding is the apparent early impact of the care model. The findings suggest an impact in the first three years with the possibility that a reduction in risk began to emerge after the first year."[10]

Another study published in this journal utilized GHP claims data for patients exposed to our diabetes system of care who met the Healthcare Effectiveness Data and Information Set criteria for diabetes and had two or more diabetes-related encounters prior to 2006. This group was compared to a second group of patients from 2006 to 2013 who were not exposed to ProvenCare Chronic. The study found that, "Over the study period, the total medical cost saving associated with bundled best practice exposure was approximately 6.9 percent. The main source of the savings was reduction in inpatient facility cost, which showed approximately 28.7 percent savings over the study period. During the first year of the bundled best practice exposure, however, there were significant increases in outpatient (13 percent) and professional (9.7 percent) costs."[11]

There were two reasons why costs were higher at the beginning. First, before any steady state was achieved in many cases, patients generally were seen more frequently either at the community practice offices, in their homes, or in skilled nursing facilities to ensure that everything was done to achieve the bundled best practice. Second, a significant amount of the benefit in achieving the best practice goals for these bundles came through improved medication adherence, which was viewed to be a worthwhile trade-off. If pharmacology costs went up but the consequence was significantly decreased need for emergency room visits, office visits, and ultimately hospitalizations, the net gain both in terms of quality of outcome for patients and decreased total cost of care was extraordinarily worthwhile. But there was a lag in the decreased hospitalization benefit until after some period of increased pharmacologic adherence was achieved. The overall benefit in quality outcome and decreased total cost of care was a twofold value increase in our diabetes population.

PATIENT CASE STUDIES

Creating better outcomes for patients was the key to energizing our doctors and team to develop and implement the reengineering innovations. The following patients presented to our PCPs with extremely poor diabetes control and consequent high risk of developing diabetes complications. By working with diabetes management clinic pharmacists and other members of the care team, the necessary medication and lifestyle adjustments were made to improve care over a relatively short period of time. As a result, none of these patients had their disease progress to nephropathy, retinopathy, neuropathy, or vascular disease.

Candice is a 34-year-old patient referred to one of our clinics for diabetes management and education. She presented with a baseline hemoglobin A1C of 11.9 and no previous education about diabetes care. She was not tolerating her only diabetes medication, experiencing stomach upset. Our physicians and pharmacists worked with Candice to switch to an extended-release version of the medication and slowly increased the dose to a tolerable and effective level. Working with our team, Candice was able to develop a meal plan and exercise routine to fit her lifestyle. After six months, her hemoglobin A1C improved to 6.5 and was at goal. Despite being at high risk for diabetes complications at a young age, Candice changed the trajectory of her health by partnering with our team.

Marie is a 44-year-old patient referred to a diabetes management clinic for disease management and education. She presented with a baseline hemoglobin A1C of 11.1 and no previous education about diabetes care. She was on Lantus insulin and glimepiride, but admitted that she was not compliant with the medications because she felt defeated by her diabetes and had gained weight since starting them. She had been on metformin in the past, but the medication was discontinued because she could not tolerate the nausea and intestinal distress. Our physicians and pharmacy team worked closely with Marie to adjust her medications. The pharmacists replaced glimepiride with Victoza and added the extended-release version of metformin, slowly titrating the dose based on Marie's tolerance. Over the next 10 months, we worked with Marie to make dietary improvements and continued to adjust her medications. Her diabetes control improved significantly, with her hemoglobin A1C decreasing to 6.6. Not only was her diabetes better controlled, she required less insulin than at baseline and was working toward continued weight loss in an effort to become less dependent on medications to maintain her health.

Matthew is a 35-year-old patient who came to one of our diabetes clinics for disease management and education. He was recently diagnosed with type 1 diabetes and had a hemoglobin A1C of 14.1. He was overwhelmed by his diagnosis, as he had just started a family of his own and suddenly life as he knew it was changing. Our physicians and pharmacists started him on intensive insulin therapy and followed him weekly to make necessary adjustments to his dosing. Our nutritionists and pharmacists provided Matthew with a thorough education of his disease state, including carbohydrate counting, exercise, sick-day rules, and self-care principles. Working with all members of the interdisciplinary primary care team, Matthew was empowered to control his diabetes by making adjustments specifically tailored to his lifestyle. After just three months, his diabetes was significantly improved with his hemoglobin A1C down to 5.5. More important, Matthew had gained an understanding of the active role he plays in his diabetes care and felt confident knowing he could now maintain his health and avoid the many complications of this disease.

LESSONS LEARNED

- It's possible to apply default best practice to how chronic disease is managed.
- Provider-led, technology-enabled commitment to a bundle of best practices for diabetes begins to change medical outcomes in one year.
- As medical outcomes improve, total cost of care decreases.
- Payers, PCPs, and hospital-based endocrinologists must work together to improve where and how care is provided.
- Patients and their families are key partners in redesigning and receiving care.
- Innovation at the highest level of institutional strategy must be transacted by providers energized to help patients to better long-term outcomes.
- Success in care reengineering creates a flywheel effect.
- Socialization of fundamental care redesign must be consistent and consistently affirmed throughout the organization.

9

ProvenHealth Navigator: Geisinger's Advanced Medical Home

Like many elderly patients, Robert had multiple chronic conditions including diabetes, lung disease, and heart failure. His heart, functioning only between 12 and 14 percent, was his main problem, but he was a Geisinger Gold Medicare HMO member and participant in our ProvenHealth Navigator® (PHN) advanced medical home program, which allowed him to stay as healthy as he could and out of the hospital for as long as possible. And for that, he was grateful.[1]

To help patients like Robert, we embed nurse care managers, who are employed by our insurance company, in the primary care office, where they become part of the patient-care team. The care manager's job is to focus on the sickest patients in the practice, such as those with congestive heart failure or diabetes, and ensure they are taking prescribed medications appropriately, keeping appointments, and following up with preventive measures. The goal is to help these patients maintain health and avoid repeated hospitalizations.

Our pioneering concept of the embedded care manager as concierge caregiver for the sickest patients is the foundation of Geisinger's version of advanced medical home. We designed this concierge care based on payer data that showed us which patients needed the most hands-on care. The embedded care manager concept came from our conviction about providing such care physically, as opposed to what has been shown in many studies, both anecdotal and formal clinical trials, that telephonic or distant care management does not work. We decided that this physical interaction with our embedded nurses as care managers was an absolute necessity for our sickest 150 or so patients per community practice, and it enables our physicians to do a different task than they were doing prior to stratification and segmentation of care. They are freed from a focus on increasing patient volume across all severity stratifications into something much more manageable.

In our version of advanced medical home, we've developed a sophisticated combination of technology and people. While our redesign of care may be technology-enabled, it is based on our view that a long-term human relationship between the patient, the patient's family, and a care manager (the healthcare quarterback paying attention to all the details) is imperative for success.

For example, when Robert stepped on a Bluetooth-enabled scale at home, his weight was transmitted to his doctor's office, where care manager Anita McCole noticed the slightest increase. Well aware of Robert's medical condition, she called to ensure he was OK. When he mentioned weakness in his legs, Anita was able to facilitate physical therapy to build strength. From their multiple conversations over time, Anita and Robert developed a rapport, and he was comfortable talking with her about his health issues.

In addition to managing chronic illness, our nurse care managers ensure that patients are safe in their homes, have the necessary transportation to get to their appointments, are eating well and taking medications as prescribed, and are complying overall with their care plans. The care managers confirm that their patients schedule tests and procedures and receive their flu, pneumonia, and shingles vaccines. In essence, the care manager becomes the patient's partner and ally to connect the patient with the healthcare team. Keeping patients as healthy as possible saves money by decreasing the need for expensive hospitalizations, but most importantly it is beneficial to our patients and their families.

Results are what matter, and we are pleased with PHN's ability to improve care while reducing hospital admissions. (See Figure 9.1.)

In addition, our advanced medical home program has demonstrated improvement in the risk of heart attack, stroke, and retinopathy in individuals with diabetes. Our three-year results for 25,000 patients found that PHN prevented 305 myocardial infarctions, 140 strokes, and 166 cases of retinopathy. While emergency department visits remained flat, acute care admissions decreased 27.5 percent and all cause 30-day readmissions decreased 34 percent. Further, 72 percent of patients say quality of care improved when they worked with a care manager.

PHN was developed as part of Geisinger's response to the national problem of not having enough primary care physicians (PCPs) available to meet patient demand, especially with the aging of the baby boom generation and the increase in patient volume associated with the 2010 Patient Protection

FIGURE 9.1 Admission and Readmission Metrics

ADMISSION METRICS

	BASELINE PREPROGRAM JAN–OCT 2006	FIRST YEAR OF PILOT JAN–OCT 2007	PERCENT REDUCTION
GHP Managed Care-Medicare	311 admissions per 1,000	311 admissions per 1,000	0%
Lewistown	365 admissions per 1,000	291 admissions per 1,000	–20%
Lewisburg	269 admissions per 1,000	232 admissions per 1,000	–13.8%

READMISSION METRICS

	BASELINE PREPROGRAM 2005 QTR 4 TO 2006 QTR 3	FIRST YEAR OF PILOT 2006 QTR 4 TO 2007 QTR 3	PERCENT REDUCTION
GHP Managed Care-Medicare	16.6%	16.5%	0%
GHP Medicare-Geisinger Sites	17%	16.6%	–2.3%
All Medical Home Sites	19.5%	15.9%	–18.5%
Lewistown (2,120 patients)	20.3%	17.8%	–12.3%
Lewisburg (645 patients)	15.2%	7.9%	–48%

and Affordable Care Act. PHN has three major components: primary care redesign, population health management, and the medical neighborhood.

PRIMARY CARE REDESIGN

The typical response to the physician shortage, attempting to train and hire more PCPs and to pay them more, is totally inadequate. Simply hiring more is impossible, because there aren't enough at the present time, and it will take 10 to 15 years for any significant increase because of training latency. Higher pay redistributes rather than solves the problem, creating market imbalance somewhere else.

Redefining the role of the PCP is another inadequate response. In various parts of the United States, we've seen the specialty-based disciplines of obstetrics/gynecology, cardiology, medical oncology, and even general surgery claim that chronic disease management for a certain component of patients is best done by the specialist. Such claims may have credibility, but this doesn't solve the problem for most patients, who need a team captain for the multitude of specialty- and subspecialty-linked medical problems generally associated with the increasing aggregation of chronic diseases of aging, such as the fragile diabetes patient or the extreme congestive heart failure patient with hypertension and reactive depression.

Geisinger fundamentally reengineered the primary care process, relocating as much of the patient's care as possible into our community-based practices and changing the relationship between our community-based primary physician team and our specialists, who more often than not are located in hospital-centric clinics. We did this by utilizing payer side data based on previous claims to identify patients who needed more hands-on care, stratifying the tasks of the community practices, adding the embedded nurse manager, and enabling that nurse to be the concierge care and triage caregiver for a group of the sickest patients in each practice. The other patients, based on decreased past utilization and expected decreased future utilization, were assigned to other members of the team for specific care. A good example is our algorithm-driven approach to managing hypertension run by a pharmacy tech, as opposed to a nonspecific accountability for helping to optimize blood pressure control that typically resided with the PCP. In the latter scenario, nothing usually was accomplished in between the patient's yearly doctor visits, and the hypertension remained a continuing problem. We also encourage and expect our nurse managers to go outside the doctors' offices as necessary, into patient homes or skilled nursing facilities where patients with the highest utilization often reside.

Four main components undergirded our primary care redesign: a PCP-led team delivering care, with all members of the team functioning at the top of their licenses; enhanced access for patients and their families; services guided by patient needs and preferences; and significantly enhanced patient and family involvement in caregiving outside of doctors' offices. Again, the payer data and stratification of patient needs is essential to redesigning not only the care itself, but also who provides it. And the expectation that our concierge care commando nurses leave the offices and visit the highest-need patients in person helps the at-home caregivers become more involved, for instance, in the daily monitoring of weight and other appropriate tasks.

Our primary care redesign was matrixed with "all-or-none" bundling of care measures for patients with prevalent chronic diseases, similar to what we used to reengineer care of type 2 diabetes patients in creating ProvenCare Chronic. We agree with Donald M. Berwick, a leading advocate of high-quality healthcare and former administrator of the Centers for Medicare and Medicaid Services, who supported the all-or-none bundle commitment because it more closely reflects the interests and desires of patients, fosters a systems approach to achieving goals, and provides a more sensitive scale for assessing improvements.[2]

In addition to activating patients and their families to become partners, we also concentrated on eliminating, automating, delegating, and incorporating what was easiest into the normal patient flow and provider caregiving. In short, we combined the redesign of the primary care based on specific payer data with the stratification of assignments to the various team members. Plus, we committed to achieving all the known best practices, as socialized by our PCPs and hospital-based specialists and subspecialists, for the most optimal outcomes for patients with type 2 diabetes, coronary artery disease, congestive heart failure, and other chronic conditions.

It was this combination of our commitment to individual high-prevalence chronic disease optimization plus our primary-care reengineering that led to Geisinger's overall decrease in hospitalization per thousand. The bundled best practice plus PHN as an integrated force changed the cost of care in two ways: getting better outcomes for chronic disease patients and reorganizing how care is provided to these patients so they are better cared for and able to avoid those all-too-frequent weekend visits to the emergency room. This ultimately decreases their need for hospitalization.

We charged everyone to go for out-of-the-box transformational change, rather than incremental redesign. To do so, we:

- Asked outrageous questions
- Made outlandish suggestions for consideration
- Became comfortable taking risks
- Anticipated, managed, and promoted emotional connections
- Celebrated successes and learned from failures

At the same time, we watched carefully and didn't readily accept the familiar reasons people use to resist change. This included making sure that routine needs were handled and communicated via the electronic health record (EHR) prior to the physician seeing the patient so the visit with the doctor could focus on solving problems as opposed to simply gathering data. It also included fundamental changes, such as the patients being brought into the examining rooms by team members not involved in actual caregiving. When these team members "room" the patients, doctors and nurses can spend their time and effort appropriately solving issues to benefit patients.

Our 20 percent of compensation based on achieving care transformation goals directly linked to top strategic innovation commitments also was doing something different than before. These goals were not related to relative value units, panel size, or the other usual fee-for-service volume-based productivity units. The providers' performance in caring for the entire universe of patients in their given practices, as well as in the overall community practice service line, is fed back almost in real time to the payer. Analysis on the payer side produces a bell-shaped curve representing how individual providers vary in their use of resources and in patient outcomes, particularly related to hospital admissions and readmissions.

Use of this two-way data flow comes into play in determining best practice. We can see who is doing the best job with type 2 diabetes, coronary artery disease, or congestive heart failure patients, or with those patients who have multiple chronic diseases. We also can see where the best job is being done among our community practice sites. The obvious systemwide commitment, particularly among the leadership and community practice, is to scale and generalize from the individual physicians and the individual practices doing the best in terms of high quality and low cost.

The initial test for community practice reengineering at Geisinger involved our sweet spot: the overlap between members of our commercial, Medicare Advantage, and Medicaid managed care insurance plans and the patients cared for by Geisinger and nonemployed panel providers in Geisinger-owned hospitals. (See Figure 9.2.)

FIGURE 9.2 Sweet Spot for Partnership and Innovation

Aligned objectives between the health plans and clinical enterprise, with each organization contributing what it does best.

Health Plan	**Joint** Population Health Population Served EHR/Infrastructure	**Clinical Enterprise**

- Population analysis
- Align reimbursement
- Finance care
- Engage member and employer
- Report population outcomes
- Take to market

- Care delivery
- Identify best practice
- Design systems of care
- Interpret clinical reports
- Continually improve
- Activate patient and family

The structural and cultural aspects of the overlap between payer and provider were fundamental in enabling the significant behavior changes necessary for both providers and patients. The two-way change in data flow and in the way that providers and payers worked together to modify the processes of care went significantly beyond simply altering how the insurance company paid the providers. Individual tasks for general internists, PCPs, nurses, nurse practitioners, physician assistants, and pharmacists all changed. Interactions also changed between those who were providing care in community settings and our specialists, who were for the most part located in the hospital-centric clinical specialty locations. An explicitly different interface between the specialists, who are most often hospital-based clinicians, and the community practitioners was required to achieve bundled best practice for patients. This was linked to the Geisinger commitment to provide care as much as possible close to where the patients live. This is in distinct contrast to simply asking the specialists to open up their hospital-based clinic scheduling so patients and their families could travel to the hub. About 75 to 80 percent of patient issues can be handled efficiently simply by having immediate open access to specialists to answer questions either electronically or by phone, obviating the physical interaction that normally means patients going to see the specialists.

In addition, all of the best practice algorithms, particularly for the bundled best practice, were socialized by having specialists work with the PCPs. For example, PCPs and endocrinologists collaborated to determine the metrics to be achieved for all type 2 diabetes patients; similarly, cardiologists worked with PCPs in determining the bundled best practice for coronary artery disease and congestive heart failure. This fundamental interaction was socialized to obtain the bundled best practice algorithms for each prevalent chronic disease and to attain buy-in from both primary care and specialist physicians.

Having a health plan employee interacting effectively as part of the care team seemed revolutionary at the start of PHN. Our experience has shown that employees paid by the insurance company function well as part of the team in the doctors' offices. The health plan representatives not only are directly responsible for managing high-utilizing patients, they are key enablers of smooth data flow between payer and provider.

We started with two beta sites, one in a Geisinger community practice in Lewistown and a second at our community practice office in Lewisburg. While the names of these two towns are similar, demographically they represent opposite ends of the socioeconomic strata. Only after we showed that we could obtain good results at both ends of the spectrum did we scale PHN throughout our entire system. In addition to learning how we could provide care and achieve results given such varying demographics, we also found that Lewisburg was close enough to the main Geisinger Medical Center hub that there was an interesting tension in determining which patients should be referred to this major hub and which should go to a non-Geisinger, but very good, community hospital within a mile of our Lewisburg practice. Lewistown, on the other hand, was more than 45 miles away from any Geisinger hub, and the only nearby hospital was a non-Geisinger facility that was, for most of the time until it joined the Geisinger family, relatively restricted in terms of resources, both human and capital. It was an interesting set of experiments with an overall commitment to keep patients as close to home as possible, even if they had significant health issues. What we learned, in essence, was that it could be done at both of these places with an early result of significant decreases in hospitalization needs and excellent patient and doctor satisfaction.

Internal scaling consisted of 42 Geisinger-owned primary care practices, 40 non-Geisinger-owned practices that were heavily reimbursed through Geisinger insurance products, and private practices that used Geisinger-owned hospitals when acute care was needed. Non-Geisinger primary care practices in California, Illinois, Maine, New York, West Virginia, Virginia, and Wisconsin have undergone similar successful PHN reengineering efforts.[3]

We learned as we scaled that unless we kept attentive to the data flow, both from payer to provider and provider to payer, and looked at variations in care almost on a real-time basis, there could be recidivism in either hitting the optimal metrics in the bundled best practice commitment for high-prevalence chronic disease or in the metrics of hospitalization per thousand. Recidivism was likely the default, which required our active participation to avoid. Another important lesson was that we could scale out to nonemployed, non-Geisinger community practices as long as those practices had an adequate volume of Geisinger insurance patients to justify getting the data into those practices and capturing the attention of the non-Geisinger practitioners. Although we had no direct leverage over their total compensation, we could add quality bonuses based on getting the same kind of population health benefit, which amounted to an increase of 15 percent or greater to their total compensation. This was certainly sufficient for them to do the same kind of PHN redesign and make the same kind of commitment to bundled best practice that we were able to achieve with a much greater and more direct leverage among employed Geisinger caregivers in our own community practices.

POPULATION HEALTH MANAGEMENT

Population health management, the second major component of PHN, involves identifying, segmenting, and risk-stratifying populations of our patients and insurance plan members by analyzing data provided by our insurance operations as close to real time as possible. Chronic disease and both primary and secondary preventive care are enhanced by clinical decision support communicated through the EHR. Gaps in care and the appropriate interventions are discovered and transmitted in real time to the provider team and also to patients and their families. We consider the EHR to be an important member of the team, but only as an enabler, not as the primary solution.

Effective population health management is founded on the ability to stratify patients with different risks based on past utilization: patients considered basically to be well; those considered at risk, with one or two chronic diseases; and chronic and complex patients with a multitude of chronic diseases and significant history of multiple acute care admissions. (See Figure 9.3.) The latter group is the chief focus of the PHN care managers.

FIGURE 9.3   Care Approach by Patient Risk Status

Well	**Advanced Primary Care** • Automated prevention care gaps and interventions • Health information technology reinforces guidelines and best practices • Patient education and activation • Care team performance management meetings
At-Risk	**Chronic Disease Care** • All of the above, plus . . . • Identify and stratify • Self-management and education • Close gaps in care • Driving to goal
Complex Chronic	**Concentrated Care** • All of the above, plus . . . • Embedded case manager • Predictive analytics • Transitions • Advanced clinical management • Care coordination

Our embedded care managers are tasked with understanding past and managing concurrent utilization. Most of the time, the care managers are registered nurses. We specify the individual chiefly responsible for frequent follow-up with each patient and his or her family. Care managers are given variable caseloads, with approximately 300 at-risk patients and 125 to 150 complex chronic disease aggregate patients assigned to each care manager.

Although employed by our insurance company, the care managers work as members of the community practice team, providing information from the insurance company that is modified for immediate use by the entire team. The care managers are chiefly responsible for everything that happens to their caseload of patients, and everything is triaged through these managers.

Most of the time, this embedded care management entails daily interaction between some member of the provider team and the patient and family. It often means linking the primary care manager with the appropriate specialists, either physically or by phone, to address acute access issues, always to be coordinated by the care managers. They often are out of the office, directly interacting with patients and their families in their homes, skilled nursing facilities, or wherever their patients are receiving care.

Care managers do condition screenings, monitor symptoms, assess the patients' or their families' ability to manage the medication regimen, and catalyze as much patient activation and engagement as possible. In addition, the care managers are tasked with closing all gaps in care, particularly with high-prevalence chronic diseases such as diabetes, asthma, hypertension, osteoporosis, coronary artery disease, chronic obstructive pulmonary disease, congestive heart failure, and reactive depression.

A Day in the Life of a Care Manager

A typical day in the life of a care manager is anything but typical. It usually starts with a review of various computer programs to check the status of hospitalized and discharged patients, but it can go in a number of directions depending on patient needs on any given day. The care manager reviews this information and prioritizes phone calls to patients.

Care managers usually contact patients discharged from the hospital first because that transition of care is hugely important. That is followed by contacting, either by phone or in person by visiting their homes or skilled nursing facilities, those patients who have been in the hospital within the past 30 days. It's important to get out into the field and see patients in person and in their home setting. Phone contact is effective, but care managers can often learn more when they actually see patients.

Care managers have the opportunity to interact with many different people throughout the day—not just patients, but also their family members. That interaction is most often favorable because patients and families identify the care manager as someone who is going to help them. Occasionally, patients and family members are not happy about something, and care managers point them in the right direction to address concerns.

Care managers also interact frequently with physicians and other care team members. This is often done via computer so as not to interrupt the physicians' workflow. For pressing matters, of course, the care manager seeks out the physician and discusses the situation. The front office staff and clinic nurses also see the care managers as important colleagues who can step in and help answer patient questions or solve problems.

In addition, the care manager interacts regularly with various people in the community including staff at nursing homes, home health agencies, area agencies on the aging, durable medical equipment suppliers, and others.

The work day is nearly done by the time the care manager's urgent calls, weekly calls, visits, and personal interactions have been completed. The end of the day is often spent returning calls received while the care manager was out of the office and reaching out to patients the care manager hasn't spoken with for some time. Although these patients usually are doing well and haven't had any issues lately, it's still important to check in with them and remind them of what they need to be doing for health and well-being.

The next day brings a new set of issues and circumstances, but the care managers' ongoing relationships with patients and familiarity with their medical histories helps them make a positive difference for people in need.

We also employ advanced care management, reserved for patients identified through predictive modeling (done on the payer side) to be at highest risk for acute care utilization. Most of the data is from medical claims and pharmacy; however, a significant amount of concurrent data also comes from the EHR and through our data warehousing and provider-side analytics. Targeted populations most often include the prevalent chronic disease aggregates: cancer, end-stage renal disease, high-risk pregnancy, special populations such as those with multiple sclerosis, cerebral palsy, and cystic fibrosis, and in general the frail elderly. The embedded advanced care managers also are asked to assess the social and behavioral issues associated with the medical diagnoses aggregations. We do this to better understand the link between physical and psychological gaps in care and to more effectively work with patients, their families, and social supports in determining how to create real behavior change in the caregiver/patient partnership.

Patients being discharged or transferred from acute care facilities are an additional target population across all of our risk stratifications and represent a particular challenge if they do not already have a PCP in our system.

The care management solution for non-Geisinger providers entails either training and onboarding care managers for the provider's system or creating care management outsourcing solutions embedded as a turnkey operation. (See Figure 9.4.)

FIGURE 9.4 Our Approach to Advanced Care Management

HIGH-RISK IDENTIFICATION	TARGETED POPULATIONS	COMPREHENSIVE ASSESSMENT	TEAM CARE
• Predictive modeling • Electronic health record data • Medical claims • Pharmacy data • Health risk assessment (HRA) data	• Heart failure, COPD, oncology • Special populations—cystic fibrosis, cerebral palsy, multiple sclerosis, high-risk pregnancy • Multiple trauma • End-stage renal disease, frail elderly • Transitions of care • Behavioral health, peds psych	• Driving issue behind case • Physical and psychosocial gaps • Readiness to change • Family/social supports • Frequent follow-up with patient and family	• Daily interaction with provider • Active team member • Patient sees care manager in practice or with specialist • Pushes access and exacerbation management

THE MEDICAL NEIGHBORHOOD

The medical neighborhood, the final core component in PHN, is an attempt to create a 360-degree care system including skilled nursing facilities, the acute care hospital before transition into the ambulatory setting, home health, and pharmacy. It involves defining resource utilization differences between employed and nonemployed physicians, selective specialty referrals, a systematic process attempting to create efficient transitions of care processes, and integration with community services.

The key is to create a fundamentally different relationship between the hospital-based specialists and the community practitioner team located near where the patients and their families live. The other equally important change is to create a relationship between the community practitioners and an enhanced care model that includes skilled nursing facilities and non-doctor's-office social resources. (See Figure 9.5.)

FIGURE 9.5   Optimizing the Primary Care Physician and Specialist Connection

NEPHROLOGY	MODES OF CARE	CARDIOLOGY
• RN, care manager on the nephrology team • Hospital and dialysis follow • Emergency department connectivity to nephrologist • Reduced admissions • Reduced readmissions • Reduced emergency department visits • Reduced per-member per-month cost	• Rheumatology and pulmonary • Methods of communication • Ask-A-Doc vs. first visit in specialty office and tele-health visit with specialist in primary care office	• Heart failure • Electronic health record enabled primary care decision support • Collaborative management plan • Acute care protocol • Care manager liaison between cardiologist and primary care physician

Two basic concepts are important. The first is that specialists and PCPs work together to determine the algorithms and the commitments to bundle best practice for patients with prevalent chronic diseases. Second, in the event of a diabetes or a congestive heart failure patient in crisis, most of the time health systems considering themselves responsive would simply figure out how to open up the daily schedules of the hospital-based specialists and subspecialists so patients could come to them and be seen the same day. Geisinger didn't think that aspiration was good enough, and what we did was have the specialists and subspecialists available 24/7 to take either phone calls or electronic communication from the PCPs. Most often this solved the issue. Only about 15 to 25 percent of the time was there still a residual need for patients to come in to be seen by the specialist or subspecialist.

In addition to keeping patients out of the hospital emergency department unless there is a true emergency, preempting chronic disease management issues that lead to emergency situations, and providing care in our doctors' offices, we also include the patients' home settings in their overall care. We create an effective medical neighborhood to further develop the continuum of care by getting to the kitchen tables of patients who have four or five chronic diseases and take 15 to 20 medications daily. We visit patients in skilled nursing facilities and intervene before they experience a 5- to 10-pound weight gain and are transferred to the local hospital emergency department to handle their fluid retention.

DRIVING SUSTAINABLE OUTCOMES

Performance metrics are straightforward, with admissions per 1,000 and reduced readmission rates our primary endpoints. Metrics focused first on patient and clinician satisfaction, then on the cost of care before and after reengineering. Decreased acute hospital utilization was the first sign of success. Specific quality metrics addressing particular high-prevalence chronic disease outcomes improved. And we looked closely at how the

FIGURE 9.6　Effective Redesign and Care Coordination Delivers
　　　　　　　Rapid Impact

ACTIVITY	EXPECTED IMPACT	TIME TO IMPACT
Short-Term Effects		
Transitions of care management	Reduce admissions	3 months
Case management for high-risk patients with targeted conditions: diabetes, heart failure, COPD	Reduce primary admissions and emergency department visits	3–6 months
Case management for other high-risk patients	Reduce primary admissions and emergency department visits	6–12 months
Pharmacy management	Increase use of generics	6–12 months
Mid-Term Effects		
Nursing home management	Reduce readmissions/ primary admissions	12–18 months
More efficient specialists and ancillary providers	Decrease cost per episode of care	12–18 months
High-end imaging	Reduce unnecessary testing	12–18 months
Longer-Term Effects		
Interventions for low-risk chronic disease patients: disease registries, chronic disease care optimization	Improved control, avoid complications	2–5 years
Preventive care, screening, lifestyle changes, wellness	Earlier identification and treatment, decrease incidence of chronic diseases	2–5+ years

reengineering could help bridge the movement from fee-for-service to pay-for-value as the dominant form of reimbursement transformation.

In our experience, success in scaling for both the Geisinger and non-Geisinger nonemployed physicians almost always has been obtained within a year, with a significant decrease in total cost of care based chiefly on decreased acute care days per 1,000 patients. Additional extraordinarily important outcome metrics include patient and physician satisfaction and improvement in chronic disease-specific process and outcome metrics. (See Figure 9.6.)

The most important benefit from the patient standpoint, in addition to a satisfying and effective relationship with the physicians in the newly reengineered community practices, is the effect on disease outcome. Some 99 percent of our patients believe working with a care manager is good, and 79 percent think the care they receive is better. For the type 2 diabetes patients who were involved in the reengineering, in fewer than three years, significant numbers of heart attacks, strokes, and retinopathy cases were prevented when compared to the practices before reengineering or to practices that had not been reengineered. (See Figure 9.7.)

FIGURE 9.7 **ProvenCare Chronic Disease Value-Driven Care Outcome Improvements**

Heart Attack	• Less than 3 years • 306 heart attacks prevented, with $8.3 million estimated savings
Stroke	• Less than 3 years • 141 strokes prevented with $412,000 estimated savings
Retinopathy	• Less than 3 years • 166 cases of retinopathy prevented; quality of life maintained • Savings—priceless!

In scaling to non-Geisinger practices in non-Geisinger markets, admissions, readmissions, and emergency department visits all were decreased significantly and sustainably within a year. Cost-of-care reductions obviously were affected by the hospital-centric finance officers' tendency to increase price per unit as volume decreased. Nevertheless, there was total reduction in cost of care per patient in a number of these scaling exercises. Finally, extension into the pioneer accountable care organizations was extraordinarily gratifying and affirmed. The value in decreasing hospital admissions was the primary benefit to both patients and their families, as well as to the financial total cost of care endpoint. We believe that a huge amount of our PHN redesign and our bundled best practice beneficial effect on chronic disease patients was, in fact, the seed for attempting to recapitulate a payer-provider interaction like the Geisinger fiduciary structure in many other types of payer-provider relationships throughout the country, most predominantly the Centers for Medicare and Medicaid Services Pioneer Accountable Care Organization (ACO) model and other ACOs.

Our most obvious gratification was not just that we were a model for this redesign, but also the fact that we had shown that we could get significantly better outcomes with a population of patients. The huge decreases in the need for hospitalization and rehospitalization were proof of the fact that quality and cost do relate (and that usually they are inversely related) so higher quality results in lower cost. Incidentally, our PHN redesign is also a win for doctors. Some 86 percent of our physicians believe they provide more comprehensive care with our advanced medical home, 82 percent believe timelier information is available regarding patients' transitions of care, and 93 percent would recommend advanced medical home to other PCPs.

LEADERSHIP ISSUES

Leadership teamwork between the payer and provider sides of Geisinger was key to PHN success. This was a transformational relationship in which both the payer and provider asked how quality and value could be improved for their mutual constituency and was significantly more than simply changing the payment incentives from insurer to provider. It started with a strategic discussion involving clinical and payer leaders defining the single highest cost group of patients in the ambulatory setting. The assumption was that these almost always were those patients with the least successful outcomes. Once the high cost/ poor outcome cohort was defined, leadership on both sides of the organization came to consensus on what would be considered an optimal outcome. Payer side analytics as well as the clinical enterprise healthcare data warehousing and analytic capabilities were employed in this exercise. How the caregiving could be redesigned for different patient groups with different severities of disease, different disease and living needs, and different utilization patterns was a fundamental benefit of payer and provider leadership working together to the benefit of their mutual constituency. This fundamentally different relationship and working partnership was never generalized to any of the non-Geisinger payers within our market areas.

Sustainability of our payer/provider sweet spot may come under stress as overall Geisinger leadership throughout the organization evolves, leaders assume additional operational duties, and clinical and insurance markets become more stringent. From our scaling experiments outside the traditional Geisinger market into Delaware, Maine, and West Virginia, clinical enterprise commitment without sustaining commitment from a dominant payer in the volume-to-value reimbursement transition has demonstrated that most positive outcomes are not sustainable long-term, despite early success.

LESSONS LEARNED

- Provide dedicated care managers enabled by both claims and clinical data.
- Implement a best practice team with proper staff allocation and be willing to change what people do.
- Be sure to have data up front.
- Provide training for all involved in advanced medical home.
- Accept that it's not just reengineering; be in it for the long haul.
- Build a strong infrastructure with guidelines for accountability.
- Pay for better patient outcomes, not filling hospital beds.
- Define outcome by individual provider and by each community practice group.
- Spread what you learn from the most successful to the least successful.
- Enable continuous innovation with some room for failure.
- ProvenHealth Navigator's success simultaneously means better health outcomes and lower total costs of care.

10

Leading and Managing a Successful Practice Transformation

The primary goal in reengineering care and implementing ProvenHealth Navigator (PHN) was enhancing patient care. That's the first question we always explore. PHN and other Geisinger innovations also have made things better for providers, an important consideration and benefit for any healthcare organization looking to innovate.

BEFORE PROVENHEALTH NAVIGATOR

The professional life of a physician 15 years ago and prior to PHN was controlled chaos. Doctors sort of had a budget, mostly dependent on the goals and ambition of the individual provider and how many patients he or she was willing to see in a day. Schedules frequently were uncontrolled, with patients added on or double-booked indiscriminately. It was difficult and stressful to spend appropriate time with each patient knowing that other patients, scheduled for the same time, were waiting.

Patient communication predominantly was via the telephone, which was overwhelming, and sometimes by fax or snail mail, which was slow and inefficient. Just imagine the mechanics of writing and mailing a note to your doctor and waiting for a response. Documentation of care was via paper chart, which served as notes for the physician to keep and review during subsequent episodes of care for the individual patient: a series of scribbles or perhaps checklists with no ability for flow charts or meaningful care plans unless manually produced and, in general, lacking organization. Office-based care then was mostly a cash business, and there was no oversight or need to review the memorialization of an office visit by outside agencies or insurance reviewers. The flow of information from inpatient to outpatient environments and vice versa was slow, inefficient, and inadequately managed, setting the stage for poor transitions of care, missed opportunities, errors, and overall care that was not as good as it could and should be.

When Geisinger implemented its electronic health record (EHR), it was used primarily as a typewriter or word processer for the first five years. Notes became more legible, accurate, and comprehensive as time passed, and we began to take advantage of additional EHR features such as prompts to ensure various tests were completed at appropriate intervals, prescription reminders, electronic referrals, and more.

But that wasn't the case in the beginning, when even the scheduling of patient appointments was uncontrolled. Paper-based schedule books commonly were used, but individual physicians had the ability to design their own templates. So doctors would have many different appointment types: 5 minutes for one, 20 minutes for another, or 60 minutes for an annual visit. There was no ability to assess or analyze the value of time spent for each of the various appointment lengths or time lost by not filling the schedule completely. There also was less control because physicians thought the phone staff and other schedulers would just add patients between the lines as needed to satisfy patient or physician requests for return visits. Due to the inability to establish firm scheduling guidelines, physicians often felt like they were running on a nonstop treadmill, trying to do the right thing, but knowing that there was always someone waiting in the next exam room.

There really was no unified direction as we attempted to provide the best evidence-based, comprehensive care. Individual doctors had their own repertoire of evidence-based care depending on the latest journal article read or educational conference attended. We all thought our unique care models were the best, but there was no ideal method to measure outcomes to provide evidence to alter practice styles or reduce variation in recommended treatment for patients with chronic conditions.

The delivery of care was laid directly on the shoulders of physicians. Support staff members answered phones, placed names on schedules, escorted patients to exam rooms, and perhaps took blood pressures, but were responsible for few other clinical interventions. That was accepted practice. The physician was expected to be in charge and in control. In many cases, the doctors didn't even want others to intervene clinically. That was their job.

There also was no accountability for quality or efficiency. No one knew outcomes, either intermediate, such as blood pressure control or diabetes management control across a practice, or endpoint, such as diabetes patients with retinal, renal, or vascular complications. Paid for volume, hospitals loved the big admitters. Pharmaceutical utilization went unchecked; for example, polypharmacy had no checks and balances and off-label use was not challenged or monitored. But we did our best, given the available tools and resources at the time. (See Figure 10.1.)

FIGURE 10.1 Life as a Family Doctor Before ProvenHealth Navigator

- Paper chart world
- Epic as typewriter
- Uncontrolled template
- Treadmill going faster and faster
- No direction
- Unknown outcomes
- Unknown quality
- All on the doctor
- No accountability

Despite these challenges, everyone thought the quality of the care they provided was superb, until our first internal chronic disease bundled care metrics were revealed in March 2006. That's when we learned that as a system we were performing dismally with only 2.4 percent (or about 450) of 20,000 diabetes patients meeting all of the agreed-upon nationally recognized measures. The care bundle is a group of evidence-based, internationally recognized treatment goals that all patients with diabetes should attain, for example, control of blood glucose, blood pressure, and lipids; periodic blood and urine testing; regular flu and pneumonia vaccination to reduce the risk of severe infection; and smoking cessation.

Before PHN, physicians often were overwhelmed, running in circles as fast as possible with no guidance, direction, or goals except to get on to the patient in the next exam room and make it through the day. All the existing responsibility and account-ability for care was placed squarely on the physician's shoulders with no expectation of assistance. There was no effective methodology to measure outcomes in a meaningful, actionable way.

As we rolled out further metrics, we learned that we were equally deficient in other areas of care. But we also learned from our insurance company's Healthcare Effectiveness Data and Information Set scores that American medicine in general was no better, and often worse, than we were on many individual measures both regionally and nationally.

AFTER PROVENHEALTH NAVIGATOR

The doctor's professional life is much improved since the development and implementation of PHN. Now there are tools and actionable reports from multiple clinical quality and resource utilization sources, which give real meaning to the differences in doctors' practice styles and help to determine whether care actually is helping patients. PHN allows us to measure and reduce unnecessary variation in care, and our team-based approach permits us to distribute functions of care delivery appropriately across all members of the team, even back-office functions, so all can contribute to high-quality evidence-based care.

A critical change in the office-based team has been the embedding of nurse care managers in all of our primary care practices. These nurses have been a godsend. Their responsibilities include a number of services all aimed at keeping patients healthier and at home rather than in the hospital.

They provide care for the frail and those with multiple chronic conditions. They review all hospital and nursing home discharges for completeness, a process called transitions of care, and they focus on answering such questions as whether resources are in place at home to continue appropriate care, whether durable medical equipment such as oxygen, a walker, or a hospital bed arrived on time, and whether the patient is taking medications correctly. They follow patients with certain conditions longitudinally as well. Those with heart failure, chronic obstructive pulmonary disease, and end-stage renal disease, for example, are known to be admitted to the hospital frequently. With appropriate access to information and medications, they can be kept healthier and out of the hospital. We developed protocols for treatment of exacerbations of these conditions that by agreement of all medical staff can be implemented by the care managers, thereby limiting the exacerbation and keeping patients at home. These nurses also monitor certain patient vital signs, such as daily weight in the case of heart failure, to provide advance notice of an upcoming problem.

In many ways, care managers are similar to health coaches. They intervene earlier in the course of many chronic conditions to provide education and access to self-care resources to provide better control of a patient's condition at a stage before complications develop. For example, newly diagnosed diabetes or hypertensive patients who need education about their condition, diet, lifestyle changes, or medication may be referred to care managers. They may provide medication reviews, community resources, telephonic monitoring, and coaching to instill good health habits in those who are early in the development of a potentially serious chronic condition; for those who need coaching in preventative health such as tobacco cessation; or for patients with chronic conditions that are not life threatening, but lifelong, such as migraines.

Another tremendous adjunct to our practice has been embedded pharmacists who provide clinical consultations to patients about medications through a medication therapeutic management (MTM) program. These pharmacists spend a greater amount of time with patients educating them about the purpose, potential side effects, and expectations of medications. A good example is the initiation of insulin for diabetes. It may take several sessions for a layperson to learn the proper technique of injecting insulin under the skin. Likewise, the use of statins for treatment of high cholesterol is fraught with rumors and hearsay about complications. Embedded pharmacists are allocated appropriate time to provide the necessary education and counseling so these medications are understood and used properly. Similarly, chronic pain management has become a specialty, and the MTM program has pharmacists devoted to this as well.

Our care gaps program that assists us in attaining the most current, recommended patient care is a good example of the value added by back-office functions. A nursing team works in the background analyzing care plans to determine whether certain evidence-based care has been completed. This may include preventative services such as cancer screening, chronic disease follow-up, or identification of patients in need of follow-up care or disease surveillance. We search for patients over age 50 who never had a colon cancer screening and females over age 50 who never had a mammogram, as well as patients on certain medications including statins for cholesterol control who require monitoring and have had no recent lab testing.

In our post-PHN world, scheduling and access have improved with the ability to spread provision of care to appropriate team partners, and templates have become more manageable and flexible to serve patient needs. Communication has been simplified to some extent, as it now is incorporated into the EHR; however, some challenges remain regarding information overload. Patient communication is more contained and streamlined because phone messages and MyGeisinger electronic messages all are contained in one place. Specialty and imaging reports also are contained and more streamlined.

The physicians, rather than being alone in responsibility for patients, serve as leaders of the care team and don't have to remember and do everything by themselves. Physician confidence in the process and willingness to let go is key to success. Some physicians initially were unwilling to relinquish control of all aspects of care, but gradually have seen the advantages, and the EHR has become a partner in care and a valuable tool to extract information that allows providers to excel. This innovation provides patients superb care for many conditions without an office visit or relying solely on the memory of their personal physician to provide needed service. (See Figure 10.2.)

FIGURE 10.2 Life as a Family Doctor After PHN

- Template controlled
- Data from Epic, CDIS, and claims
- Information from the EHR
- Disease management goals
- Defined outcomes
- Defined actionable quality
- Team-based care delivery
- Team-based accountability

Even as providers remain somewhat overwhelmed with access, communication, and sheer volume of patients, finally, there is a measurable, improved sense of pride and professional satisfaction in the care we provide. We now see measurable aspects of quality and endpoint clinical outcomes improvement, which truly is what PHN and all of Geisinger's innovations are designed to accomplish.

THE FORESIGHT OF DR. BILL NEWMAN

Dr. William (Bill) Newman practiced family medicine near Scranton, Pennsylvania, for decades. As the senior partner of a three-physician group that joined Geisinger, he knew that care had to become more efficient with greater support for the physician. One of his rationales for leaving the traditional small group practice model and taking the leap of faith as a pioneer in the evolving integrated health system model was that he clearly recognized his model of care delivery was essentially the same, fundamentally, as that of his grandfather, who founded his practice almost 100 years previously.

Dr. Newman and his colleagues saw patients one at a time, listened to their stories, performed physical exams to assimilate the findings into a list of differential diagnoses, and then narrowed the list down to the most likely etiology. He recognized that the available tools certainly were different.

Dr. Newman expressed confidence that Geisinger, as an integrated system, would help him develop a more efficient practice style, provide greater support for physicians, offer linkages to medical and surgical specialists, and reduce duplication of services and waste. He spoke of the technology that Geisinger offered as a huge improvement in his practice style and ability to serve patients better. What we originally offered him related more to electronic registration, billing, and revenue cycle services rather than true clinical support, but we ultimately supported him with team-based care that includes physicians, advanced practitioners, nurses, pharmacists, and the EHR, which allows us to provide excellence in care.

THE COMPLEXITIES OF PRACTICE TRANSFORMATION

There are numerous moving parts in any medical practice, and they must move in conjunction with one another to truly change patient care, improve work flows, and enhance the overall patient experience. There was significant tactical planning at the outset of PHN, and with no one to show us the way as plans evolved, we needed to work collaboratively to determine how work flows and clinic operations could support new ideas. We vetted ideas clinically to gain understanding of whether they truly were doable. If they passed this test, ideas then were vetted at the site where the care was actually provided for a reality check. Finally, ideas were vetted even further at a site PHN meeting before they were adopted. See Figure 10.3 for information on managing a ProvenHealth network.

Early on, we learned to pilot all of our initiatives at one or two sites, selected based on the adaptability and change management style of lead physicians, and often one large site and one small site to assess scalability. We learned that physicians may fall into the category of early adopter for one change process and late adopter for another.

Once a concept was proven clinically, we addressed work flows, both clinically and electronically. Because the EHR was a necessary partner in practice transformation and successful PHN implementation, information technology (IT) support

FIGURE 10.3   Managing a ProvenHealth Network

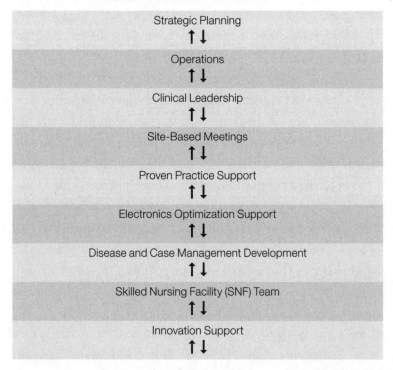

and optimization were imperative. We had a full-time IT optimization team focused on getting the EHR to think like a doctor, rather than asking doctors to think like IT professionals.

Our nurse care managers were another critical partner; it's important to engage nurses throughout the improvement process. Additional fundamental partners include our "SNFists," advanced practice providers who work in skilled nursing facilities (SNFs) to optimize care provided to our patients who require skilled nursing services. These important team members understand that while post-acute patients years ago would stay in the hospital until their disease improved and they were able to ambulate safely and conduct their activities of daily living in a safe environment, this is not the case today. Most inpatient stays now are approximately three to four days, then patients are transferred to a post-acute care facility for the remainder of convalescence.

Last, we put together what we called a Delta Team to ensure ongoing support for innovation efforts and to continue developing ideas to help outpatients. This team consists of doctors and advanced practitioners, nurses, operations managers, representatives from public affairs, and financial and regional managers from both the clinical enterprise and health plan.

We stay on top of how we are doing with a monthly 90-minute meeting at every site that focuses on ensuring that processes are effective. These meetings, which are attended by as many of the practice staff as possible, include case presentations by physicians and care managers so the team can continually review and learn. We strive to discuss saves as well as misses to learn about better patient centricity. A steady flow of utilization measures also is studied, including health plan membership, admissions, readmissions, length of stay, high-end imaging, and generic prescriptions. As a result of the discussion and inquiries about the basic data, these efforts ultimately have evolved into a comprehensive report with many levels of detail about each practice.

LEADERSHIP ISSUES

We understood early that PHN is critically dependent on the partnership between the clinical enterprise and our health plan, which meant we had another layer of leadership to consider in planning and implementation. For example, executive leaders in our community practice service line and health plan, including our population health leader, had to unite in the common goal of making things better for patients. This involved not only partnering for accountability, but also a command of change management skills and the ability to interact and relate well with the service line leads and health plan managers. Our service line structure includes regional medical directors and geographically dispersed operations managers, clinic supervisors, and managers. This ensures geographic support to the site medical leads and staff, an important factor in confirming that PHN is working at each individual site.

As the practice transformation occurs, the nonclinical management staff effect the changes in terms of facility space, staffing, phones, and other front desk services, so it is imperative that they are involved in the planning and management of the overall program. They also must assist the physician leaders, as there inevitably is some pushback from less innovative physicians and late adopters.

Strong physician leadership is critical at all levels, from systemwide to geographic regions to the office sites themselves. The site lead physicians must buy in to the concept of improved patient outcomes, decreased unnecessary or hurtful costs, and improved patient satisfaction (our Geisinger version of the Institute for Healthcare Improvement Triple Aim),[1] be local thought leaders, and have effective people skills and good relationships with the office staff (medical, nursing, and support) to effect the necessary change. On the payer side, there must be an engaged medical director to lead and mediate clinical issues. The care managers and regional managers must interact with clinic staff at several levels including physicians, advanced practitioners, nurses, and support team members. They must clearly represent the payer and their employer and relate closely to the physician leads.

LESSONS LEARNED

- Recognize that the physician can't do it alone and needs team members to support effective patient care and office operations.
- Use technology to its fullest capabilities.
- Pilot programs at one or two sites to determine scalability.
- Expand the role of each care team member.
- Remove as much care as possible from the hospital, emergency department, and doctors' offices.
- Ensure that new care pathways are easier than old care pathways for both patients and providers.
- Benefit to patients always increases both patient and provider satisfaction.
- Continual performance data feedback drives results and enables ongoing reengineering to achieve best results for patients.

11

ProvenCare Biologics

Overweight with lower back and knee pain, Karen was grossly misusing her Soma, Klonopin, and Vicodin prescriptions, taking a 30-day supply of medication in 20 days or fewer every month for years. Her untreated mental health issues contributed to her medication abuse. Through close monitoring and pill count, her Geisinger caregivers identified the misuse and developed a plan to taper Karen off the medications and prevent withdrawal. No longer on Soma or Vicodin, she now appropriately takes a much lower dose of Klonopin. She is in mental health treatment and actively working on unresolved issues.

Karen walks regularly, eats better foods, has more energy, is losing weight, and even went to an amusement park, which was totally out of the question in the past. She proactively checks in with her caregivers and is an active partner in working on her health. Her husband sees a big difference and says she is much better off without all the medications she previously was abusing. She still has pain, but it's tolerable, and her level of activity and ability to derive pleasure from it are much improved. Karen finally feels good about herself, and is more invested in her life and health.

Mary is a breast cancer patient with a jejunostomy feeding tube, known as a J-tube, taking capecitabine, an oral chemotherapy drug. Our team worked carefully with her husband, explaining how her medication needs to be dissolved in water and flushed through her feeding tube. We have followed her care for six months, and her cancer is responding to the properly administered treatment. At one of her recent appointments, Mary's husband hugged her providers and thanked them for their caring.

Geisinger's ProvenCare initiatives are built on a foundation of enhancing patient care in ways that eliminate unjustified variation and capitalize on best practice efficiencies, resulting in quality and value for patients, providers, and payers. For innovation to succeed, there must be a service or product to reengineer, the providers, patients, and patients' families must agree to the changes, and we must be able to demonstrate that the changes actually make life better for all of these important stakeholders.

As we developed ProvenCare Acute and ProvenCare Chronic, it became clear that biological medications,[1] one of the most medically compelling, yet expensive, areas of ambiguous utilization (medical practice pattern variation that cannot be explained by illness, medical need, or the dictates of evidence-based medicine) today, were a natural next step for the application of our reengineering processes. ProvenCare Biologics was the result.

The numbers supported this next step: 1 to 2 percent of the population used specialty medications in 2015, or 37 percent of U.S. drug spend.[2] Specialty drug spending is increasing 25 to 40 percent annually and will represent more than half of the total U.S. drug spend within two years, with the average monthly cost of a specialty medication at $3,384 and ranging from $600 to $30,000.[3]

Biologics account for 70 percent of all U.S. Food and Drug Administration (FDA) medication approvals, with many more presently in clinical trials.[4] The good news is that many of these new therapies, although extremely expensive, are extremely effective. The bad news is that for most applications, indications in treatment protocols remain ambiguous, or treatments are transacted ambiguously. While price per unit was a legitimate point of attack for our move to value, our primary goal here was to eliminate unnecessary or hurtful use of biologicals and to establish the most efficient treatment protocols and most accessible and optimal treatment venue when the indication for treatment was, in fact, unassailable.

Determining the right thing to do for patients in all Proven-Care Biologics value reengineering initiatives is primarily the job of disease-specific experts, enabled by pharmacist-led expert programming teams. Whether it's something as straightforward as erythropoietin (EPO) for the treatment of anemia or something as complex as multiple sclerosis (MS) management algorithms and subalgorithms, design of the initial best practice pathway, as well as the more dynamic adherence monitoring and practices pathway updating, could not be accomplished without this team approach and sociology. At Geisinger, it doesn't matter whether the insurance side or the clinical enterprise/provider side wins financially as long as patients benefit and the total cost of care is decreased. And more often than not, the two go together.

The clinical pathway development is as follows:

- Gather collective experts and support staff (physicians, nurses, pharmacists, allied health professionals) from across the system.
- Explain process and goals.

- Research the current literature.
- Obtain best practice clinical consensus for ensuring safety, reducing variation, and enhancing education and collaboration.

As with all of our ProvenCare processes, the team is responsible for developing the clinical pathways and maintaining and updating each of the reengineered best practice algorithms. While the composition of our reengineering teams varies depending on disease state and stage, they typically include physicians, specialists, and subspecialists who are subject matter experts; clinical pharmacists with particular expertise in the disease; care managers; nurse coordinators; physician assistants; primary care physician leads in community practice sites; health plan medical officers; data analytics and information technology staff from our Epic electronic health record (EHR) support group; and, in most cases, patients with the disease and/or their family members. They are joined by health economists from both the payer and provider sides of our organization. Team members understand that their accountabilities and involvement do not end when optimal care templates initially are put into place. Rather, the process is dynamic and continues because knowledge is changing constantly and rapidly, and we expect to learn and iterate as we go.

The primary component of the formalized reengineering process planning road map is defining which patients have the appropriate condition to begin treatment. For the most prevalent diseases, generally 20 to 30 percent of treatments are not indicated or are indicated only ambiguously. Unnecessary treatment has more than economic consequence; more important, it can be hurtful, causing complications and, in many cases with the use of biologicals, major quality-of-life compromises.

The second component of the planning road map is to determine the default optimal treatment algorithm. The third is to put the clinical pathway into action, and the fourth is to assess performance, both process adherence and patient outcome metrics. The final component is to determine how the template should be continuously improved based on new knowledge, treatment transaction issues, and outcomes.

ALTERNATIVES FOR TREATMENT FOR ANEMIA, MULTIPLE SCLEROSIS (MS), HEPATITIS C, AND PSORIASIS

At Geisinger, the most prevalently prescribed biologics are Harvoni for hepatitis C; Humira for rheumatoid arthritis, inflammatory bowel disease, or psoriasis; Enbrel for rheumatoid arthritis or psoriasis; Tecfidera for MS; and Revlimid for multiple myeloma. We have teams in place to optimize treatment templates and transaction for the following therapeutic areas: anemia, MS, psoriasis, hepatitis C, Crohn's disease, ulcerative colitis, and oral chemotherapies for cancer.

Anemia

More than 20 percent of our patients with anemia associated with chronic renal failures were being treated inappropriately with EPO, which makes a huge difference both in terms of cost and the frequency of disease-related complications. For non-oncology anemia therapy (such as presurgical or chronic renal disease treatment), the minimum EPO dose costs $1,417. Oral iron, more appropriate treatment for up to 20 percent of anemia patients, costs about $3.80. If the better treatment were intravenous iron dextran, the cost would range from $325 to $514 per patient and would entail a single treatment. Iron sucrose is yet another EPO alternative indicated for some of the 20 percent of patients now being treated with a biological and would entail three to four patient encounters at a total cost between $272 and $347 for the entire course. More important than the financial considerations, though, is that EPO is known to exacerbate central and peripheral vascular disease symptoms, particularly in older patients. Even before establishing efficient treatment protocols, and prior to designating centralized sites for biological treatments (for example, no longer permitting EPO treatment in nephrologists' offices), more than 20 percent of unnecessary costs and potentially hurtful outcomes can be avoided simply by applying stringent, standardized indications for treatment.

Under our reengineering of anemia treatment with EPO, there has been a 30 percent total cost savings while improving care. Some 20 percent of cost was eliminated immediately because it represented patients who didn't need to be treated with EPO. An additional 10 percent cost efficiency occurred due to Geisinger's reengineering to an improved treatment of the anemia using EPO, with no overshoot or undershoot of red blood cell optimization. Red blood cell optimization was extremely volatile when treatment was decentralized in nephrologists' offices, and it improved dramatically with implementation of a centralized treatment location supervised by specialists, but transacted by pharma techs.

Multiple Sclerosis (MS)

For MS, the most common disabling neurologic disease of young adults, biological disease-modifying treatments have

FIGURE 11.1 MS Protocol Example

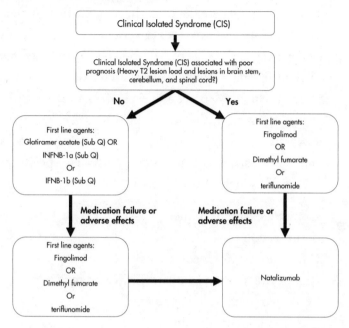

proven beneficial only for the relapsing-remitting types of the disease. Geisinger cares for more than 2,600 patients classified as having MS. Documentation of which MS patients should receive a specified treatment is the first and probably most critical step in establishing best practice treatment protocols. We have determined how this complex information can be used to quickly identify appropriate patients, physician prescribing habits, and starting points for the various disease management algorithms. (See Figure 11.1.)

Our reengineering teams not only developed the treatment protocols for MS at various stages in the patient's symptomatological journey, but also created metrics to measure the reliability of treatment and reassigned various clinical tasks. Monitoring these redesigned roles and ensuring performance of the various protocols and subprotocols, as well as capturing the initial patient data, are done via the Epic EHR system and analyzed through Geisinger's data warehousing and analytics. Geisinger payer data, as well as prospective management through the Geisinger provider data, are critical in both the redesign and the iterative process of evaluating adherence to the redesign and updating of the various protocols.

The overall intent of the MS ProvenCare Biologics program is that only the most appropriate candidates receive specific biologic therapy. This includes:

- Comprehensive drug therapy assessment and optimization
- Proper delivery of medications
- Monitoring of therapeutic response and toxicity
- Support of medication adherence
- Effective patient education
- Communication throughout the entire care team

Patient-reported data is captured by iPads distributed through the neurology clinics or through touchscreen monitors at clinic physical locations. Identifying appropriate clinical content, building questionnaires into Geisinger's survey software, and interfacing the survey software capture with the patients, their families, and the EHR are what enables initial identification of patients for specific biological therapies and also the effective monitoring of adherence to the various protocols.

A decision tree app was created to enhance the reliability of and adherence to specific MS treatment protocols. Features include:

- A program launched directly from within the EHR
- Evidence-based algorithms embedded in the program

- Electronic aids to help select medication, laboratory tests, imaging studies, and referral orders within the specific EHR-embedded protocol
- Ability to capture end-user interactions and incorporate adherence and possible toxicities into the EHR
- Interaction with existing data to provide program adherence metrics to the accountable provider, either the neurologist or the pharmacist
- Maintenance of all clinical content performed by non-discipline-based technical staff

For many patients, home-based monitoring of symptoms is sufficient for certain aspects of the algorithm-directed care. Structured patient-reported questionnaires, if not done at the time of the office visit, can be completed via the Epic-based patient portal, MyGeisinger. It has been an important interface in the communication between primary care physicians, specialists, subspecialists, and our patient population for the past 15 years. Most recently, physicians' progress notes have been made accessible to patients and families, which has fundamentally changed the level of patient activation in relationship with providers. Responses to MyGeisinger questionnaires by patients diagnosed with MS are managed similarly to laboratory results, routed to appropriate EHR-based "in baskets" for clinical management by either the primary physician, the neurologist, or the appropriate disease-specific pharmacist expert.

The MS ProvenCare initiative is evaluated across a number of clinical and financial domains. Evaluation was designed in partnership with clinical leadership in neurology, pharmacology leadership with special expertise in neurologic disorders, and biostatisticians and health economists from our payer and provider sides. Clinical outcomes measured include:

- Radiologic remission focused on lesion burden and whether new MRI lesions are occurring
- Progression versus relapse of MS symptomatology
- Exacerbation of MS symptomatology
- Disability progression
- Adverse medication reactions
- Differential diagnosis of comorbid conditions (like infection) versus relapse of MS
- Progression of comorbid conditions
- Effect on other concomitant diseases and their management

The application of the intervention for MS is exemplified in Figure 11.2.[5]

The net financial benefit estimate for reengineering the MS biologics treatment process and the monitoring of the 2,600 patients in our MS population is considerable, not to mention the benefits in avoiding unnecessary complications, unknown increases in comorbid diseases including cancer, and unacceptable quality of life compromises. These additional benefits are difficult to quantify, but are without a doubt more valuable than the financial savings. (See Figure 11.3.)

FIGURE 11.2 Risks and Adverse Effects

KEY RISKS AND ADVERSE EVENTS OF MULTIPLE SCLEROSIS DISEASE-MODIFYING THERAPIES: MONITORING, DETECTION, AND EVALUATION

DISEASE-MODIFYING THERAPY	PREGNANCY CATEGORY	NEUTRALIZING ANTIBODIES	ROUTINE MONITORING	ADVERSE EVENTS	EVALUATION AND MANAGEMENT STRATEGIES
Interferon beta preperations	C	Yes	Baseline and regular CBC, LFTs	Injection-site reactions	Dose titration, topical methods (eg, ice); usually self-limited
				Flu-like symptoms	Dose titration, NSAIDs/acetaminophen, usually self-limited
				LFT elevation	Review other potential hepatotoxic medications, consider temporary interferon beta suspension, rechallenge at lower dose
				Leukopenia	Lower dose or temporarily discontinue drug and then rechallenge
				Depression	Consider psychiatric evaluation and antidepressant therapy; if severe, consider discontinuing interferon beta
Glatiramer acetate	B	No	None	Injection-site reactions	Topical methods
				Benign systemic reaction (dyspnea, palpitations)	None (self-limited, usually nonrecurrent)
Mitoxantrone	D	No	Baseline and regular (eg, every 6 mo) CBC, LFT	Cardiac toxicity	Predose echocardiogram or MUGA scan; annual follow-up scans even after course completion to detect delayed cardiac toxicity
			Baseline echocardiography; repeat before each dose	Leukemia	Regular CBC; follow-up recommended for years after course completion

(continued)

175

FIGURE 11.2 Risks and Adverse Effects, *continued*

DISEASE-MODIFYING THERAPY	PREGNANCY CATEGORY	NEUTRALIZING ANTIBODIES	ROUTINE MONITORING	ADVERSE EVENTS	EVALUATION AND MANAGEMENT STRATEGIES
Natalizumab	C	Yes	Baseline and routine (eg, every 6 mo) CBC, LFTs	Infusion reactions	If recurrent, check neutralizing antibody titer
			JCV serology and brain MRI every 6 mo in JCV seronegative patients	PML	TOUCH program surveillance; if suspected, discontinue natalizumab and complete clinical, MRI, and CSF evaluation
Fingolimod	C	No	Baseline and regular (eg, every 6 mo) CBC, LFTs	Bradyarrhythmia	First-dose observation protocol (6-h monitoring of heart rate and blood pressure)
			Baseline ECG and VZV serology		Cardiology consultation if risk factors or abnormal baseline ECG results
			Baseline and 3-mo ophthalmological examination (minimum)		Prolonged cardiac monitoring if risk factors or events during first-dose observation
				Macular edema	Ophthalmological monitoring; consider indefinitely in patients with diabetes mellitus or history of uveitis
				Herpes virus infections (especially VZV)	Prompt antiviral therapy; consider prophylaxis in patients with recurrence

FIGURE 11.2   Risks and Adverse Effects, *continued*

DISEASE-MODIFYING THERAPY	PREGNANCY CATEGORY	NEUTRALIZING ANTIBODIES	ROUTINE MONITORING	ADVERSE EVENTS	EVALUATION AND MANAGEMENT STRATEGIES
Teriflunomide	X	No	Baseline and regular (eg, every 6 mo) CBC	Teratogenic risk	Emphasize need for reliable contraception; discontinue drug and use accelerated drug washout protocol if pregnancy occurs while on drug or is planned after discontinuation
			Baseline and monthly LFTs for 6 mo, then every 6 mo		
			Baseline pregnancy test, tuberculosis test		
			Baseline and regular blood pressure	Hepatotoxicity	Monthly LFT monitoring, for 6 mo, then every 6 mo; discontinue drug and use accelerated washout protocol for moderate or severe toxicity
Dimethyl fumarate/ BG-12	C	No	Baseline and regular (eg, every 6 mo) CBC	Flushing (dose-related)	Self-limited; may take with food or aspirin
				Gastrointestinal symptoms and gastrointestinal side effects	Self-limited; symptomatic
				Leukopenia	Laboratory monitoring
Alemtuzumab	C	No	Baseline and regular (eg, every 6 mo) thyroid function and monthly platelet (and possibly urinalysis) monitoring	Secondary autoimmunity	Laboratory monitoring

FIGURE 11.3   Cost and Benefit Estimates for MS ProvenCare Biologics
Reengineering

	YEAR ONE	YEAR TWO
Cost of Intervention	$307,014	$34,830
Financial Benefit	$913,920	$913,920
Net Savings	$606,906	$879,090

Psoriasis and Hepatitis C

As with our other ProvenCare reengineering efforts, we chose to start with cases that were high frequency, high cost, and high variability in both indications and in how and where the specialty drugs were administered. We focused first on what was most likely to succeed in improving patient outcomes. Not surprising, application of the ProvenCare approach to high-use, high-cost biologicals produced two outcomes: better treatment effects for patients and lower costs—both lower expense and lower toxicity. Two additional ProvenCare Biologics pathways are shown in Figures 11.4 and 11.5.

Compared to MS, the best practice algorithms are straightforward for both the psoriasis and hepatitis C pathways. Implementation of the care paths includes development of tools embedded into the transactional EHR; organization of suitable patient and family support; and appropriate patient flow into centrally located treatment sites. Most sites are managed by pharmacists who utilize supervised pharmacology technicians to transact the best practice algorithms. The technicians' adherence to these algorithms is the basis for the care redesign benefit to our patients.

Applicable ongoing support includes defining the roles for clinical oversight, which is shared among pharmacists, care managers, and nurse coordinators, all focused on the patient

FIGURE 11.4 Dermatology: Psoriasis Treatment Care Path

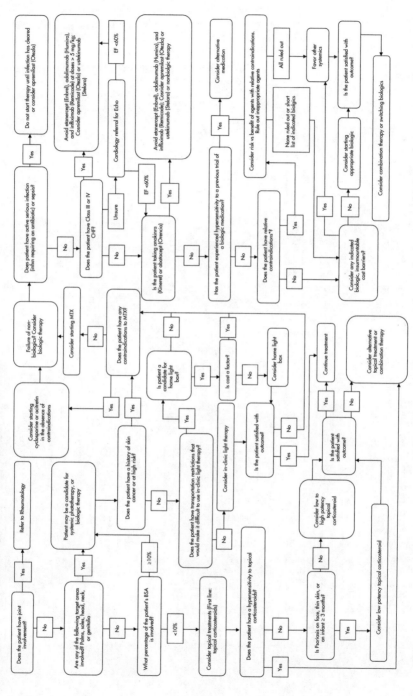

FIGURE 11.5 Hepatitis C Treatment Care Path

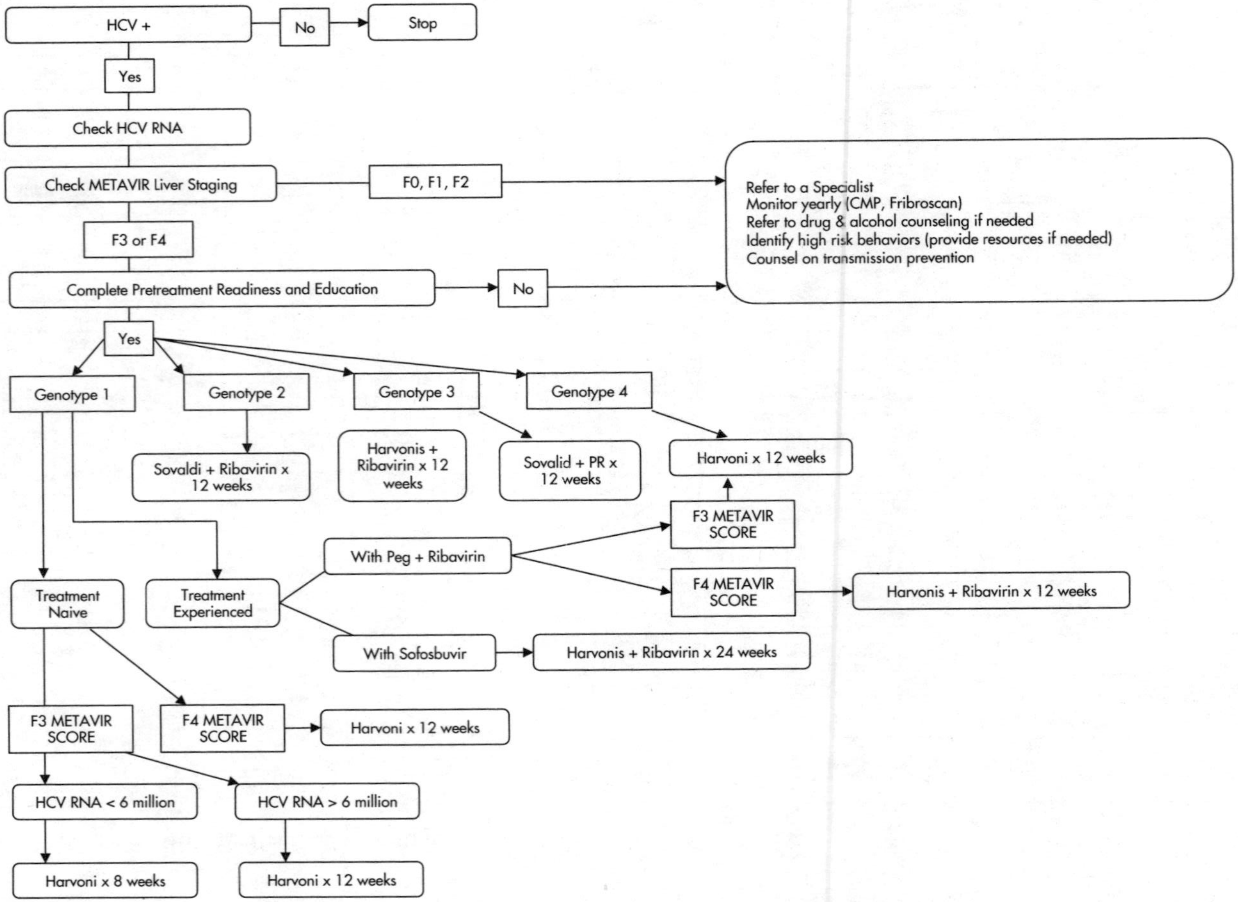

postdiagnosis after physician referral. Prescriptions are directed to the Geisinger specialty pharmacy for medications dispensing and monitoring, including education, patient adherence and medication tolerance, compliance issues, and any required lab monitoring. Scheduling appointments and reviewing lab test results, answering basic patient and/or family questions, and providing overall support including transportation all are part of this wraparound effort, with follow-up scheduled monthly. "Missed to follow-up" monitors are generated by Epic, and patients on this list are reviewed and scheduled manually as needed. This "lost to follow-up" process consists of the following:

- Structured, uniform diagnosis-naming conventions
- Population identification processes
- Monthly monitoring of missed to follow-up reports
- Patients contacted and scheduled as needed

Additional implementation targets include achieving the maximum leverage possible to drive down unit price by coordination of contracting and purchasing through the specialty pharmacy supply chain on both our payer and provider sides. Finally, key input by patients and their families is transacted primarily through the web-based EHR portal. We queried convenience, general access, and patient satisfaction, and designed the ProvenCare Biologics insurance product to be appropriately incentivized and financially advantageous for patients as well as the purchasers.

Early evidence for patients with psoriasis is promising. Some 15 percent of psoriasis patients in Geisinger Health Plan could be treated just as well with daily exposure to ultraviolet light, with a start-up cost of $3,000, versus approximately $80,000 to $100,000 a year for a continuing course of biologics. (See Figure 11.6.) The difference in cost is projected over six years, the average life span of a UV light source. Our year one actual savings for treating psoriasis patients was $2,139,867.

FIGURE 11.6 Dermatology: Psoriasis

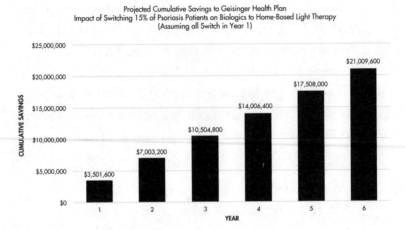

Projected Cumulative Savings to Geisinger Health Plan
Impact of Switching 15% of Psoriasis Patients on Biologics to Home-Based Light Therapy
(Assuming all Switch in Year 1)

A significant issue encountered in planning for a more appropriate psoriasis treatment was a necessary review and modification of the current insurance benefits. Originally the UV light box was an out-of-pocket expense for the patient, while insurance covered the full cost of the more expensive biological treatment for the entire patient population, whether it was appropriate and indicated or not. We mitigated the out-of-pocket cost so it would not be a barrier to patient acceptance of the much more reasonable therapeutic alternative.

Even more important than the financial consequence, though, is the issue of long-term comorbidity in treatment with biologicals, particularly if the treatment is unnecessary. For the approximately 7.5 million Americans with psoriasis, those treated with long-term biologicals not only have an unjustified huge economic consequence, but also an increased cancer risk.

During the period September 2014 to September 2015, among nearly 39,000 patients with all types of psoriasis taking biologicals and reporting adverse events 1,315 cases (3.4 percent) were identified as having cancer diagnoses. This contrasts sharply with no increased cancer risk in psoriasis patients using UV light boxes compared to the population at large with or without psoriasis and having normal exposure to sunlight.[6]

BIOLOGICALS AND CANCER TREATMENT

The high-frequency use of biologicals for treatment of a variety of cancers represents about 70 percent of the biologicals pipeline now at the FDA. Spending on oncology drugs is expected to increase 20 percent annually for the next several years, reaching almost $173 billion by 2020.[7] Use for cancer treatment is expected to quadruple over the next eight years, and development of algorithms for reengineering many cancer care treatments is highly complex. Much of this use not only is unjustified, it's potentially harmful. But cancer patients often want whatever treatments are available to them, providers get paid more when they prescribe more, and pharmaceutical companies get paid regardless of whether patients benefit from the prescribed treatments.

In 2014, the following number of medicines were in development for cancer:[8]

- 168 for breast cancer
- 96 for colorectal cancer
- 176 for lung cancer
- 155 for lymphoma

- 120 for prostate cancer
- 121 for skin cancer

Attempting to standardize this array of biological treatments is fraught with peril regarding patient preference and the sociology of the oncology specialty providers, especially with inadequate evidence and significant specialty oncology advocacy for widespread application. Throughout the United States, there is direct professional incentive to use many of these high-priced and perhaps effective treatments. The current pharma business model enables the treatment of significant numbers of patients with a given drug, whether or not it's biological, even though good results occur only in a minority of patients treated. All patients, however, are charged, and payment is from some combination of insurance or out-of-pocket expensing. Future business models for professional providers and pharma must change, as undoubtedly evidence will increase regarding which biologicals are effective for specific cancers and cancer stages. But at the present time, all remains very much in flux. Hence Geisinger's decision to move into other disease-use cases to target more standardized and high-value approaches, leaving the compelling area of oncology treatments with biologics perhaps to a future ProvenCare program.

GEISINGER CARESITE SPECIALTY PHARMACY

ProvenCare Biologics reengineering includes a more formalized use of indications and treatment protocols, redesign of accountabilities in the treatment transaction, and the reporting of treatment adherence, as well as a change in location of the actual treatment itself. This is more convenient for our patients, as opposed to treatment being provided in individual specialty or subspecialty doctors' offices. We are able to utilize Geisinger's CareSite specialty pharmacies, in various locations throughout our geography, which has worked very well. A summary of the effects of reengineering and relocating the biologic treatments is detailed in Figure 11.7.

FIGURE 11.7 CareSite Specialty Pharmacy (dollars in 1,000s)

FINANCIAL SUMMARY

	FY13	FY14	FY15	FY16 OCT. YTD ANNUALIZED
Revenue	$33,346	$51,341	$75,434	$100,302
Expense	$32,945	$50,352	$73,198	$97,563
Contribution Margin	$401	$989	$2,236	$2,739
CM %	1.2%	1.93%	3.0%	2.7%
Scripts	11,491	14,933	17,987	21,258
GHP mix	72.4%	78.5%	75.9%	76.6%
340B savings on GMC	$1,278	$5,187	$5,335	$4,831

RX REVENUE GROWTH

	FY13	FY14	FY15	FY16 OCT. YTD ANNUALIZED
GHP	$24,138	$40,276	$57,292	$76,800
Other	$9,210	$11,065	$18,142	$23,502
Total	$33,348	$51,341	$75,434	$100,302

LESSONS LEARNED

- Overuse of biological medications causes unjustified financial and clinical ill consequences.
- Reengineering of biologics usage can be done to the benefit of patients.
- You must redefine indications, application, accountability, and patient and family input to optimize the use of biologicals.
- The process is dynamic and iterative and takes advantage of a changing knowledge base.
- Changes must be made regarding who is accountable for the treatment, how it is managed, and where it is given.
- As is the case with all of our reengineering and innovation, patient and physician satisfaction is key to success.

12

ProvenExperience

Six-year-old Maddy is a fan of Elsa, the queen in Disney's animated film *Frozen*. When Maddy was admitted to Geisinger's Janet Weis Children's Hospital, it was Elsa who helped make her feel better. Maddy's concerned father, James, a member of the armed services and unable to be at her side, wanted to do something special. "Could the character Elsa from *Frozen* visit Maddy?" he asked his friend Tiffany Noll, nurse team leader for Geisinger's Mountain Top outpatient clinic. She immediately knew who could help: her friend Kim Duffy, operations manager of the children's hospital.

Kim just happened to have an Elsa costume from the previous Halloween. Donning it the next morning and braiding her long blond hair to be fully in character, she was at Maddy's bedside when she awoke. Mother Nature contributed to the surprise: it snowed overnight. Maddy's favorite Disney character brought a message of cheer from her Daddy: "He wanted you to know what a special little girl you are and how much he loves and misses you. Look! There's snow outside, just for you."

This is the essence of Geisinger ProvenExperience: treating patients like family, empathizing that they are in a tough situation, and doing our best to make it easier for them. We endeavor to do this for all patients, 100 percent of the time, and offer a money-back guarantee when we fall short.

Before Dr. David Feinberg officially started as CEO in May 2015, he spent a month visiting every Geisinger clinic and hospital, meeting with patients such as Maddy and staff and team members such as Tiffany Noll and Kim Duffy. He also visited patients in their homes and continues to do so regularly.

As he sat on patients' beds and asked about their care, he learned that people had mixed feelings about Geisinger. Patients were thrilled beyond belief that they had such great medical care in their part of the country, but they said there was still much we could do to help them to get better.

They told us that it was loud in the hospital at night, which disturbed their rest and recuperation. In addition, patients were confused about their care when transitioning from the hospital to skilled nursing facilities or their homes.

Patients endured a lot of waiting. It could take weeks to get an appointment, and the scheduling process itself was daunting. They observed that our physician office hours were not especially convenient for people working or going to school. Parking structures and buildings were difficult to navigate. Patients didn't understand their bills.

Although well-intentioned, employees were not uniformly friendly, nice, or caring. Patients wanted our healers to listen better, understand their situations, and partner with them to come up with a plan for their care. They often were bothered more about the process of care than their diagnosis.

Geisinger patients are very trusting of their healthcare provider. Much of our service area is rural and small-town U.S.A., with hardworking and family-oriented citizens who know and care about one another and have a true sense of community. In his regular rounding on patients in their homes, Dr. Feinberg has checked on an elderly woman injured chasing away a bear who stole a freezer off her porch. He's visited a man receiving in-home infusion for cancer treatment who likes to watch TV, but limits how much because of the cost of electricity. When we recently built a four-story parking garage, which is free of charge, patients avoided it because they didn't know how to use it, so we positioned staff in the garage to help them understand how to navigate it.

Patients were accustomed to restricted access to care because of geography. Remarkably, they were content to wait until we could see them. And they would wait weeks for an appointment with us rather than drive two hours to Philadelphia to be seen more quickly. We were providing incredibly high-quality care for this trusting community, but we were not always easily accessible and not consistently compassionate.

For nearly 15 years, Geisinger reengineered our processes to achieve world-class care, quality, safety, and value. Every aspect of this effort began by asking how patients' outcomes were to be improved, and we often included input from patients and their families in the care redesign. Our strategy was to take as much care as possible out to where our patients lived and worked, and even out of the doctors' offices and into our patients' homes, so we could provide the right care at the right time in the right place.

As we built our ProvenCare portfolio, the capacity for our service lines to do everything to which they aspired often pushed them against the boundaries of their capability. We always were concerned that too much innovation might diminish the all-important provider/patient interaction, and we viewed decreased patient satisfaction as the first warning signal. Rapid expansion through merger and acquisition made this challenge even more formidable, as we blended people and organizational cultures. While we kept our focus on our patients and their families, we were only partially successful in mitigating our over-aspiration and continuing to achieve the highest levels of patient satisfaction.

Now with many ProvenCare services in place, we are building on our innovation energies and our intention by elevating the patient experience to historic levels. We are applying Geisinger's renowned ProvenCare model and methodology, perfected over years of development and experience, to the patient satisfaction issues of responsiveness and compassion. The goal is to offer the high-quality, high-value, safe care for which Geisinger is famous in a more culturally sensitive, compassionate, private, connected human way patients don't expect. We will not settle to be simply the best in the healthcare industry. Geisinger won't rest until all patients are satisfied 100 percent of the time, and we have the best customer service in *any* industry.

PROVENEXPERIENCE BEST PRACTICES

There's a long history of patient-experience initiatives at Geisinger that foreshadowed the launch of ProvenExperience in late 2015. For example, for 20 years, we've been surveying patient satisfaction, learning from that feedback, and teaching professionalism to all new staff members, programs spearheaded by Victor J. Marks when he was director of dermatology. Since around 2000, all Geisinger physicians and advanced practitioners have participated in a four-hour course covering one-on-one patient communication skills. Medical residents work with actors posing as patients to practice skills and learn how to handle communication challenges.

In 2014, Dr. Steele named internal medicine associate Greg F. Burke and chief nursing officer Susan M. Robel chief patient experience officers. Geisinger needed to get the entire organization on board to recapture the more patient-centric feeling present when the system had just two hospitals. The goal: to do things right for patients and treat them like family all the time.

A systemwide Patient Experience Steering Committee, broadly reflective of key caregivers and geographies, was formed to develop Geisinger's standards for the patient experience. We used the acronym ABIGAIL, a touchstone to founder Abigail Geisinger, to reintroduce the patient experience mission and establish behavioral standards or expectations: Accountable, Befriend, Inform, Genuine, Acknowledge, Involve, and Listen. (See Figure 12.1.) Because employees and their families are also patients, they strongly connect with Mrs. Geisinger's "Make my hospital right, make it the best" admonition to her founding medical director. Some 99.7 percent of all physicians and most staff completed the initial ABIGAIL training, and all new employees complete online training and are required to agree to adhere to the standards.

From involvement in developing the ProvenCare lumbar spine surgery procedure, Dr. Burke had nurtured the idea to "Geisinger-ize" the patient experience, to establish a level of service guaranteed to meet a rigorous set of patient-experience best practices. We would eliminate variation and make it happen every time. We would certify patient satisfaction, just as certain medical procedures and services are under the Proven-Care model, and call it ProvenExperience. The idea gained momentum with Dr. Feinberg's arrival in mid-2015, when he

FIGURE 12.1 ABIGAIL Standards

Accountable	• I deliver the best patient experience by striving to manage, meet, and even exceed expectations.
	• I exemplify my profession's standards and competencies.
	• I ensure all patient issues are resolved.
Befriend	• I treat everyone with courtesy, dignity, and respect.
	• I provide assistance to those in need of help.
	• I help and collaborate with my colleagues.
Inform	• I am clear with patients about their care, speaking in terms they understand.
	• I provide reassurance, information, or answers in a timely manner.
	• I communicate fully with my colleagues to ensure a positive patient experience.
Genuine	• I treat everyone with respect, as unique individuals.
	• I convey kindness and courtesy in my words and actions.
	• I show gratitude to all who choose Geisinger.
Acknowledge	• I make the best first impression and leave a lasting positive impression.
	• I acknowledge others with a smile and a greeting.
	• I anticipate and address everyone's needs.
Involve	• I involve patients in decisions regarding their plan of care.
	• I communicate with family members when appropriate.
	• I collaborate with my colleagues to produce positive patient outcomes.
Listen	• I am "present"—actively listening without interrupting.
	• I listen to concerns and demonstrate empathy.
	• I listen without judgment.

further challenged the organization to a money-back commitment: patients unhappy with a service or procedure could request reimbursement of all or part of their copay.

We identified best practices for broad implementation, starting in late 2015:

- Consistent patient communication, using the C.I. CARE (pronounced see-I-care) communication framework
- Transparency in reporting quality metrics
- Leadership rounding
- A consistent professional appearance
- Bedside shift report, hourly rounding, and white-boards in hospital rooms to improve communication and service
- Calls the night before surgery and patient rounding on demand
- Transition to home care
- Same-day appointments with phones answered by human beings
- Notes pushed to the patient
- A redesigned, easy-to-understand bill
- Standardized continuous service recovery

Many healthcare systems select one or two patient-experience best practices to implement, but Geisinger is endeavoring to make them all happen every time with every patient. Implementation is under way on each campus across the system.

The C.I.CARE Patient Communication Framework

Geisinger is implementing the C.I.CARE communication framework, developed at UCLA Health and now used at Stanford Medicine and other healthcare systems. The framework is designed to ensure consistent employee communication with patients and colleagues. The C.I.CARE acronym stands for:

- *Connect* with the patient or family member using Mr./Ms. or the preferred name.
- *Introduce* yourself and your role.
- *Communicate* what you are going to do, how it will affect the patient, and other needed information.
- *Ask and Anticipate* patient and/or family needs, questions, or concerns.
- *Respond* to patient and/or family questions and requests with immediacy.
- *End with Excellence*, courteously explaining what will come next or when you will return.

C.I.CARE reflects a broad set of communication actions that everyone throughout the organization can practice, from dietary and housekeeping workers to administration and volunteers, as well as clinical healers. We expect each employee to use C.I.CARE in every interaction throughout Geisinger, in person and on the phone.

This communications framework was operationalized with a broad, systematic rollout as a major training process in every level of the organization. All 30,000 employees received training from their leaders and completed an online course. C.I. CARE was established as a competency, just as cleaning an IV or inserting a catheter are for nurses. Crucial for follow-up and reinforcing this approach, we created a tool for leaders or peers to observe others and document whether and how the behaviors are being performed.

Transparency in Reporting Quality Metrics

Geisinger is among the first dozen U.S. health systems to be transparent about caregiver ratings. Geisinger patients searching for caregivers on our website will find that their profiles show patient satisfaction scores and patient comments. The patient satisfaction rating is an average of all responses on the nationally recognized 10-question Press Ganey Patient Satisfaction Survey.[1] Responses are measured on a scale of 1 to 5, with 5 being best.

Press Ganey randomly selects patients seen at Geisinger outpatient clinics to receive a survey, sent via U.S. mail or e-mail within a few weeks of appointments. We receive more than 165,000 survey responses annually, a response rate of around 18 percent. We share the ratings on our website to help patients and families make informed decisions about healers, and we use the data for continuous improvement in patient care and for constructive feedback to healers and staff.

Ratings are updated monthly, and comments are posted weekly, with a one-year archive. We post both positive and negative comments, but remove offensive, abusive, or malicious language; names or detailed information that jeopardize patient confidentiality or privacy; and comments exclusively about other clinicians. Only about 2 percent of comments are not displayed. Patients may also request to remove a comment.

In addition, we do not display ratings or comments for clinicians with fewer than 40 survey responses, due to lack of statistical validity. Transparency currently is available only for outpatient clinic healers. In addition, we don't survey the experiences of patients seeing nonemployed Geisinger clinicians, residents, and fellows.

Future improvements may include enabling our healers to respond to a comment and innovative psychoanalytic tools to more closely match healer and patient compatibility.

Leadership Rounding

Geisinger instituted consistent, coordinated leadership rounding in 2015. Between 20 and 150 leaders representing administrative and clinical departments and the Geisinger board of directors meet monthly on each campus for several hours. They fan out to visit inpatients on units other than their own, knocking on doors, washing their hands, and asking about the care. They address anything that needs immediate attention, and treat the patients as they would their own family member, correcting food delivered in error, getting a pillow, or helping a patient to the bathroom.

During one early leadership round, for example, Joi Siebecker, medical-surgical operations manager, and Angelo Venditti, chief nursing officer, discovered that one floor of Geisinger Community Medical Center in Scranton lacked sufficient thermometers, so they went to a local CVS Pharmacy, purchased seven, and had them in clinical staff hands within 30 minutes.

The leaders also find out what is going well and convey the appropriate compliment, plus go upstream with a thank you, for example, to the person who hired the nurse and the unit IT and facility managers who support the nurse's work.

Regrouping to debrief, the leaders share both the positive and the negative. We assign ownership for addressing systemic issues and report on follow-up items from prior rounds.

An unprecedented simultaneous rounding episode at all 11 hospitals in late 2015 connected leaders by live videoconference. Deemed "the largest leadership rounding taking place in America," more than 500 executives from across Geisinger gathered at their respective hospitals, simultaneously embarking on a walking tour to engage patients and caregivers and listen to their praise and concerns. The assignment was to fix anything they could and to take care of issues right then.

A Consistent Professional Appearance

To ensure that patients can identify various team members and their roles readily, Geisinger has enacted a new professional appearance policy. Starting January 1, 2016, all 3,000-plus registered nurses wear pewter-colored uniforms displaying an embroidered Geisinger logo, along with a newly designed name tag spelling out "registered nurse," as patients don't always know what R.N. means.

The neutral pewter, or dark gray, uniform color existed at a hospital joining the Geisinger system in 2015 and is appropriate for both male and female nurses. The pewter scrubs may be worn with an alternative color, such as white pants. A more pediatric-friendly secondary color, ceil blue, is worn instead of white by healers working with children.

Geisinger works with one supplier to size and provide the uniforms to nurses in various styles of their choice. Financial support of $150 was granted to each nurse, sufficient to purchase a week's supply of uniforms, and supplier discounts help with subsequent purchases.

Studies show that patients associate clean, well-pressed white lab coats with professionalism in physicians. Geisinger supplies and encourages all doctors, physician assistants, and nurse practitioners to wear white coats when interacting with patients. Underneath, we ask our healers to dress as if presenting for a job interview. We view that medicine is not a casual business, so dress should not be casual.

New professional appearance standards eventually will cover all healers, including physicians. Those with the same job title will be dressed in the same color. Environmental services workers already wear navy. Uniforms for licensed practical nurses will be rolled out next.

The first impression of our healers is determined not only by tone and expertise but also by appearance and demeanor. The identical attire helps bring order to the complexity of our environment, offers a calming effect, and visually demonstrates professionalism.

Bedside Shift Report, Hourly Rounding, and Whiteboards

We are implementing a bundle of nursing best practices simultaneously at all Geisinger hospitals; three of the components are bedside shift report, nurse hourly rounding, and communication boards (whiteboards).

At all hospitals, we've changed the handoff process so that discussions occur at patients' bedsides, where nurses coming on and off shift discuss the status of the patient's care and include the patient and/or family in the discussion. For decades, traditional nursing shift report took place in a conference room, at the nurse's station, or even in the hall or via tape-recorded message.

Bedside shift report involves patients in their care and leads to a higher level of safety.[2] Any inaccurate or incomplete information is corrected on the spot by the patient or family members. Nurses look at IVs and examine wounds together, double-checking that everything is correct. In semiprivate rooms, we take precautions to safeguard privacy and not share protected health information.

Hourly rounding is an evidence-based intervention in which nurses purposefully visit a patient about every hour to check the "Five Ps": pain, potty, position, PO^3, and placement. The series of questions includes "Are you having any pain? Can I assist you to the bathroom while I'm here? Are you comfortable? Would you like a drink or fresh ice? Do you have everything you need within your reach?" Nurses are scripted to say that someone will be back in about an hour, but if something is needed urgently before, the patient should ring the call bell. They also conduct an environmental sweep, ensuring that there are no safety issues such as tripping hazards. Hourly rounding generates trust and establishes caring through presence and partnering with patients. Further, it demonstrates Geisinger's promise to patients and their families to anticipate and meet their needs. Hourly rounding decreases falls, reduces pressure ulcers, and improves patient satisfaction, and it also enhances nursing satisfaction owing to fewer call bells and less distance walked each day.[4]

Whiteboards have been installed in every inpatient room systemwide. The information noted on this important communication tool is highly standardized and updated at shift change. The boards identify the patient's doctor, nurse, nursing assistant, and unit operations manager; outline the patient's plan of care for the day; show the patient's phone number and anticipated discharge date; note the last time the patient had pain medication; record the patient's fall risk; and indicate whether the patient needs assistance getting out of bed and whether one or two assistants are needed based upon steadiness and mobility.

For all three best practices, we measure patient perceptions through Press Ganey surveys. In 2015, Geisinger added custom survey questions, asking whether nurses came in to check about every hour and whether we checked frequently enough. In addition, nurse managers round on every patient to check that hourly rounding and bedside shift reports are occurring and that whiteboards are updated, validating with patients in real time that the practices are taking place. Training occurs on all aspects of the bundle, and every nurse is evaluated annually on the practices, which are considered a nursing competency.

Calls the Night Before Surgery and Patient Rounding on Demand

Geisinger is implementing new physician processes to enhance inpatient satisfaction. For example, the surgeon, as captain of the ship, calls patients the night before surgery (or on Friday before a Monday appointment) to go over last-minute questions, reinforce pre-op quality measures such as cleansing the surgical site, and convey anxiety-reducing messages, such as she will be getting a good night's rest, is confident that the procedure will go well, and will see the patient before he undergoes anesthesia.

Not only do the calls contribute to increased quality surgical outcomes, they enhance engagement, with patients anecdotally demonstrating a significant amount of appreciation for the contact showing that the surgeon sincerely cares. Challenges have included not reaching patients and missing their returned calls, rehashing questions already covered during pre-op visits, and allocating time for the calls when a large number of patients are scheduled the next day.

The idea of surgeons calling patients stemmed from an Orthopaedics Institute faculty meeting focused on increasing patient satisfaction. Forms of individual outreach were discussed, including calling the night before, and the surgeons were encouraged to try it and see what happened. Some jumped right in, while others initially said, "Forget it." The concept was promoted to other surgeons, and it's becoming a routine part of the day.

In addition, the patient's family members are consulted about a time window during which they would prefer the physician to round on their loved one. This is caring and efficient for patients and their families and helps build effective partnerships with their healers. We've done similarly with food service, offering an à la carte menu available by phone request, like hotel room service.

Transition to Home Care

Geisinger has improved the process for making the transition to home after hospitalization, anticipating patient and family needs in that stressful time. Our 70 nurse case managers, termed health navigators, focus on transition of care from hospital to home or nursing home. Representing a partnership between our healers and Geisinger Health Plan, the navigators are notified about every admission, identify patients with chronic conditions, and put strategies in place to prevent readmission for pneumonia, heart failure, cellulitis, and urinary tract infection.

When patients come home from surgery, a box is waiting for them at home containing the medical equipment they need and have ordered, from a shower stool to a bedside commode, accompanied by clear instructions for the new care setting.

The idea for the boxes originated in the Orthopaedics Institute, where as part of preparation for total knee or hip replacement, patients participate in a program that manages expectations. They view a video and attend a class during which they learn the steps in total joint replacement, what to expect in the hospital, how their pain will be managed, the type of physical therapy they'll require, and the level of care needed at home postsurgery.

Also included is discussion regarding what equipment is helpful postoperatively, including a walker, knee brace, or ice therapy device. This allows patients to preorder such items so they are delivered before surgery, not two weeks later.

Same-Day Appointments and Phones Answered by Human Beings

Lack of healthcare access is not compassionate. When your third grader is drawing disturbing pictures with red yarn around his neck, when you've found a lump, or when your father falls in the bathroom and is bleeding, but doesn't call you until the morning because he didn't want to disturb you, you don't want to go through an 800 number and wait six weeks for an appointment. Geisinger offers a warranty to patients that a person will answer the phone and that same-day appointments are available in any specialty, any day of the week.

We have a twofold tactic for managing access. For primary care services, there are large blocks of volume, lots of clinicians, and always someone available with capacity for urgently needed care, and we make room.

With specialists such as otolaryngologists or neurologists, it works differently. There always have been specialists on call overnight in the emergency department, so part of a specialist's day now starts in the daytime, and when a need arises, there's a system to make the physician available at night.

We recently upgraded to a state-of-the-art phone system, answered by humans who use a script prompting callers regarding whether they'd like to be seen that day. About 20 percent take us up on the offer.

We have same-day appointments every day of the week, especially on the weekends, because it's easier for patients who are working or going to school to see a doctor then. The goal is to create an awareness in our patients that we're like a big-box store or a restaurant: you know we're open, and we're ready and happy to serve you.

Notes Pushed to the Patient

Geisinger collaborated in the development of OpenNotes and was one of three original study sites in 2010. Today, more than 1,400 of our team members routinely share notes with more than 300,000 outpatients, inpatients, and emergency-department patients. Since the inception of OpenNotes, we've pioneered an evolution: OurNotes for patient activation to enhance the patient/provider relationship.

OurNotes not only documents the visit but also pushes the note to the patient and employs an agenda, a previsit application that creates a patient-generated problem list. OurNotes also enables us to communicate more effectively what our healers are thinking, to tell a real story that makes sense in language a layperson can understand.

Via e-mail link, OurNotes pushes to patients not only lab results and medication lists but the entire note from the most recent and all prior visits. This improves patients' compliance and helps them better understand their medical reports and be more involved in their health decisions. Patients use the agenda application to prepare for a visit, prioritizing what they want to cover. The note cannot be closed until the healer addresses the concerns identified by the patient when creating the agenda.

In the first large-scale study of its kind, our researchers confirmed that patient access via a web portal to doctors' notes is associated with increased adherence to a medication regimen, improving overall health while reducing use of healthcare services, leading to a lower overall cost of care.[5]

A Redesigned Bill

The way we pay for healthcare is irritating, confusing, and unintelligible to consumers. Everyone understands the other things they pay for in life, such as a mortgage, a restaurant meal, or groceries—all of these the common individual can explain. But few can explain health insurance coverage and medical billing.

Having a health insurer as part of our system, Geisinger is uniquely qualified to make revolutionary improvements in this area. Geisinger and Geisinger Health Plan work hand in hand to understand what patients want on their statements and explanations of benefits (EOBs). We've found that what matters to patients isn't what insurance covers, but what they owe.

In 2005, we were among the first to develop a combined statement, the document we use to bill patients. It contains charges for all providers and delivers information regarding what is expected of patients, their options for payment, and alternatives for financial assistance if needed. (See Figure 12.2.)

Geisinger doesn't send statements to patients until their insurance has satisfied the bills. We tell patients their liability and give them options for paying in full or over time. We are one of the few health systems in the nation to have EOBs correlate to the patient statement; most systems send out estimated bills. We ensure that the EOB and statement match and that they are simple for patients to understand.

We're improving this statement with clearer, more familiar wording about the services provided to help the patient better connect with what occurred at the visit. We also are spelling out more plainly how much insurance paid and the patient's obligation.

FIGURE 12.2 Geisinger Patient Statement

Keys To Understanding Your Geisinger Patient Statement

Numbered Areas Point Out Where Important Information Can Be Found On Your Statement

STATEMENT EXPLANATIONS

1. Date Statement was printed

2. Name and address of person recorded as responsible party for account (guarantor)

3. Identifies specific facilities having activity on this statement (Geisinger Medical Center, Geisinger Clinic, and/or Geisinger Wyoming Valley Medical Center)

4. Patient Information

5. How to reach us

6. Patient Balance

7. Area to complete when paying by Discover Card, MasterCard or American Express

8. Fill in amount you are paying this statement

(continued)

FIGURE 12.2 Geisinger Patient Statement, *continued*

9. **Previous Charges** reflect services which have appeared on a prior Account Overview, but have not been paid. Charges are listed by facility.

10. **New Charges** reflect services having a patient balance which have not before been listed on an Account Overview. Charges are listed by facility.

11. **What you owe now** indicates the total patient balance for both previous and new charges. Amount reflects total for all facilities listed.

Patient Name: John Q. Patient
Medical Record Number: 99999999
Page 3 of 3
October 13, 2015   32283

Geisinger Health System
Account Overview

9. Previous Charges: For care received at Geisinger Clinic

This table shows the status of your previous charges by visit date.

Visit Date	Description	Total Charges	What we billed to insurance	What ins. covered/ other	Your payments	What you owe now
11/06/2014	MV~LABORATORY	79.00	79.00	-74.00	-0.73	4.27
06/26/2015	MV~LABORATORY	79.00	79.00	-74.00	0.00	5.00
06/29/2015	LB~NEUROLOGY	799.00	799.00	-794.00	0.00	5.00
Total for Geisinger Clinic		**$957.00**	**$957.00**	**-$942.00**	**-$0.73**	**$14.27**

New Charges: For care received at Geisinger Medical Center   10.

Your insurance company will send you a document explaining the amount your insurance covered.

Products, medications, equipment and rooms

11.

Visit Date	Description	Total Charges	What we billed to insurance	What ins. covered/ other	Your payments	What you owe now
09/02/2015	Clinical Laboratory	765.00				
SubTotal		$765.00	$765.00	-$760.00	$0.00	$5.00
Total for Geisinger Medical Center		$765.00	$765.00	-$760.00	$0.00	$5.00

New Charges: For care received at Geisinger Clinic

Your insurance company will send you a document explaining the amount your insurance covered.

Physician and other professionals

Visit Date	Description	Total Charges	What we billed to insurance	What ins. covered/ other	Your payments	What you owe now

0203

(continued)

FIGURE 12.2   Geisinger Patient Statement, *continued*

12. **What you may owe later**
indicates services provided
but not yet processed.

Patient Name: John Q. Patient
Medical Record Number: 99999999
Page 3 of 3
October 13, 2015   32283

09/15/2015	DV-GENERAL SURGERY	247.00	247.00	-227.00	0.00	20.00

Total for Geisinger Clinic $247.00 $247.00   -$227.00 $0.00 $20.00

What you may owe later: 12.

There may be charges for services provided that have not yet been processed by our system and/or your insurance carrier.
Once these are processed, we may send you a bill for the portion not covered.

To Pay Your Bills On-Line, Go To: www.geisingerwebpay.org

Thank you for selecting Geisinger Health System for your healthcare needs.

(continued)

FIGURE 12.2 **Geisinger Patient Statement,** *continued*

STATEMENT EXPLANATIONS

13. Provided for your information are additional instructions regarding our billing practices, answers to some frequently asked questions, and our uncompensated care guidelines

14. This area is provided to indicate any changes to address information

13.

Geisinger Health System- Committed to Caring.

Providing Healthcare for those in need
Geisinger Health System is committed to providing medically necessary healthcare to those in need, regardless of their ability to pay. The following is our financial assistance policy and how to qualify and apply for financial assistance.

Our financial assistance policy
- Your financial circumstances will not affect the care you receive. All patients are treated with respect and fairness.
- Assistance is available for medically necessary care. Patients may apply for financial assistance at any time – before, during or after their care.
- If you have no health insurance or limited insurance benefits and/or limited financial resources, you may be eligible for assistance. Uninsured patients are required to apply for Pennsylvania Medical Assistance or enroll in the Federal or State Health Insurance Marketplace.
- Approval of financial assistance is determined by Geisinger's policy guidelines, which are explained on this statement.
- Depending on the amount of your bill and your financial circumstances, interest-free re-payment plans are available with minimum monthly payments as low as $25.
- If you do not qualify for financial assistance but believe you have special circumstances, you can request that your case be reviewed by a Geisinger Financial Counselor.
- To apply for financial assistance you must provide us with all information necessary to apply for other funding sources that may be available to you such as Medical Assistance, Medicare Disability or other Federal or State programs.
- You are financially responsible for your healthcare and for applying for financial assistance. Geisinger will make application materials easily available. To request an application please visit our website at geisinger.org or call 800.640.4206.

Do you qualify for financial assistance?

Eligibility for financial assistance is based upon the U.S. Government's Federal Poverty Guidelines. These guidelines are updated annually. You may qualify for assistance if your household income is 300% or less of the current Federal Poverty Guidelines. To determine if you qualify for financial assistance, use the income matrix below as a guide to determine whether your household size and income is less than 300% of the Federal Poverty Level.

Household Size	300% of Federal Poverty Level
1	$35,640
2	$48,060
3	$60,480
4	$72,900
5	$85,320
6	$97,740
7	$110,190

Final determination is based on an evaluation of income, information provided on the financial application, and assets compared to patient liability. Patients deemed eligible under Geisinger's financial assistance program will receive 100% discount on medically necessary charges.
Exclusions
While Geisinger's Financial Assistance Program covers most services, there are some exclusions, such as, but not limited to:
- Cosmetic services
- Elective reproductive services
- Transplant-related services
- Bariatric-related services
- Routine dental care or cosmetic dental reconstruction
- Other services, at Geisinger's discretion

To reach a financial counselor call 800.640.4206

How Do I apply for financial assistance?

Our goal is to make applying for patient financial assistance as easy as possible. Here is the process, step by step:

Step 1: Request an Application Form.
These forms are available at no charge by visiting our website at geisinger.org or by calling 800.640.4206. In addition, these forms are available at all Geisinger Hospital emergency departments and admission areas and Clinic locations.

Step 2: Complete and return the form.
Once you have completed the application, mail to:
Geisinger Uncompensated Care Services 49-38
100 N. Academy Avenue
Danville, PA 17822-4938

Step 3: We review your application.
We will review your application to determine if you qualify for assistance according to the guidelines outlined on this statement. If there are special circumstances that affect your ability to pay, these will be reviewed by one of our Financial Counselors.

Step 4: You receive a decision.
You will receive a written decision promptly, usually within 30 days of applying. If you are denied assistance, we will provide the reason for denial. The decision will also provide you with information on how to set up a payment plan.

All applications for financial assistance are kept completely confidential. The information on your application is shared only with those responsible for determining your eligibility. Financial assistance forms are available in the following languages upon request: Spanish, Arabic, Vietnamese, Chinese, and Nepali.

Need more detail?
If you need more detailed information than this Billing Statement provides, call a Patient Service Coordinator at 1-800-640-4206, 8:00 AM to 5:30 PM M-F. In the event where no financial assistance application is received, Geisinger may use presumptive analytic tools to assess your eligibility for financial assistance.
Check Conversion Process
When you provide a check as payment, you authorize us to use information from your check to make a one-time electronic fund transfer from your account as a check transaction. When we use information from your check to make an electronic fund transfer, funds may be withdrawn from your account as soon as the same day we receive your payment, and you will not receive your check back from your financial institution.
Insufficient Funds
If your check is returned to Geisinger due to insufficient funds, it will be re-presented to your bank electronically and your account will be debited the amount of the check plus the state allowed fee.
Phone Scam Alert
Please be alert for a phone scam with the caller claiming to represent Geisinger and offering a retail gift card if you send a small payment. If you receive a call such as this, hang up and do not call back. While Geisinger at times does offer gift cards for completing surveys or participation in research projects, Geisinger would never ask for a payment from a patient to receive a gift card. Thank you.

14.

Change of address?

If your address on page one is incorrect, check the box on the other side of this slip and fill in your new address below.

Name _____

Address _____

City, State _____

Zip _____

Telephone Number _____

We are exploring how better to convey what insurance covered to help dispel misunderstanding between insurance coverage and insurance benefits paid. We also are working on guaranteeing a price estimate for when we counsel patients in advance regarding how much a service will cost.

The U.S. Department of Health and Human Services has invited Geisinger to collaborate with other vanguard health systems regarding development of national best practices in easy-to-understand medical provider bills and EOBs, with recommendations expected in 2017.

STANDARDIZED CONTINUOUS SERVICE RECOVERY

How do we handle situations such as these?

- There's a bad trauma incident tonight on I-80, and some of those with elective surgery tomorrow are being rescheduled.
- An ICU doctor is "so amazing" that when his patients are ill, he sleeps in the room with them, giving up his personal life. Then he is cranky with others because he's tired.
- You show up for an appointment that was confirmed via telephone, but find out you're not on the schedule until tomorrow.

The opportunity is always there to be recovering, and our brand loyalty depends on it.

Our 30,000 healers are trained to notice if something's not right with a patient, to ask about it, and to do what it takes to make things right. Geisinger healers all are accountable, and leadership has their backs.

We empower our staff to fix compelling, rational, and real problems within 24 hours, not requiring them to seek permission multiple levels up the organization. At our Geisinger Marworth Alcohol and Chemical Dependency Treatment Center, Gina Cicio, director of food and environmental services, learned that patients found their plastic-encased bed pillows uncomfortable and hot, making it difficult to sleep. Many patients there have sleep disorders, and the pillows were making their conditions worse. Ms. Cicio went to a local big-box store and bought 70 pillows for the patients.

Walking through the Geisinger Medical Center lobby, Alison Mowery, nurse practitioner specializing in cardiovascular disease, discovered a tearful patient and her mother. Asking how she could help, Ms. Mowery learned that the patient had been in substantial pain for quite a while and had driven more than an hour to the hospital, expecting an MRI at 7:00 a.m. But the precertification hadn't been completed, so the patient was turned away, and follow-up appointments that day had been cancelled. Finding the patient distraught and not knowing what to do, Ms. Mowery escorted her and her mother to neurology, where the grateful patient was seen, her case discussed, and the MRI rescheduled.

We're very hands-on in terms of training to recognize and deal with service recovery and empowering employees who have direct contact with patients, and we've created tool kits to make it easier for team members and patients to respond. For example, the checkout staff ask how the experience was today, and if there is a problem, they are authorized to remedy the situation on the spot.

Like an airline giving you free miles or a ticket to atone for a mechanical delay or overbooking situation, if Geisinger doesn't live up to its promise anywhere along the line, we compensate for the dissatisfaction by apologizing, providing parking and meal vouchers, and offering to refund all or part of the copay.

Our patient advocacy team subsequently springs into action, ensuring that whatever occurred is relayed to the operations team. To ensure that it doesn't happen next time, we've implemented back-end processes to close loops and effect change. The goal is to minimize the number of bad experiences through an environment of continuous improvement so that, over time, the need for remediation will be low.

THE PROVENEXPERIENCE APP

The concept of giving a refund certainly isn't new; our innovation is ensuring it's as clear and easy as requesting a refund from Amazon.com or Zappos.com, making it a one-touch process, promoting it, and in a sense entreating patients to request the refund.

We developed a free, simple smartphone application for ProvenExperience to measure patient experience and offer a refund as part of our service recovery with our patients. It was built and rolled out in about three months, using a clinician-led team to ensure relevancy, with vital administrative support for project management, technical skills, subject matter expertise, and regulatory compliance.

We piloted the app with bariatric and lumbar spine surgery patients, considered knowledgeable about technology and having substantial copays of $1,000 and $2,000, respectively. We learned that patients wanted to tell us their stories about what went well and didn't and to have a sliding scale for the refund request.

Patients receive a one-page handout instructing them how to access the app and are encouraged via e-mail to respond one week after surgery. The app prompts, "Tell us about your experience," triaging between "I'm happy" and "I'm unhappy." Happy patients indicate with check boxes which aspects of their care were outstanding; unhappy patients are asked where the experience went wrong. The app records how the patient would like to proceed, either talking to us or sending a message, getting a copay refund, or submitting information about the experience. Patients without smartphones respond in more classic ways, on paper, by phone, or using our website.

LESSONS LEARNED

Geisinger is disrupting the entire healthcare service model, making it as customer-centric as the Ritz-Carlton, keeping prices down like Walmart, and knowing you as well as Amazon.com. ProvenExperience puts our money where our mouth is. We are writing refund checks, but they are valuable, because our patients are telling their friends and neighbors how we made it right.

- Treat patients like family.
- Lack of access is not compassionate.
- Empower all employees to make it right, and have their backs.
- Get leaders into the clinical areas frequently.
- Don't study innovations forever. Pilot, learn, and roll out.
- If healthcare doesn't disrupt itself, someone will do it to us.

13

Future Vision

The 16-year-old soccer player collapsed on the field from apparent dehydration and was brought to one of our emergency departments. While receiving fluids, she agreed to participate in our genomic sequencing study, and we found gene profiles associated with young athletes dying during practice. Collapsing during exercise was probably the first sign of her deadly condition.

Follow-up with 30 family members revealed that her uncle died at age 20, ostensibly from choking, but now more likely from a heart attack. Subsequent testing revealed several who needed a drug regime or pacemaker and a half dozen additional relatives who would be closely monitored.

This striking case represents the future of care and caring at Geisinger and emphasizes the excellence of our overarching value-reengineering path: using data, identifying the best practice pathways, and engaging the patient in the process. Thanks to our longstanding commitment to research and the MyCode® community health initiative, patients are volunteering to have their blood and saliva samples stored in our system-wide biobank and studied. Our ultimate goal is to find ways to make healthcare better, as we fortunately did for the young soccer player and her family. In this respect and many others, the future is now at Geisinger.

IT'S ALL ABOUT CARING

While research and technology continue to advance medical science, in some ways healthcare as an industry has become deficient in caring. Healthcare professionals overwhelmingly enter the field because they want to help patients, but for a variety of reasons this hallmark of interacting with patients and their loved ones falls short. So while we are in the business of caring, we often miss the mark, which marks us for disruption. Someone else will come up with a better way if we don't take charge of it ourselves. Recall what happened to the railroad, print publishing, photography, and video rental industries. We've long been known for being ahead of the curve at Geisinger, as early adopters of the electronic health record (EHR), through our various ProvenCare innovations and chronic disease management, and with our vision and progress toward precision medicine based on solid medical research. It's the same with our commitment to making sure that, even with all of these advances, our foundation always will be built on doing what is right and best for our patients and doing so in a caring, compassionate manner. Our reengineering efforts always have focused on higher quality at lower cost, and we define lower cost not just as less expensive care but as less aggravation to patients and their families.

It's not caring, though, when we make patients wait, speak in a language they don't understand, or provide services that aren't necessary and, in fact, may be harmful. Caring must go beyond meeting the accepted standards of care, and our caring imperative is a logical extension and growth of our desire to continually make things better for the people we serve. To return to caring, healthcare requires radical change, and once again Geisinger intends to be the model. But we aren't going to be satisfied with being the best in healthcare; our goal is to be the most caring organization anywhere. It is through striving to be a model for others that we can elevate our caring to new heights.

Let's put this caring imperative in context with where healthcare now is nationally and where we want it to be. Despite good progress, there still is considerable unjustified variation in quality, access, and cost in healthcare today. There continues to be unwarranted and fragmented caregiving and an addiction to perverse payment incentives that not only encourage but reward units of work, or volume, rather than better care and improved outcomes, or value.

It isn't caring when we put 35 to 40 percent of our patients through procedures or treatments that are unnecessary and perhaps detrimental, especially when we know that the high cost associated with this unnecessary care almost always represents a quantitative surrogate for poor quality. It isn't caring when we are inconsistent in providing best practice care to everyone. And it certainly isn't caring when patients experience higher costs because their providers focus on volume, not value. With the implementation of the Affordable Care Act (ACA) and ongoing post-ACA turbulence, we need to remember why we are in healthcare in the first place—to care for others—and increase our energy, commitment, and hard work toward our ultimate aspiration of where healthcare should be in this country. To be truly caring, healthcare must quickly evolve and be characterized by:

- Affordable coverage for all
- Payment for value
- Coordinated care
- Continuous improvement and innovation
- Empowered patients who take an active role in their good health
- National health goals, leadership, and accountability
- Professional, compassionate service every time for every patient

We have been and remain active at Geisinger in defining this new post-ACA environment and anticipating a huge number of the changes that must occur in hospital-associated care reengineering with our various ProvenCare, ProvenHealth Navigator, and ProvenExperience innovations. Reengineering care has two outcomes that are absolutely essential for us to move healthcare in the United States forward. The first is a focus on improving quality outcomes for patients and their families and the other, almost always correlated, is a decrease in cost.

Further, we have chosen to take as much of our intellectual property as possible into scaling and generalizing experiments that include our own expansion into new markets, our insurance operations expansion into other states with non-Geisinger providers in other non-Geisinger markets, and the founding and nurturing of xG Health Solutions, which is committed to spreading as much of the Geisinger innovations as possible to as many organizations on both the payer and provider side of healthcare as we can.

PATIENTS, PROVIDERS, PAYERS, AND PURCHASERS

What we're doing at Geisinger and the aftermath of the ACA affect the four major "Ps" in healthcare: patients, providers, payers, and purchasers. The influx of 20 million more Americans with access to healthcare through the increased availability of Medicaid, and the new rules regarding who can provide that care, place added pressure on the structures and business models of providers, payers, purchasers, and all other stakeholders involved in creating various products and services. As Medicaid and Medicare expand, the only reasonable solution for both the federal and state governments' portion of the cost is to continue the move away from fee for service and toward expansion of Medicaid managed care organizations. The Health Care Payment Learning and Action Network has produced a series of white papers with implementation suggestions regarding how to fundamentally change the behaviors of the four Ps and shares a commitment for Medicare to move to 50 percent non-fee-for-service payment by 2018 and 80 percent non-fee-for-service by 2020.[1]

Medicare conversion to population-based payment and managed care will extract cost only if the relationship between the payer and provider is fundamentally changed to decrease price per unit and remove unnecessary care. If this is not done, the combination of increased access to care through expanded insurance and the increased ability to give great care using great new drugs and devices will quickly bankrupt not just the healthcare system, but the entire country. There continues to be much pressure on the federal health insurance exchange and speculation that the ACA will be repealed. If that occurs, it likely will be replaced ultimately by some type of expanded public plan (something like Medicare for all) that would probably put even more pressure on healthcare organizations to adopt a reengineering of care approach and a fundamentally different relationship between payer and provider.

Continued mergers and acquisitions activity is likely among the payers and providers, with the justification of providing higher quality at lower cost. But until payment incentives are changed to move away from fee for service, such volume-driven activity will continue and even increase, at least in the short term.

With greater regulatory and other cost pressures, small practices won't be able to afford to stay in business and will disappear. Providers will adjust and respond appropriately to whatever the payment incentives are, but in every scenario the key is to extract unnecessary or hurtful care and cost in a way that Geisinger has modeled for the past 20 years.

Caring has been at the center of all our reengineering and innovation and will be more important than ever, given fundamental change in the relationship between doctors and their colleagues taking care of patients together and also in the doctor-patient relationship. Patients will be much more equal in relationships with providers and will be more accountable for long-term outcomes. A major responsibility in these relationships will be effective communication with patients and their families about important healthcare outcomes. Providers always hear about the temperature of the food and the cleanliness and quietness of the hospital room, and these concerns must be addressed. But patients must also be more educated about and involved with their actual care. With their increased knowledge and active participation, earning patient satisfaction will be more demanding than ever before.

There will be winners and losers in this healthcare industry evolution. The winners will be those payers and providers who work together to obtain the best outcomes for their mutual constituencies, keeping members and patients so healthy that they need less acute care and less hospitalization and experience less aggravation. Purchasers also will initiate a transformed partnership with selected providers who commit to working continuously with large employers to achieve significantly improved outcomes for employees. Businesses that partner with entities such as the Health Transformation Alliance or the Pacific Business Group on Health to work with payers, providers, device makers, pharmaceutical companies, and intermediaries to keep employees healthier will have a significant competitive advantage. Healthcare costs represent about a third of total compensation expenses for businesses, and the amount of revenue required to accommodate such expense is considerable, especially when those resources could be used for innovation. The winners will be able to approach healthcare in a way that benefits employees and their health status to help offset this huge indirect cost.

The fundamental issues always center on behavior change, and the behaviors of patients, providers, payers, and purchasers will be changing over the next decade. It is imperative to understand and respond effectively to patient and family satisfaction, and success will depend on effectively communicating how working together can create better health for our society.

PREVENTATIVE CARING

Healthcare has a unique opportunity to make things better for populations of people, for example, those with similar health challenges, those in a specific industry, and the members of a community. One way Geisinger plans to return to caring is by taking exceptional care of the communities we serve through prevention. There are many illnesses, demographic challenges, and lifestyle choices causing tremendous suffering across our nation. But healthcare systems often are designed around conditions hospitals can make money on, such as chemotherapy and heart and brain surgery. Essentially, this outdated medicine capitalizes on the old pay-for-volume model by identifying certain illnesses and procedures that pay better than others and doing plenty of them. Advances in these areas are miraculous, but they don't take care of large populations and aren't focused on preventing illness.

Geisinger, like other health systems, has a long history of collaborating with other organizations to complete regular community health needs assessments, and we are committed to taking this effort even further and truly focusing on prevention. With that in mind, we will assess the health needs in all the communities we serve to determine whom we're caring for and how needs differ by geography. The priority might be obesity in one area, lack of immunization in another, and opioid addiction in a third, or, more likely, a combination of conditions and challenges.

In the current payment system, these are losers. No one is advertising about them. This is a different mindset from our outdated sickness care system. The old way is neither preventative nor patient-focused, and it's wasteful. For example, no one ever advertises to the elderly American male on Medicaid who has congestive heart failure, diabetes, and moderate alcohol use. He is challenging to treat and providers aren't paid well to do so, but if he represents our community, we have an obligation to find him and care for him in a way that is culturally sensitive, compassionate, private, and connected. Much of our Proven-Care innovations are designed to support payment for value rather than volume, which improves care for such patients and rewards providers appropriately.

UNBELIEVABLE ACCESS

With millions of additional Americans getting health insurance, and the aging of the baby boom generation, demand will continue to challenge healthcare organizations throughout the country. All providers need to commit to providing unprecedented access. Despite everyone's best prevention efforts, bad things will still happen to people. You develop an irregular heartbeat or get hit by a car, or a family member becomes suicidal. Life changes overnight as something happens environmentally, genetically, or in some combination of both, and you become a patient. When you show up at the hospital or clinic, we'll be ready because we know you.

U.S. healthcare systems are not good at this right now, and they must improve. They check your name and allergies multiple times, sending the message that they don't know who you are. They also don't know much about how you like to receive information or prefer to be treated. Amazon.com knows you better than your doctor does, and that, too, must change.

In the future, we will know who you are and keep that information readily available using the best practices of customer relationship management (CRM), so we can be more patient-centered, knowing and understanding patient preferences. Our newest facilities are moving toward open, social space in place of waiting rooms, and our ultimate goal should be never to make our patients wait.

Rather than a generic approach, we will employ personalized care models that take motivation and behavior into account to help patients follow their care plans and be as healthy as possible. We'll know whether you prefer frank discussions or a gentler approach, want us to always include your daughter, communicate via Skype, or welcome e-mail messages. We'll know whether or not you want to try new medications or cutting-edge treatments. And we'll know how to shift those preferences depending on what's happening with your health in any given situation.

Thanks to our early adoption and implementation of the EHR and a largely stable patient population at Geisinger, we have 20 years of data we are building upon to make this depth and breadth of knowledge a reality.

Additionally, anytime you touch our system, you'll understand your financial responsibility accurately. Industrywide, this has been difficult to achieve, as insurance copay, coinsurance, and deductibles are rolling continuously. Because we have an embedded health insurance company, we are building a system that pulls from multiple data streams and can answer the financial responsibility question in real time with total accuracy. Billing for doctor visits and tests will be free from complex terminology that no one understands and will be as clear as though you're paying for a gallon of gas.

ANTICIPATORY, PRECISION MEDICINE

In addition to being well-prepared for patients when bad things happen, we will also know in advance that something might happen. Thanks to a major DNA study we began in 2014 in collaboration with Regeneron Pharmaceuticals, we are getting to know our patients very precisely at Geisinger. We're well on our way to collecting patient blood samples from 250,000 consenting volunteers for analysis, sequencing of genetic material, and comparison to long-term health outcomes. With one of the largest U.S. populations of participants, the study's size and scope will allow great precision in identifying and validating the associations between genes and human disease.

Geisinger brings state-of-the-art sample collection and storage capabilities, our MyCode biorepository, extensive EHRs, and a stable patient population that trusts us and is willing to participate in collaborations, while Regeneron provides the infrastructure to support sequencing and genotyping. The intent is to build a high-throughput platform for discovering and validating genetic factors that cause or influence a range of diseases where there are major unmet medical needs. The partnership is meant to further Geisinger's ongoing mission to improve population health and individualized care through clinical innovation and cutting-edge, world-class research.

Our rate of participation is more than 85 percent of those invited to join the study, remarkably high for this type of research and a tribute to our loyal patient population. Included in that group is a woman we identified with the BRCA1 gene and its associated increased risk for early breast and ovarian cancer. When presented with this information, she elected for prophylactic removal of her ovaries and fallopian tubes. During the procedure a tumor was detected and removed.

With two decades of clinical data on our stable, multigenerational patient population, from both inside and outside of our clinical enterprise because of our integrated insurance company, we know a tremendous amount about our patients.

Presently, there are only about 70 conditions of genetic abnormality for which there is an effective medical treatment. We've taken the stance that we're going to tell patients of a genetic abnormality only when we can do something about it, because DNA test results are stress-provoking if not actionable. Our initial findings show that results are positive for genetic abnormality about 3 percent of the time, with at least three to four first-degree relatives additionally affected.

If a DNA study comes back with potentially treatable conditions, the information is relayed to the primary care physician, who has five days to communicate with the patient. Meanwhile, the physician can access a 30-minute online primer about the condition and how best to discuss it with the patient. We also have an army of genetic counselors on staff for follow-up.

Does this type of precision medicine make a difference? Projecting from our early experience, we are confident that we will be able to reduce the risk of breast cancer in women under 40 in our population by the identification of high-risk individuals and improved surveillance and treatment. Familial hypercholesterolemia appears to be found in one in 250 of our patients. According to the American Academy of Pediatrics, children in such families should be evaluated and statin treatment started by age eight to reduce the early heart damage and risk of early heart attacks.[2] So we add value in this area, too.

We expect that many patients will benefit directly from participation in this research because of our ability to validate and return clinically actionable results to them, such as starting appropriate youngsters on statins. In addition, all patients will benefit from the knowledge we gain regarding setting standards for genome-informed care. The study will transform our ability to foresee disease before the onset of symptoms, diagnose chronic and potentially fatal conditions before it's too late to intervene, and determine how best to optimize the health and well-being of each patient.

CARE IN PLACE

We believe that every time a patient arrives at a provider for care, the organization should apologize that he or she had to come. Our goal is to treat patients at home, at work, or in the classroom, rather than in the hospital or clinic, and moving forward, providing the right care in the right place will be more important than ever.

For example, a heart failure patient arriving at one of our emergency departments will be started on diuresis, and then "admitted" to his home where hands-on, in-place professional follow-up care will be administered until he's recovered. A person experiencing a heart attack will be "admitted" to home with a paramedic, who will take care of her for the next three or four days as a "hospital" patient. Her cardiologist will round regularly via Skype until the patient is indeed "discharged" to home.

A recent study demonstrated that for the typical medical appointment, patients drive about 40 minutes, wait approximately an hour to be seen, and spend 20 minutes with the doctor.[3] The cost to the American economy of this nonproductive travel and waiting is astronomical. According to Geisinger, being patient-centered and caring means coming to you, either virtually or physically.

If you've shown up at one of our facilities, we will make the best use of your time, first by eliminating the wait. In our clinics, there will be no waiting rooms, as they have no value; they will be converted to clinical space. As you enter the parking lot or garage, a transponder on your dashboard will alert us that you're on site and will arrive in the clinic in three to eight minutes. We'll get the exam room ready, and the physician will be there waiting with the cardiologist you've anticipated seeing for a second opinion because of your heart concern. They know all about you, thanks to our CRM system and clinical and genetic records, and they've prepared for your visit ahead of time via the OurNotes system that allows patients to help set the agenda. If you've asked a question this morning about needing a dermatologist, one will link in via telemedicine shortly.

The doctor will not spend all of her time entering information into a computer, so the focus will be entirely on you. The computer is there to serve the doctor and provide prompts regarding what she may be missing. For example, the doctor may review your last five blood pressure readings from the EHR using a device that enables her to keep the focus on you personally. An assistant or intelligent system will record the visit notes, and you're on your way in 15 to 20 minutes, feeling that your time and money were well spent.

We've built physical spaces for such innovations, with pilots under way and patients being invited to participate. But it's not just a physical location that makes it possible; it's a completely different service mentality: we exist to serve you, and we value your time.

FAMILY AS CAREGIVERS

Consider all of the disruptions in the travel industry during the past decade. You're now the travel agent and the airline check-in employee. Airline innovations such as online flight booking and check-in were ways to transition labor to the customer and lower costs. Similarly, we will transition care to patients and family members by training them to be part of the care team, but the goal here is to improve the quality of outcomes.

With inpatients, we typically never ask the family member whether they'd like to provide food for the patient or whether someone would like to be the nursing assistant and change dressings. In our future vision, however, families will help care for patients. As we've explored this innovation, we've found that family members are willing and able to provide care to their loved ones.

For example, one weekend Dr. Feinberg went to visit a patient at home, an Amish farmer who had fractured nine ribs when he was pinned by a large bull in his barn. Despite suffering significant pain and having trouble breathing, he initially refused to seek care and only relented when a physician friend urged him to go to the hospital, where he was admitted to relieve his pain and prevent pneumonia. The patient insisted on being released after two days because he preferred to be treated at home.

Asked about his care in the hospital, the patient noted that he was treating his pain by applying to his ribs an herbal remedy made from plants in his yard, which to him was a more comfortable approach. He also observed that when our healers moved him they were "work hardened," remarking that his wife was "more delicate" when she moved him. His wife, baking pies nearby, had never moved a trauma patient before, but she did it perfectly. While there were benefits to the patient being in the hospital where we could monitor him more closely, his family was taking better care of him because they were not "work hardened."

Healthcare often gets so caught up in regulations that the family can't lay a hand on inpatients. But when they go home, their families become their nurses and often do a better job of caring. We presently are building an experimental inpatient unit to pilot the concept of having family members on the care team and working through the associated regulatory issues.

A RALLYING CRY FOR CARE AND CARING

Geisinger nurse Cassandra Thomas was enjoying a vacation in Florida with her family when the sky darkened and lightning struck the beach. Looking out the window, she saw someone down on the sand, and her nursing instincts told her something was terribly wrong. She ran down 16 flights of stairs and out onto the beach where, with lightning still in the area, she performed CPR on 15-year-old Cameron. Assisted by a police officer who was also on vacation and others, Cassandra continued CPR until paramedics arrived. Little did Cameron know how lucky he was to have someone, who is not only a nurse but a CPR instructor, put herself in harm's way to help him. Cassandra's efforts were heroic, but she didn't think she was doing anything out of the ordinary.[4] That is what care and caring are all about.

Today, Geisinger is one of the most scientifically advanced and innovative healthcare organizations in America. But we also know that to be the best, we must care the best. We must never forget what got us here: the values we share with our neighbors, friends, patients, and loved ones. We're committed to the good health of our community, with compassionate, kindhearted caring along with our advanced, innovative care.

We're also committed to sharing what we're learning and doing in our journey. Our solutions are highly reliable, based on processes and tools refined in our clinical settings. Many of our best practices came from studying the ways of others, and we're eager in turn to share our methods, trials, and results through published research and medical education. Numerous other health systems are replicating our improved patient outcomes, enhanced efficiencies, and reduced costs.

We invite you to join them and us in this quest to be the best in care and caring.

LESSONS LEARNED

- Innovation in healthcare never ends.
- Geisinger is continuing to challenge itself to improve in every way.
- Scaling Geisinger's innovations is one of our most important strategic commitments.
- Caring is fundamental to caregiving.
- Caring must go beyond meeting the accepted standards of care.
- Know your patients better than Amazon.com knows its customers.

NOTES

ACKNOWLEDGMENTS

1. J. Wennberg and Alan Gittelsohn, "Small Area Variations in Health Care Delivery," *Science* 182, no. 4117 (December 14, 1973): 1102-08, https://www.ncbi.nlm.nih.gov/pubmed/4750608.
2. Robert E. Andrews et al., *Towards a New Model of Health Care: Employer-Facilitated Care* (Washington, DC: American Health Policy Institute, 2016), http://www.americanhealthpolicy.org/Content/documents/resources/Towards_a_New_Model_of_Health_Care.pdf.

CHAPTER 1

1. Miliard, Mike, "Geisinger CEO David Feinberg, MD, on patient satisfaction, population health, genomics and more", *Healthcare IT News*, (2016, April 12), http://www.healthcareitnews.com/news/geisinger-ceo-david-feinberg-md-patient-satisfaction-population-health-genomics-and-more
2. Anthony Shih, Karen Davis, Stephen C. Schoenbaum, Anne Gauthier, Rachel Nuzum, and Douglas McCarthy, "Organizing the U.S. Health Care Delivery System for High Performance," *Commission on a High Performance Health System* (New York: The Commonwealth Fund, August 2008), http://www.commonwealthfund.org/usr_doc/Shih_organizingushltcaredeliverysys_1155.pdf.
3. Reed Abelson, "In Bid for Better Care, Surgery with a Warranty," *New York Times,* May 17, 2007, http://www.nytimes.com/2007/05/17/business/17quality.html?_r=0.
4. President Barack Obama, address, Joint Session of Congress on Healthcare, September 9, 2009, https://obamawhitehouse.archives.gov/the-press-office/remarks-president-a-joint-session-congress-health-care

5. President Barack Obama, remarks, town hall meeting, Southwest High School, Green Bay, Wisconsin, July 11, 2009, https://www.whitehouse.gov/blog/2009/06/11/a-town-hall-and-a-health-care-model-green-bay.

6. Joe Klein, "The Long Goodbye," *TIME*, June 11, 2012, http://time.com/735/the-long-goodbye/.

7. Steve Sternberg, "Unsatisfied With Your Surgery? Get (Some of) Your Money Back," *U.S. News & World Report*, November 11, 2015, http://www.usnews.com/news/articles/2015/11/11/unsatisfied-with-your-surgery-get-your-money-back.

CHAPTER 2

1. Gerard Anderson, *Chronic Care: Making the Case for Ongoing Care* (Princeton, New Jersey: Robert Wood Johnson Foundation, 2010), http://www.rwjf.org/en/research-publications/find-rwjf-research/2010/01/chronic-care.html.

2. Elizabeth A. McGlynn et al., "The Quality of Health Care Delivered to Adults in the United States," *New England Journal of Medicine*, June 26, 2003, http://www.nejm.org/doi/full/10.1056/NEJMsa022615.

3. Arnold Milstein, "Perspective: Managing Utilization Management: A Purchaser's View," *Health Affairs* 16, no. 3 (1997): 87–90, http://content.healthaffairs.org/content/16/3/87.full.pdf+html.

CHAPTER 4

1. Glenn Steele Jr., *Reinventing Health Care: The Geisinger Health System 2001–2015* (Danville, PA: privately published, 2015), 352.

2. Ibid, 353.

3. Ibid, 361–62.

4. Ibid. 364, 365, 371.

5. Lawrence F. Wolper, *Healthcare Administration: Managing Organized Delivery Systems*, 5th ed. (Burlington, MA: Jones & Bartlett Learning, 2010), 86.

6. *Reinventing Health Care*, 357–59.

CHAPTER 5

1. Pennsylvania Health Care Cost Containment Council, www.phc4.org.

2. A. S. Casale et al., "ProvenCare: A Provider-Driven Pay-for-Performance Program for Acute Episodic Cardiac Surgical Care," *Annals of Surgery* 246, no. 4 (2007): 613–21.
3. G. Pang, "Central Teachers Gain $7,000 Average: Health Care Savings Balance Raises in Contract," *Press Enterprise* (July 6, 2009).
4. Reed Abelson, "In Bid for Better Care, Surgery with a Warranty," *New York Times*, May 17, 2007, http://www.nytimes.com/2007/05/17/business/17quality.html?_r=0.
5. Ibid.

CHAPTER 6

1. Glenn Steele Jr., MD, PhD, *Reinventing Health Care: The Geisinger Health System 2001–2015*, ©2015 Geisinger Health System.
2. Steele, *Reinventing Health Care.*
3. Steele, *Reinventing Health Care.*
4. Steele, *Reinventing Health Care.*

CHAPTER 7

1. Alexander Kulik, Marc Ruel, Hani Jneid, T. Bruce Ferguson, Loren F. Hiratzka, John S. Ikonomidis, Francisco Lopez-Jimenez, Sheila M. McNallan, Mahesh Patel, Véronique L. Roger, Frank W. Sellke, Domenic A. Sica, and Lani Zimmerman on behalf of the American Heart Association Council on Cardiovascular Surgery and Anesthesia, "Secondary Prevention After Coronary Artery Bypass Graft Surgery: A Scientific Statement From the American Heart Association," *Circulation* (February 9, 2015): published online ahead of print, http://circ.ahajournals.org/content/early/2015/02/09/CIR.0000000000000182.
2. Mark R. Katlic, Matthew A. Facktor, Scott A. Berry, Karen E. McKinley, Albert Bothe Jr., Glenn D. Steele Jr., "ProvenCare Lung Cancer: A Multi-Institutional Improvement Collaborative," *CA: A Cancer Journal for Clinicians* 61 no.6 (November–December 2011): 382–96.

CHAPTER 8

1. 2010 Diabetes Burden Report, Pennsylvania Department of Health, http://www.statistics.health.pa.gov/HealthStatistics/OtherHealthStatistics/Documents/2010_Diabetes_Burden_Report.pdf.

2. Thomas Nolan and Donald M. Berwick, "All-or-None Measurement Raises the Bar on Performance," *JAMA* 295, no. 10 (2006): 1168–70, http://ow.ly/4n7Ktt.

3. Frederick J. Bloom Jr. et al., "Primary Care Diabetes Bundle Management: Three-Year Outcomes for Microvascular and Macrovascular Events," *American Journal of Managed Care* 20, no. 6 (June 26, 2014), http://ow.ly/4n7I8m.

4. Daniel D. Maeng et al., "Value of Primary Care Diabetes Management: Long-Term Cost Impacts," *American Journal of Managed Care* 22, no. 3 (February 29, 2016), http://ow.ly/4n7J5p.

5. xG Health Solutions, *ProvenCare Process Guide, Chronic Disease Methodology Diabetes Mellitus Management.*

6. Ibid.

7. ProvenCare codes are customized, best practice clinical codes. Their purpose is to optimize care plans, health management reminders, performance monitoring, and evidence-based alerts. These codes are not billing codes and are not used for any reimbursement purpose.

8. xG Health Solutions, *ProvenCare Process Guide, Chronic Disease Methodology Diabetes Mellitus Management.*

9. Jan Walker et al., "The Road Toward Fully Transparent Medical Records," *New England Journal of Medicine* 370 (January 2, 2014), http://ow.ly/4n7JXG.

10. Bloom et al.

11. Maeng et al.

CHAPTER 9

1. "Reinventing American Healthcare," WVIA original feature presentation, 56:44, April 23, 2015, http://on-demand.wvia.org/video/2365467227/.

2. Thomas Nolan and Donald M. Berwick, "All-or-None Measurement Raises the Bar on Performance," *JAMA* 295, no. 10 (2006): 1168–70, http://ow.ly/4n7Ktt.

3. See Figures 6.1 and 6.2.

CHAPTER 10

1. The Institute for Healthcare Improvement's "Triple Aim" is to improve the patient's experience of care (including quality and satisfaction); to improve the health of populations; and to reduce the

per capita cost of healthcare. See *IHI Triple Aim Initiative*, http:
//www.ihi.org/engage/initiatives/tripleaim/pages/default.aspx,
accessed September 27, 2016.

CHAPTER 11

1. For a concise explanation of biological products and how they differ
   from conventional drugs, see "'What Are Biologics' Questions
   and Answers," U.S. Food and Drug Administration, accessed
   August 8, 2016, http://www.fda.gov/AboutFDA/CentersOffices/
   OfficeofMedicalProductsandTobacco/CBER/ucm133077.htm.
2. Express Scripts Holding Company, *Express Scripts 2015 Drug
   Trend Report*. St. Louis: Express Scripts Holding Company, 2016,
   http://lab.express-scripts.com/lab/drug-trend-report.
3. Steven G. Ivey (vice president, specialty pharmacy programs, Med-
   Impact Healthcare Systems, Inc.), in discussion with Geisinger
   Health Plan, November 19, 2015.
4. Aimee Tharaldson, "Specialty Drug Approvals in 2013," (blog),
   Express Scripts Holding Company, March 26, 2014, http://lab
   .express-scripts.com/lab/insights/drug-options/specialty-drug
   -approvals-in-2013.
5. Dean M. Wingerchuk and Jonathan L. Carter, "Multiple Sclerosis:
   Current and Emerging Disease-Modifying Therapies and Treatment Strategies," *Mayo Clinic Proceedings* 89, no. 2 (February 2014):
   225–40.
6. Institute for Safe Medication Practices, "Cancer Risks of Biological Products for Psoriasis," *QuarterWatch* (April 6, 2016), http://
   www.ismp.org/QuarterWatch/Default.aspx.
7. Deena Beasley, "Analysis: Drug Costs Become Bigger Issue in
   Cancer Care," *Reuters*, June 14, 2012, http://www.reuters.com/
   article/us-cancer-cost-idUSBRE85E05B20120615.
8. Pharmaceutical Research and Manufacturers of America, "Cancer
   Chart Pack, Cancer Medicines: Value in Context," 2014, http://
   www.phrma.org/sites/default/files/pdf/cancer-chart-pack-5-22-14
   .pdf.

CHAPTER 12

1. Press Ganey Associates works with more than 10,000 health care
   organizations nationwide, including more than half of U.S. hospitals, to improve patient care and experience.

2. Wendy Chaboyer, Anne McMurray, and Marianne Wallis, "Bedside Nursing Handover: A Case Study," *International Journal of Nursing Practice* 16, no. 1 (January 2010): 27–34. See also Wendy Chaboyer, Anne McMurray, Joanne Johnson, et al., "Bedside Handover: Quality Improvement Strategy to 'Transform Care at the Bedside'," *Journal of Nursing Care Quality* 24, no. 2 (April 2009): 136–42.

3. From the Latin *per os*, or by mouth.

4. Margo A. Halm, "Hourly Rounds: What Does the Evidence Indicate?," *American Journal of Critical Care* 18, no. 6 (November 2009): 581–84.

5. Geisinger study, "Access to Doctors' Notes Increases Med Adherence," *PRNewswire*, November 2, 2015, http://www.prnewswire.com/news-releases/geisinger-study-access-to-doctors-notes-increases-med-adherence-300170282.html.

CHAPTER 13

1. Health Care Payment Learning and Action Network, Alternative Payment Model Framework and Progress Tracking Work Group, "Alternative Payment Model Framework Final White Paper," January 1, 2016, https://hcp-lan.org/workproducts/apm-whitepaper.pdf.

2. American Academy of Pediatrics, "Expert Panel on Integrated Guidelines for Cardiovascular Health and Risk Reduction in Children and Adolescents: Summary Report," *Pediatrics* 128, supplement 5, December 2011, http://pediatrics.aappublications.org/content/128/Supplement_5/S213.

3. Kristin N. Ray, Amalavoyal V. Chari, John Engberg, Marnie Bertolet, and Ateev Mehrotra, "Opportunity Costs of Ambulatory Medical Care in the United States," *American Journal of Managed Care*, August 18, 2015, http://www.ajmc.com/journals/issue/2015/2015-vol21-n8/Opportunity-Costs-of-Ambulatory-Medical-Care-in-the-United-States.

4. Chris Krepich, "Geisinger Staff Honors Hero; Nurse Bonds with Lightning-Strike Victim, His Family," *Bloomsburg Press Enterprise*, July 29, 2016.

INDEX

Abelson, Reed, 59
ABIGAIL standards (patient experience), 191, 192
ACA (*see* Patient Protection and Affordable Care Act)
Access, quality, and cost triangle, xi
Access to care, 189, 221–222
  managing, 202
  phones answered by humans, 202
  same-day appointments, 202–203
Access to health insurance, xvii, 221
Accountability, 23, 153, 210
Accountable care organizations (ACOs), xiii–xiv, 148
Acute services:
  fee for, 2–3
  typical American acute care, 82
  (*See also* ProvenCare Acute)
Administrative partners, xiv, 23, 65
Advanced care management, 142–143
Advanced medical home (*see* ProvenHealth Navigator (PHN))
Advocacy, linking mission to, 35
Alexander, William, 47
Allina Health System, 43

All-or-none bundle of care commitment, 132
Ambulatory care, 54, 57 (*See also* ProvenHealth Navigator (PHN))
American Academy of Pediatrics, 224
American Association of Hip and Knee Surgeons, 53
American Journal of Managed Care, 122–123
American Surgical Association, 55
Anemia, 117, 169–170
Anticipatory medicine, 222–224
Anticoagulation therapy management service, 3
App, for ProvenExperience, 211–212
Appearance of professionals, policy for, 197–198
Appointments:
  nonproductive time related to, 225
  same-day, 202–203
AtlantiCare, 40
AT&T, 67
Autism care, 55, 117

Baseline data, 68, 81–82
Bedside shift report, 198
Behavior change, 219

Bell Telephone Laboratories, 66–67

Berwick, Donald M., 132

Best practices:
choosing elements of, 84
default, 100
establishing, 91–92
information on, 52–53
modification of proposals for, 69
monitoring of patient compliance with, 87
for patient experience, 192–193
in ProvenCare, 81 (*See also specific areas of care*)

Bills, redesigned, 204–209

Biologics (*see* ProvenCare Biologics)

Blue Cross of Northeastern Pennsylvania, 22

Boards of directors:
agenda for, 45–46
composition of, 45, 46
foundation board, 39–40, 45
insurance board, 43–45
leadership of, 41
in Penn State Hershey Medical Center merger, 40, 41
presentations for perspective in, 42–43
selection of chair for, 6
structure of, 41–42
(*See also* Governance)

Bravman, John, 47

Budgeting process, 67–68

Bundled care:
all-or-none commitment to, 132
for CABG, 90

for chronic diseases, xxii, 10, 36, 54, 57, 132, 133, 136–138, 144, 148, 154 (*See also* ProvenCare Chronic)
for nursing practices, 198, 200

Bundled payment package, 84, 88–89

Burke, Greg F., 191

C sections, 3

CABG (*see* Coronary artery bypass graft surgery)

Cancer:
biologicals for, 183–184
lung cancer treatment, 102–104
oral chemotherapies, 169
risk with biologics, 182–183

Capital BlueCross, 22, 26

Cardiology care:
as beta test, 51, 53, 54
congestive heart failure, 109–110

Care gaps program, 157

Care in place, 225–226

Care managers (PHN), 127–130, 139–142, 155–156, 161

Care reengineering, xv, 29–32
choosing targets for, 51–54
enabling (*see* Enabling change)
initiating (*see* Initiating change)
linking incentives and fundamental change, 32–35
and operational trajectory, 35–36
outcomes of, 215
professionals' motivation for, 21
strategic vision for, 34–36
(*See also* ProvenCare)

Caregiver–patient relationship, xv

Caregivers:
  in clinical pathway, 55
  embedded nurse care
    managers, 127–130
  family as, 226–227
  transparent reporting of quality
    ratings for, 194–195
Caregiving, preference for
  innovations over, 69
CareSite specialty pharmacies,
  184–185
Caring:
  becoming the best in, 228–229
  as central to reengineering and
    innovation, 218
  characteristics of, 216
  imperative for, 214–216
  preventative, 219–221
Cataract surgery, 56
Centers for Medicare and
  Medicaid Services
    Pioneer Accountable Care
    Organization (ACO) model,
    148
Centers of excellence, xii
CEO:
  as chair of insurance board, 44
  in innovation budgeting, 68
  partnering between board
    chairman and, 41–42,
    46–47
  visibility of, 38
Cerner, 6
Certified trauma center
  designation, 6
Chief information officer, 70
Chief medical informatics officer,
  70
Chief of innovation, 67

Chief scientific officer, 70
Chronic diseases, 15–16
Chronic pain management, 157
Chronic service:
  fee for, 2–3
  reengineering (*see* ProvenCare
    Chronic)
Cicio, Gina, 210
Clinical leaders, xiv, 23
  choosing initial targets to
    appeal to, 51–52
  at head of transformation
    effort, 64
  in operationalizing innovation,
    68–69
Clinical orders, in ProvenCare
  Chronic, 119, 121
Clinical pathway:
  including caregivers in, 55
  responsibility for developing,
    168
Clinical service reengineering
  targets, 51–53
Clinician satisfaction, 145, 147
Collaborating on change, 107–110
Commission on Cancer
  ProvenCare Lung Cancer
    Collaborative, 103
Commonwealth Fund, 11
Communication, 38
  in chronic disease care, 121–122
  C.I.CARE communication
    framework, 193–194
  concerning genetic
    abnormalities, 223–224
  information overload, 158
  OurNotes to patients, 203
  in physician practices prior to
    PHN, 152

Communication strategy,
strategic vision in, 35
Communication technology,
65–66
Community practice
reengineering, 134–138
Community Practice Service
Line (CPSL), 54
Compensation:
fundamental change in, 42, 57
linking incentives to
fundamental change,
32–35, 57–58
linking incentives to strategic
goals, 89, 101, 134
Compliance monitoring, 87
Concierge care, 128, 132
Congestive heart failure, 109–
110, 144–145
Consolidation of providers, prior
to ACA, 18
Continuous service recovery,
209–211
Cookbook medicine, 87
Copays, refunded to dissatisfied
patients, 12
Coronary artery bypass graft
surgery (CABG), 3, 11
as beta test, 22, 53, 54, 90–91
long-term outcomes of, 107
ProvenCare Acute for, 90–95
Dr. Steele Jr.'s experience with,
79–80, 92–94
Dr. Steele Sr.'s experience with,
49–50
variations in care, 86
Cost of care, 219
access, quality, and cost
triangle, xi

for anemia, 169–170
benefit of reducing, 26–27 (*See
also* Care reengineering)
decreased by care
reengineering, 216
flat fee services, 2–3
as fundamental, xvii
at Geisinger, 2
oncology drugs, 183, 184
for psoriasis, 181–182
and quality of outcome, x, 20,
21 (*See also* ProvenCare)
specialty medications, 166–167
Cost shifting, xii
Coventry Health Care, 22
CPSL (Community Practice
Service Line), 54
Crohn's disease, 169
Culture of innovation, 5–6, 27–29

Data:
availability of, 31–32
baseline, 68, 81–82
on MS treatments, 172
Davis, Karen, 45
Delivery of care:
care in place, 225–226
determining unjustified
variation in, 81–82
hospital-centric integrated
networks, xiii
hub-and-spoke delivery
system, 8
hurtful or useless cost in, 21, 59
non-Geisinger systems for, 71
in physician practices after
PHN, 155
in physician practices prior to
PHN, 153

(*See also* Care reengineering;
   Integrated
   delivery networks;
   ProvenExperience)
Delta Team, 162
Design of system:
   driving principles for enabling
      change, 64–66
   structural design elements,
      55–68
Diabetes care, 144–145
   diagnoses in, 117–118, 121
   medication therapeutic
      management program in,
      157
   patient case studies, 124–125
   patients' role in, 121–122
   summary report in, 118–119
   (*See also* Type 2 diabetes care)
Dissatisfied patients, refunding
   copays to, 12
Doctor-patient relationship, 218
Documentation:
   of MS patient treatment, 171
   in physician practices prior to
      PHN, 152
   (*See also* Electronic health
      records [EHR])
Dominance of day-to-day
   operational crisis, 65–66
Duffy, Kim, 187

Education initiatives, 22
Electronic health records (EHR),
   6–7
   in diabetes care, 117–119, 121
   early use of, 152
   IT support for, 160, 161
   in MS treatment, 172–173

in population health
   management, 138
in psoriasis and hepatitis C
   care, 181
value of near real-time data
   from, 31
Embedded nurse care managers
   (PHN), 127–130, 139–142,
   155–156, 161
Embedded pharmacists, 157
Employers, self-insured, xii, xvi
Enabling change, 63–77
   design principles for, 64–66
   operationalizing innovation
      function, 68–70
   scaling outside of Geisinger,
      71–73
   structural design elements,
      55–68
   xG Health Solutions, 74–76
Enbrel, 169
EOBs (explanations of benefits),
   204–209
Epic, 6, 113, 122 (*See also*
   Electronic health records
   (EHR))
Erythopoietin (EPO), 169, 170
Evidence-based practices:
   and care gaps program, 157
   hourly rounding, 198–199
   information on, 52–53
   of physicians prior to PHN,
      153
   in ProvenCare, 81
   (*See also specific areas of care*)
Executive vice president for
   strategy and strategic
   program development, 66,
   68

Explanations of benefits (EOBs),
204–209
External affirmation of
ProvenCare, 59

Failure:
learning from, 55, 56
permitting and recovering
from, 8–9
False polarities, 58
Families:
in care delivery reengineering
processes, 112–113
as caregivers, 226–227
as essential partners, 86–87
interactions with care
managers, 140–142
and patient rounding on
demand, 201
Federal health insurance
exchange, 217
Fee-for-service reimbursement,
ix
under ACA, xi
returns to insurance companies
from, 16–17
revenue generation under, 16
Feinberg, David T., xv, 4, 42, 47,
188, 189, 191, 192, 227
Finance committee, 42
Financial experts/leaders, xiv–xv,
23, 65
Financial responsibility data,
204–209, 222
"Five Ps," 199
Five-year strategies, 25–38
care reengineering, 29–36
extending previous strategic
aims, 36–38

vertically integrated payer/
provider model, 26–29
Flywheel effect, 51, 53, 55, 106
Foss, Harold, 5, 46, 47
Four "Ps" in healthcare, 217–219
Future vision for healthcare,
213–229
access to care, 221–222
anticipatory, precision
medicine, 222–224
care in place, 225–226
caring imperative, 214–216
family as caregivers, 226–227
four "Ps," 217–219
preventative caring, 219–221

Geisinger, 1–13
acclaim for ProvenCare model,
10–13
board of directors chair at, 6
evolution of, 4
five-year strategies of, 25–38
healthcare value reengineering
at, 4–10
insurance company of, 9–10, 19
leadership concept at, xiv–xv
problems in developing new
approach at, 15–24
ProvenCare approach at, 2–4
ProvenCare innovations at, xii
scaling innovation at, xvii
shared mission and staff morale
at, xiii
vertical integration at, xiii–xiv
(See also specific topics)
Geisinger, Abigail, 5, 34, 35,
46–47, 191
Geisinger Accelerated
Performance Program, 69

Geisinger Commonwealth
   School of Medicine, 4
Geisinger Community Practice
   Service Line (CPSL), 54
Geisinger Gold, 18–19
Geisinger Gold Medicare HMO,
   28
Geisinger Health Foundation
   Board, 39
Geisinger Health Plan (GHP),
   5, 9–10
   board for, 43–45
   decision to retain, 27
   evolution of, 27–29
   in northeast Pennsylvania, 71
   in other states, 72–73
Geisinger Health System
   Foundation Board, 39
Geisinger Innovations, 67, 68
Geisinger Marworth Alcohol
   and Chemical Dependency
   Treatment Center, 210
Geisinger Medical Center, 2, 3,
   7–8
Geisinger Transformation,
   69–70
Generalizing, 216
   engines of, 37–38
   innovation, 54, 59–60
   outside of Geisinger, 71
Genetic abnormalities, 223–224
Genomic sequencing, 213, 223
Genotyping, 223
George F. Geisinger Hospital,
   4, 5
GHP (*see* Geisinger Health Plan)
Governance, 8, 39–48
   agenda for board, 45–46
   board leadership, 41

board structure, 41–42
composition of board, 45
of insurance company, 43–45
leadership relationship in,
   46–47
during Penn State Hershey
   Medical Center merger,
   40
presentations for perspective in,
   42–43
Guidelines for care, establishing,
   91–92

Harvoni, 169
HCCs (Hierarchical Condition
   Categories), 28
Health Care Payment Learning
   and Action Network, 217
Health economists, interaction
   with, 67
Health insurance:
   and ACA, 17
   access to, xvii, 221
   (*See also* Insurance companies)
Health navigators, 3, 201 (*See
   also* ProvenHealth Navigator
   (PHN))
Health Transformation Alliance,
   xii, 219
Healthcare Effectiveness Data
   and Information Set, 155
Healthcare environment:
   future vision for, 213–229
   at Geisinger, prior to ACA,
   18–19
   national, chaos in, 16–18
   needs for transformation of,
   17
   sickness care system, 220

Healthcare spending, x
    on chronic diseases, 16
    main components of, xi
    (*See also* Cost of care)
Healthcare value, 17, 22 (*See
    also* Value creation; Value
    reengineering)
Henry, Frank, 47
Hepatitis C, 169, 178, 180, 181
Hierarchical Condition
    Categories (HCCs), 28
Highmark, 22
High-performance systems,
    attributes of, 83
High-performing provider
    networks, xii
Hip surgery, 94, 96–102
HMO plan, 27, 28
Holy Spirit Health System, 40
Home care:
    care in place, 225–226
    families as caregivers, 226–227
    transition to, 201–202
Hood, Henry, 5–6
Hospital admissions, 148, 156
Hospital for Special Surgery, 53
Hospital readmissions, 148
Hospital-centric integrated
    delivery networks, xiii
Hub-and-spoke delivery system, 8
Humira, 169
Hypertension management,
    131–132

Incentives:
    in improving healthcare value,
    22
    linking fundamental change
    with, 32–35, 57–58

linking strategic goals with, 89,
    101, 134
    seeing patients do better as,
    57–58
    (*See also* Compensation)
Information overload, 158
Infrastructure, 63 (*See also*
    Enabling change)
Initiating change, 49–61
    choosing engineering targets,
    51–54
    success factors in
    operationalizing and
    scaling, 54–60
Innovation:
    beta test for, 51–53
    choosing targets for, 65
    critical factors in, 20–24
    culture of, 5–6, 27–29
    Delta Team for, 162
    demand for, 106–107
    evolution of structure for, 70
    in future vision for healthcare,
    213–229
    Geisinger's definition of, 32
    generalizing, 54, 60
    linking incentives to, 32–35
    models of, 66–67
    monitoring negative effect on
    patients, 189–190
    operationalizing, 68–70
    scaling, xvii, 54–60
    sustaining, 36
Institute for Advanced
    Application, 70
Institute for Advanced Study, 66
Institute for Healthcare
    Improvement Triple Aim,
    163

Insurance companies:
doctor groups and hospitals
purchased by, xiii
Geisinger, 9–10, 19 (*See also*
Geisinger Health Plan
[GHP])
from hospital-centric integrated
delivery networks, xiii
returns in fee-for-service
system for, 16–17
(*See also* Vertically integrated
payer/provider model)
Insurance coverage, 17, 221
access to, xvii
on patient statements, 204–209
Insurance operations, scaling and
generalizing, 37
Integrated delivery networks:
as financial contrivances, xiii
hospital-centric, xiii
visit requests from, 74
Integrated health system:
definition of, xii–xiii
physicians' rationales for
moving to, 159–160
Intellectual property, 76, 216
Internal transfer pricing, 10, 30, 57
Intravenous iron dextran, 170
Investment committee, 42
Iron sucrose, 170
IT:
enabling reengineering,
161–117
in support of EHRs, 160, 161
IT experts, 67

Janet Weis Children's Hospital
and Level One Pediatric
Trauma Center, 1–2, 187

Joint replacement surgeries:
hip surgery, 94, 96–102
patient information about,
201–202
JP Morgan, 76

Klein, Joe, 11

Leadership:
concept of, xiv–xv
effect of change in, 72
of foundation board, 41
in physicians' practices,
162–163
in ProvenHealth Navigator,
148–149
recruiting, 23
role of, 64
rounding by, 196–197
triad leadership partnerships,
23, 65
Legacy, securing, 36
Lewisburg community practice,
136–137
Lewistown community practice,
136–137
License agreements, 76
Life Flight, 2
Lockheed Martin Corporation
Skunk Works, 67
Lung cancer, 102–104

Maffei, Frank, 1–2
Management and compensation
committee, 42
Market growth, 36–37, 71
Marks, Victor J., 190
Mayo Clinic, 5
McCole, Anita, 128–129

Medicaid, ix, xi
increased availability of, 217
in patient, provider, and payer
triad, xvi
Medicaid managed care, 56,
134–135
Medical affairs committee,
42–43
Medical neighborhood, in
ProvenHealth Navigator,
143–145
Medical practices (*see* Physicians'
practice(s))
Medicare, ix, xi
expansion of, 217
non-fee-for-service payment
under, 217
in patient, provider, and payer
triad, xvi
Medicare Advantage, 27, 28,
134–135
Medicare managed care, 56
Medicare Modernization Act
(MMA), 28
Medication therapeutic
management (MTM)
program, 157
Medications:
biologics, 166–167 (*See also*
ProvenCare Biologics)
in development for cancer,
183–184
management of, 165–166
oncology drug spending, 183
specialty, use of and spending
on, 166–167
Mergers and acquisitions, 37, 218
(*See also* Penn State Hershey
Medical Center)

Metrics:
for chronic disease care, 154
in compensation setting, 89
literature search for, 91
modification of proposals for,
69
from PHC4, 52
preventive care, 114
for ProvenHealth Navigator,
145–148
of quality, transparency in
reporting, 194–195
(*See also* Performance measures
and metrics)
Milstein, Arnold, 20, 21
Mission, xiii
applied to new endeavors,
34–35
of improving healthcare value,
22
joint, of payers and providers,
xiv
MMA (Medicare Modernization
Act), 28
Mount Sinai, 18
Mowery, Alison, 210
MS (multiple sclerosis), 169–178
MTM (medication therapeutic
management) program, 157
Multidisciplinary teams, 84–85,
91, 168
Multiple sclerosis (MS), 169–178
MyCode, 213

Name tags, 197
National recognition, 36, 59–60
National representation on
board, 45
Neonatal intensive care, 3

New York Times, 11
New York University, 18
Newman, William (Bill),
159–160
Noll, Tiffany, 187
Nonclinical management staff
(PHN), 163
Non-fee-for-service payment,
217
Nonfiduciary partnering, xiii
Nurse care managers (PHN),
127–130, 139–142, 155–156,
161, 201
Nurse leaders, 67
Nurse practitioners, white lab
coats for, 197
Nurses:
nursing best practices, 198–200
uniforms for, 197

Oak Investment Partners, 76
Obama, Barack, 11, 60
Obamacare (*see* Patient
Protection and Affordable
Care Act (ACA))
Objections to change, 85–86
Operational return, 9
Operationalization:
of innovation function, 68–70
success factors in, 54–60
Operations:
in care reengineering, 35–36
continuing pull of, 70
dominance of day-to-day
operational crisis, 65–66
mitigating focus on, 66
scaling and generalizing
engines, 37
Oral iron, 169–170

Orthopaedics Institute, 200
Orthopedics:
best practices in, 53
hip surgery, 94, 96–102
OurNotes system, 203, 226
Outcomes of care, ix, x
and cost of care, x, 20, 21 (*See
also* ProvenCare)
performance metrics, 145–148
populations with worst
outcomes, 21
professional pride in, x–xi
(*See also* Quality of care)

Pacific Business Group on
Health, xii, 219
Partners HealthCare, 18
Partnership model, 23
Partnerships, linking mission
to, 35
Patient compact, 87
Patient compliance monitoring,
87
Patient experience:
best practices for, 192–193
personalized care models,
221–222
pre-ProvenCare initiatives for,
190–191
(*See also* ProvenExperience)
Patient Experience Steering
Committee, 191
Patient outreach, in ProvenCare
Chronic, 121–122
Patient population, of Geisinger,
7–8
Patient Protection and
Affordable Care Act (ACA),
xi, xii, 17, 56, 59–60, 217

Patient risk status, 139
Patient satisfaction, xv, 145, 147
  refunds for dissatisfaction with
    services, 192, 211–212
  reporting ratings of, 195
  (*See also* ProvenExperience)
Patient-centered care, 8, 225
Patients:
  in care delivery reengineering
    processes, 112–113
  communications with, 158
  doctor-patient relationship,
    218
  as essential partners, 86–87
  interactions with care
    managers, 140–142
  OurNotes to, 203
  research participation by, 223,
    224
Payer-provider structure, xiii–xiv,
  148–149, 217–219 (*See also*
  Vertically integrated payer/
  provider model)
Pay-for-volume model, 220
PCPs (*see* Primary care
  physicians; Primary care
  providers)
Penn State Hershey Medical
  Center, 8, 18–19, 40, 41
Pennsylvania Health Care
  Cost Containment Council
  (PHC4), 52
Performance measures and
  metrics:
  for ProvenCare Acute, 84
  for ProvenCare Chronic,
    110–117
  for ProvenHealth Navigator,
    145–148

Personalized care models,
  221–222
Pharmacists, embedded, 157
PHC4 (Pennsylvania Health
  Care Cost Containment
  Council), 52
PHN (*see* ProvenHealth
  Navigator)
Phones answered by humans,
  202
Physician assistants:
  leadership by, 67
  white lab coats for, 197
Physician groups:
  rationales for moving to
    integrated system model
    from, 159–160
  stability of, 8
Physician leaders, xiv
  in leadership triad, 23
  in PHN, 163
Physicians:
  doctor-patient relationship,
    218
  fundamental personality traits
    of, 51
  patient rounding on demand
    by, 201
  pre-surgery calls by, 200
  white lab coats for, 197
  (*See also* Providers)
Physicians' practice(s), 151–164
  after ProvenHealth Navigator,
    155–159
  complexities in transformation
    of, 160–162
  leadership issues with,
    162–163
  of William Newman, 159–160

before ProvenHealth
Navigator, 151–155
regulatory and cost pressures
on, 218
Population health management,
in ProvenHealth Navigator,
138–143
Practice transformation (*see*
Physicians' practice(s))
Precision medicine, 222–224
Predictive analytics, 31–32
Press Ganey Patient Satisfaction
Survey, 195, 199
Preventable complications,
warranty for risk of financial
effects of, 83
Prevention:
focus on, 17
preventative caring, 129,
219–221
Prices for care, xi
bundled, 84, 88–89
internal transfer pricing, 10,
30, 57
(*See also* Cost of care)
PRIDE (Proven Innovation
Drive for Excellence), 69
Primary care leaders, 107
Primary care physicians (PCPs):
optimizing connection
between specialists and,
144–145
redefining role of, 131
shortage of, 129–131
Primary care providers (PCPs),
107–110, 136
Primary care redesign, in
ProvenHealth Navigator,
130–138

Problem resolution, standardized
continuous service recovery
for, 209–211
Problems in developing
Geisinger approach, 15–24
chaos in U.S. healthcare
environment, 16–18
critical factors in innovation,
20–24
turmoil within Geisinger,
18–19
Productivity, 89
Professional appearance policy,
197–198
Proven Innovation Drive for
Excellence (PRIDE), 69
ProvenCare, 2–4, 83
acclaim for, 10–13
achievements of, 3–4
care pathways in, 101, 102
components of best outcome
in, 81
five-year strategies in
developing, 25–38
problems underlying
development of, 15–24
return on investment in, 81
(*See also specific topics, e.g.:*
Initiating change)
ProvenCare Acute, 79–104
attributes of high-performance
system, 83
bundled payment package in,
88–89
for CABG, 90–95
core components of, 83–84
determining unjustified
variation in caregiving,
81–82

ProvenCare Acute, *continued*
early success of, 90–94
for hip surgery, 94, 96–102
implementation stages for,
84–87
initial heart care targets for,
51–54
for lung cancer, 102–104
modification of proposals for,
69
typical acute care today, 82
ProvenCare Biologics, 165–186
anemia alternatives, 169–170
cancer treatments, 183–184
CareSite specialty pharmacies,
184–185
hepatitis C alternatives, 178,
180, 181
multiple sclerosis alternatives,
170–178
psoriasis alternatives, 178–179,
181–183
ProvenCare Chronic, 105–126
clinical orders in, 119, 121
collaborating on change for,
107–110
expanding value reengineering
portfolio to, 106–107
impact of, 122–123
initial type 2 diabetes targets
for, 54–55
patient case studies, 124–125
patient outreach in, 121–122
performance measure set for,
110–117
provider process in, 117–120
ProvenCare Heart, 54
ProvenCare Knee, 3
ProvenCare Perinatal, 3

ProvenExperience, 187–212
bedside shift report, 198
best practices in, 190–209
calls to patients before surgery,
200
C.I.CARE communication
framework, 193–194
hourly rounding, 198–199
leadership rounding, 196–197
OurNotes to patients, 203
patient rounding on demand,
201
phones answered by humans,
202
professional appearance policy,
197–198
redesigned bills, 204–209
same-day appointments,
202–203
smartphone app for, 211–212
standardized continuous
service recovery, 209–211
transition to home care,
201–202
transparency in quality metrics
reporting, 194–195
whiteboards, 199–200
ProvenHealth Navigator (PHN),
127–164
embedded nurse care managers
in, 127–130, 139–142, 155–
156, 161
focus of, 32
leadership issues in, 148–149,
162–163
medical neighborhood in,
143–145
performance metrics for,
145–148

physicians' practices after, 155–159

physicians' practices before, 151–155

population health management in, 138–143

practice transformation complexities with, 160–162

primary care redesign in, 130–138

primary goal in, 151

Provider process, in ProvenCare Chronic, 117–120

Providers:

consolidation of, prior to ACA, 18

high-performing provider networks, xii

in patient, provider, and payer triad, xvi

patient relationships with, 218

payment incentives for, 218

(*See also* Nurses; Physicians; Vertically integrated payer/provider model)

Psoriasis, 178–179, 181–183

Public payer, ix–x, xvi

Purchaser of care, in patient, provider, and payer triad, xvi

Quality metrics, transparency in reporting, 194–195

Quality of care:

access, quality, and cost triangle, xi

and cost of care, x, 20, 21 (*See also* Care reengineering)

as fundamental, xvii

at Geisinger, 2

Geisinger's definition of, 32–33

linking mission to, 35

as outcome of care reengineering, 216

striving for perfection in, 36

RAND study, 20–21

Recruiting, 23, 60, 66, 106

Reengineering (*see* Care reengineering; Value reengineering)

Refunds, for dissatisfaction with services, 211–212

Regeneron Pharmaceuticals, 222, 223

Research initiatives, 22

Research participation, 223, 224

Review team, 92

Revlimid, 169

Robel, Susan M., 191

Rounding:

on demand, 201

hourly, 198–199

by leadership, 196–197

Same-day appointments, 202–203

Scaling, 216

for community practices, 137–138

engines of, 37–38

innovation in, xvii

outside of Geisinger, 71–73

success factors in, 54–50

team members devoted specifically to, 75

Self-insured employers, xii, xvi

Service recovery, 209–211

Shared mission, xiii

Shift reports, 198
Sickness care system, 220
Siebecker, Joi, 196
Single parent fiduciary structure, xiii–xiv, 39–40 (*See also* Governance; Vertically integrated payer/provider model)
Smartphone app, for ProvenExperience, 211–212
"SNFists" (skilled nursing facilities providers), 151–162
Society of Thoracic Surgery National Database, 103
Specialists:
  collaboration with primary care providers, 107–110, 136
  and community practitioner team, 144
  optimizing PCP connection with, 144–145
  in ProvenHealth Navigator, 131
Specialty pharmacies, 184–185
Staff morale, xiii
Standardized continuous service recovery, 209–211
Stanford Medicine, 193
Stanford University, 18
Statements, billing, 204–209
Steele, Glenn D., xiii, xv, 20, 34, 42, 47, 70, 79–80, 113, 191
Steele, Glenn D., Jr., 4, 49–50, 79-80, 92-94
Steele, Glenn D., Sr., 49–50
Strategic prioritization process, 31–32
Strategic vision, for care reengineering, 34–36

Structural design elements, 55–68
Success:
  in operationalizing and scaling, 54–60
  from tailoring expectations to strengths and structural/cultural aspects, 34
Surgery:
  at-home equipment boxes for patients following, 201
  calls to patients before, 200

Tecfidera, 169
Technology:
  communication, 65–66
  IT enabling reengineering, 161–117
  IT in support of EHRs, 160, 161
  in ProvenHealth Navigator, 128–129
  (*See also* Electronic health records [EHR])
Thomas, Cassandra, 228
TIME magazine, 11
Transition to home care, 201–202
Transitions of care, 156
Transparency, in reporting quality metrics, 194–195
Type 2 diabetes care, 57–58
  best practice goals for, 10–11
  outcome measures, 147
  performance measures for, 112–117
  ProvenCare reengineering for, 108–109

UCLA Health, 193
Ulcerative colitis, 169

Ultraviolet light (UV) treatment, 181–183
Uniforms, 197–198
University of California San Francisco, 18
U.S. Department of Health and Human Services, 209
U.S. News & World Report, 12
Utilization measures, 162
UV (ultraviolet light) treatment, 181–183

Value:
  linking mission to, 35
  payment for, 220–221
  unlocking, 53
Value creation:
  direct benefit from, xvi
  redistribution of profits from, 30
Value reengineering, 4–10
  culture of innovation for, 5–6
  with electronic health records, 6–7
  enabling (*see* Enabling change)
  expanding to ProvenCare Chronic, 106–107
  high-probability early wins in, 22
  initiating (*see* Initiating change)
  and patient population, 7–8
  permitting and recovering from failure in, 8–9

  in ProvenCare Biologics, 167
  sweet spot in, 9–10
Variation in care/performance:
  with biological medications, 166
  inventorying breadths and depths of, 86
  justified, 87
  in physicians' practices, 155
  unjustified, 81–82
Venditti, Angelo, 196
Vertical integration, xiii, xiv
Vertically integrated payer/ provider model, 26–27
  criticisms of, 26
  legal challenge to, 43
  moving culture toward, 27–29
  (*See also* ProvenCare)
Virginia Mason Health System, 27

Warranties, 83, 89, 202
Web portal, 203
Wellness, focus on, 17
Whiteboards, 199–200
Wilensky, Gail, 45

xG Health Solutions, xvii, 74–76, 216
  rationale for creating, 75
  scaling and generalizing, 37–38
  in scaling outside of Geisinger, 71–72

ABOUT THE AUTHORS

Glenn D. Steele Jr., MD, PhD, serves as chairman of xG Health Solutions, an independently operated venture Geisinger launched to help healthcare organizations create value and improve quality, leveraging Geisinger intellectual property and expertise on issues such as population-health data analytics, care management, and health IT. He is the former president and chief executive officer of Geisinger Health System (2001–2015). Dr. Steele previously served as the dean of the Biological Sciences Division and the Pritzker School of Medicine and vice president for medical affairs at the University of Chicago, as well as the Richard T. Crane Professor in the Department of Surgery. Prior to that, he was the William V. McDermott Professor of Surgery at Harvard Medical School, president and chief executive officer of Deaconess Professional Practice Group, and chairman of the Department of Surgery at New England Deaconess Hospital. Dr. Steele is past chairman of the American Board of Surgery.

His investigations have focused on the cell biology of gastrointestinal cancer and precancer and most recently on innovations in healthcare delivery and financing. A prolific writer, he is the author or coauthor of nearly 500 scientific and professional articles.

Dr. Steele received his bachelor's degree in history and literature from Harvard University and his medical degree from New York University School of Medicine. He completed his internship and residency in surgery at the University of

Colorado, where he was also a fellow of the American Cancer Society. He earned his PhD in microbiology at Lund University in Sweden.

A member of the National Academy of Medicine, Dr. Steele serves on the Roundtable on Value and Science-Driven Healthcare, the Committee on the Governance and Financing of Graduate Medical Education, and the Vital Directions for Health and Health Care Steering Committee, and previously served on the Committee on Reviewing Evidence to Identify Highly Effective Clinical Services (HECS). A fellow of the American College of Surgeons, Dr. Steele is a member of the American Surgical Association, the American Society of Clinical Oncology, and past president of the Society of Surgical Oncology.

Dr. Steele serves on the following boards and national committees: Health Transformation Alliance (vice chair), City of Hope board of directors, Ingenious Med board of directors, PTC Therapeutics board of directors, Stratus Video board of directors, Synaptive Medical board of directors, Wellcare Health Plans Inc. board of directors, Healthcare Innovation Program (HIP) external advisory board (Emory University), and the Peterson Center on Healthcare advisory board. Dr. Steele formerly served on the following boards: Agency for Integrated Care (AIC) Singapore, Bucknell University board of trustees, Cepheid board of directors, Harvard Medical Faculty physicians board at Beth Israel Deaconess Medical Center, Premier, Inc. board (chairman 2011–2013), Temple University School of Medicine board of visitors, Weis Markets, Inc., Congressional Budget Office panel of health advisers, Commonwealth Fund's Commission on a High Performance Health System, and American Hospital Association (AHA) board of trustees.

Dr. Steele is the recipient of several awards, NYU School of Medicine's Solomon A. Berson Medical Alumni Achievement Award in Health Science, Medicine and the Arts (2016); AHA's Justin Ford Kimball Innovators Award (2015); NCHL Gail L. Warden Healthcare Leadership Award (2014); HFMA Board of Directors' Award (2011); AHA Health Research & Education Trust Award (2010); AHA's Grassroots Champion Award (2007); and CEO IT Achievement Award (2006). He has been named consecutive times to the following lists: *Modern Healthcare*'s 50 Most Powerful Physician Executives in Healthcare, *Modern Healthcare*'s 100 Most Powerful People in Healthcare, and *Becker's Hospital Review*'s 100 Nonprofit Hospital Health System CEOs to Know.

David T. Feinberg, MD, MBA, is president and chief executive officer of Geisinger, one of the nation's largest health services organizations known for reinventing medical care. Geisinger is an integrated healthcare organization consisting of 13 hospital campuses, two research centers, a school of medicine, over 30,000 employees, 1,600 employed physicians, 420 residents and fellows, and a 583,000-member health plan, all serving and caring for more than 3 million residents in Pennsylvania and New Jersey.

A longtime champion of the patient experience, Dr. Feinberg has caught the industry's attention by introducing Geisinger's latest evolution of its renowned ProvenCare portfolio: ProvenExperience, which allows patients to request a refund based on the outcome of their patient experience.

Prior to joining Geisinger, Dr. Feinberg served as CEO of UCLA's hospitals and associate vice chancellor of UCLA Health Sciences, as well as president of UCLA Health System.

Dr. Feinberg earned his undergraduate degree at the University of California, Berkeley, and graduated with distinction from the University of Health Sciences/Chicago Medical School. He earned a master of business administration from Pepperdine University.

Recognized among the 100 Most Influential People in Healthcare as well as in the top 3 of the 50 Most Influential Physician Executives and Leaders by *Modern Healthcare*, Dr. Feinberg's numerous awards and recognitions include Alpha Omega Alpha Medical Honor Society; Medical Center CEO of the Year Healthcare Leadership Award; Leadership, Vision, and Commitment Honoree by the National Health Foundation; Distinguished Fellow of the American Psychiatric Association; and the Cancro Academic Leadership Award from the American Academy of Child and Adolescent Psychiatry. Dr. Feinberg is a well-known national speaker, especially on the subject of patient experience, and has published numerous articles.

ABOUT GEISINGER

Geisinger is a leading integrated health services organization widely recognized for its unwavering commitment to caring and innovation, including the development of pioneering care delivery models, such as ProvenCare, ProvenExperience, and ProvenHealth Navigator.

Everything Geisinger does is about caring—for its patients, its members, the Geisinger family of physicians and employees, and its communities. As an organization, Geisinger values:

- **Kindness**: We strive to treat everyone as we would hope to be treated ourselves.
- **Excellence**: We treasure colleagues who humbly strive for excellence.
- **Learning**: We share our knowledge with the best and brightest to better prepare the caregivers of tomorrow.
- **Innovation**: We constantly seek new and better ways to care for our patients, our members, our communities and the nation.

In addition to fulfilling its patient care mission, Geisinger has a long-standing commitment to medical education, research, and community service. The MyCode Community Health Initiative at Geisinger includes one of the world's largest biobanks designed to store blood and other samples for DNA analysis research use by Geisinger and Geisinger collaborators.

Geisinger serves more than three million residents throughout central, south-central, and northeast Pennsylvania, and in

New Jersey at AtlantiCare, a Malcolm Baldrige National Quality Award recipient. The physician-led organization includes approximately 30,000 employees, 1,600 employed physicians, 13 hospital campuses, two research centers, a 580,000+ member health plan, and Geisinger Commonwealth School of Medicine, all of which leverage an estimated $12.7 positive annual impact on the Pennsylvania and New Jersey economies.

Geisinger has repeatedly garnered national accolades for integration, service, quality, and value. For more information, visit www.geisinger.org or connect on Facebook, Instagram, LinkedIn, and Twitter.

ABOUT
XG HEALTH SOLUTIONS

With roots in Geisinger—one of America's most innovative and successful integrated delivery systems—xG Health Solutions® enables healthcare organizations to optimize clinical and value-based performance through proven care redesign and management, actionable analytics, and industry-leading content.

Its team of clinically-led experts and its solutions accelerate and sustain value transformation through:

- **Care Redesign and Workflow Optimization**: improve outpatient, inpatient, and transition of care through care designs and workflows that have been successful at Geisinger and other high-functioning organizations
- **Care Management:** organizational structures, policies, procedures, clinical protocols, workflows, training via xG Learn™, and supervision, so providers can implement effective care management programs
- **Actionable Data Analytics:** data analytic expertise and clinical and financial management experience to help organizations identify and prioritize opportunities to improve quality of care and reduce cost
- **xG Intelligent Care Management™:** adult and pediatric care management assessments that automatically suggest patient-specific care plans for Medicare,

Medicaid, and commercial patients based on evidence-based guidelines and social determinants of health.

xG Health Solutions works with leading healthcare organizations from Maine to Singapore. Its clients and partners include:

- **Providers**: hospitals, health systems, and physician groups that are currently taking or planning to take financial risk
- **Health Insurers**: who work collaboratively with providers to achieve success in value-based payment arrangements
- **Employers**: who seek to work with health providers and insurers in a fundamentally different way to achieve better outcomes and value
- **EHR and HIT Vendors**: who incorporate its intellectual property into their products

xG Health Solutions is the leader in optimizing care delivery and care management, driving the behavioral change necessary to achieve and sustain value transformation reliably. For more information, please visit www.xghealth.com.